HENRIK IBSEN'S
THEATRE AESTHETIC
AND DRAMATIC ART

JANE ELLERT TAMMANY

Henrik Ibsen's Theatre Aesthetic and Dramatic Art

a Reflection
of Kierkegaardian Consciousness —
its significance for Modern Dramatic
Interpretation
and the American Theatre

Dobbeltreflexion i Øieblikket

PHILOSOPHICAL LIBRARY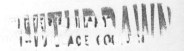

NEW YORK

To

"hiin Enkelte"

that Individual

who cries and laughs
at the same time ——

— Captain Hans Ludvig Mortensen and Fru Inger,
Magda and Karolina
— Karen and Susan Elin, et al. —

TABLE OF CONTENTS

---

* two-way switch

† Johann—*n* dialectical inference, J. E. T.

* a side-glance at
** The Moment
*** The possibility made actual

viii

LIST OF ILLUSTRATIONS

xiii

COLOR ILLUSTRATIONS

AUTHOR'S NOTE &
ACKNOWLEDGMENTS

"Takk skal du har!"*

To thank someone is to acknowledge in a special way the existence of that person. Those people who have been generous with their gifts are *special* and it is my privilege to acknowledge them; each one of them is "hiin Enkelte," that individual to whom this book is dedicated. It has been my experience that the creative activity an author generates and enjoys and sometimes is aghast at — is positive, and it separates the women and the men from the girls and the boys. The people specified here have one bond in common: they are creative individuals and they are adults.

It is difficult to say when the author's "moment" of conception takes place — the point of *professional commitment* is more easily recognized; that point for me — *in part* an outgrowth of a Northern background, theatrical discipline and the formalization imposed by critical study of drama and theatre — occurred in 1964. At the Catholic University of America, I was exposed to what I am wont to call the "Hartke" aesthetic and to a program that *believed* in "crea-

---

* "Thanks shall you have!"

xix

tive intuition" and regarded professionalism as natural to the art of theatre. This kind of sensitivity I could understand. Special thanks to Leo Brady who accompanied me through a labyrinthine exploration of Old Norse drama and theatre and supervised my Master's thesis; and thanks to Joseph Lewis who lent a willing ear and whose seminars in playwriting structured my creative voice; and to John Brown who urged me to pursue my bent.

In Norway at the University of Oslo, I was fortunate in meeting persons of deep dedication and talent and one scholar in particular, a man who presented the depth and breadth of Norwegian art dynamically and responsibly, Dr. Knut Berg, director of the National Gallery of Art in Oslo.

My doctoral committee at the University of Wisconsin was supportive of my interests in Northern drama and theatre. In the department of Theatre and Drama, A. C. Scott directed my doctoral work and his aesthetic sensibility provided a force that was constructive to my perspective (his Asian Theatre seminars were an expression of this kind of sensitivity); Jonathan Curvin placed the vitality of the American dramatic scene in a context that permitted critical judgment of the American stage; and in John Ezell's design course *Øieblikket* was created "in concreto"; Ordean Ness lent another ear. In Scandinavian studies, *my thanks to* Harald S. Naess for his interest in the Northern dramatic perspective of my study, his discernment and his linguistic remarks regarding "seeming" inconsistencies in Norwegian/Danish spelling; *and to* Niels Ingwersen, "thanks." His innate understanding of the Kierkegaardian dialectic clarified many concepts "existentially" and his response generated insights.

The walls of a university are not high and the theatre, the world, towers above it and it was my life experience — professionally and personally — that allowed for a unique perspective. The means by which one recognizes kindred spirits is intuitive in many ways. In any event, my thanks to Howard V. Hong for his generosity in connection with Kierkegaard and for introducing me to the Copenhagen principle. A note of appreciation to Robert Brustein and Robert Corrigan for notes of encouragement that came at an appropriate time, and a note to William Adams for his good will and helpful support in England. A thank you to Rolf Fjelde who invited me to participate at the Ibsen Sesquicentennial in New York where I gave a paper — *The Wild Duck* — that reflected the interpretative focus of this book *and* also to Birgitta Steene and John Allee for similar instances — a paper on the theatricality of Ingmar Bergman and one on Old Norse drama and Ibsen (both given in connection with The Society for the Advancement of Scandinavian Studies), and also appreciation to the Norwegian government for grant assistance. And to Einar Haugen a word — in connection with the Eddaic/Ibsen correspondence central to my paper at the University of Massachusetts — he confirmed the possibility that Ibsen had been exposed to Eddic material — in translation.

Artists are intuitively blessed and beautiful people — such has been my experience with the open and generous natures of Maggie Smith, Ingmar Bergman and Liv Ullmann. Their professional talents are admired and their photographs have a place in *Henrik Ibsen's Theatre Aesthetic and Dramatic Art — underscoring the text.* Thanks to each one of them for special permission, and to I. B. Singer for just "being" and to Walter Kerr — a succinct and responsible essayist and writer, a man who knows whereof he writes.

"The cultural watch" — the guardians of art (who have to be artists to know art), Mr. and Mrs. Lionel Epstein, thank you for the Munch illustrations that are from your collection. Thanks to the National Gallery of Art (Washington, D.C.) and to Editions Beyelser (Basel), the Dover Archives Series, Norstedt & Söners Forlag — for permission to reproduce some of the illustrations, and to the Munch Museum where I was overwhelmed in 1970 by Munch's several versions of the "Syk Pike," (Sick girl), which lined the walls, and gratitude to Ibsen's birthplace and Grimstad for their homage to Ibsen and also to the National Library in Oslo, the Bergen Theatre Museum "det første norske Theater" et al.

"Their names are legion" it is written, and to Mrs. Rose Morse of the Philosophical Library — praise for her expertise, consideration and patience. Other "individuals" to whom I wish to say thank you are just ordinary people of a rather extraordinary kind and I refer to them by initials; they will know who they are: M.C.; B.G.; J.Q.; C.S.; C.G.; I.C.; E.B.; D.H.; j.; B.B.D.; C.U.S.; T.W.; T.E.K., D.S̲.V.; R.B.; D.R.; L.R.E., et al. See illustration listings also.

J/E/T.

An aside: "Takk" to S.E.T. for the drawings.

GLOSSARY

1. Christendom   — pseudo Christianity
2. Christenhed   — true Christianity
3. den Enkelte   — the individual
4. Existents-Sphaer   — spheres of existence
5. Gjentagelsen   — repetition
6. Maengden   — the crowd
7. Metamorfose   — metamorphosis
8. Ofringen   — the Sacrifice
9. ØIEBLIKKET   — *the Moment*
10. Springet   — the leap
11. Valget   — the choice

The Premise

a "tankestreg," in modern drama*

The underlying principle of my focus is that *Søren Kierke-gaard's existentialism — Henrik Ibsen's theatre aesthetic and dramatic art* function as a *tankestreg,* a dash, a thought-mark in modern drama.

Their personae pursue an existence which is at once real and fictitious. The organic unity of their work is marked by crises which are necessary and unpredictable. They present a progressive realization, carefully considered from every point of view, which eventually converges. Each step seduces their audience on to the next. To present the truth as it is discovered is their purpose. Because each of them wants to reveal men to themselves, they pose questions which are ambiguous; replies are dialectical in that they re-echo the question. In not drawing conclusions, they permit the individual to conclude, "to untie the knot," thereby achieving his own existence. Form and content are inseparable and doubly reflected, whereby the finite is presented in an ordinary context, and then by indirect communication, a second expression emerges in which method and meaning are one. Consequently, the idea, doubly reflected, approximates Reality.

---

* A thought-mark

Ibsen, as did Kierkegaard, wanted to unmask and expose the conflict between truth and delusion. In one play after another, Ibsen presents crucial instances in an individual life that illuminate the moment of being, the *Moment* when the present is shown to contain the past within it whether that Moment occurs for the character or for the audience.

HENRIK IBSEN'S
THEATRE AESTHETIC
AND DRAMATIC ART

The Prologue

The Existentialist and
The Playwright

Søren Aabye Kierkegaard –

Henrik Johann Ibsen

The Proposal

The intention of this study is to focus on Henrik Ibsen's dramatic work so as to reveal the organic nature of his art as dictated by a special kind of *inner consciousness,* a Kierke-gaardian consciousness. The nature of this awareness, although it has its origin in the unconscious, is a state of intellectual actuation wherein the concentration is maximal. It is expected that the revelation of this inner consciousness as germane to Ibsen's art will allow for another dimension of his work to emerge, a dimension Yeats described as "the artifice of eternity." That is, the made and the eternal are given an immediacy consonant with the theatrical and the metaphysical. This concept also indicates that what is dealt with in drama is not essences in themselves but essences embodied in concrete reality. One does not have its *being* without the other. Consequently, drama/theatre, which is being considered as one entity, is the only art form appropriate to the existential vision that Kierkegaard and Ibsen possessed.[1] The artistic sensibility of Henrik Ibsen is not regarded as being imitative of Kierkegaard. What is more interesting and illuminating is that Ibsen's theatre aesthetic and dramatic art in relation to Kierkegaard is being thought of as a refracted image, the consciousness reflecting "a thought that falls in well with mine."[2] The expression of each man is a unique dialectic.

Further, the inner coherence of Ibsen's work is considered to be *that essence* which expresses its *individuality*. And, while it is not appropriate to this study to assert that this *special* consciousness is the "quintessence of Ibsenism," it does posit the thought. Viewed academically and theatrically, that is, professionally, the expectation is that a Kierkegaardian frame of reference will provide the fulcrum that will give significance to studies of Ibsen and to the consideration of "modernism" in modern drama.

Søren Kierkegaard's philosophical percepts, and most particularly *Øieblikket,** as the referential point will provide the interpretative basis that will permit the philosophical and mythical core of Ibsen's drama to be discerned, and it is from this center that the *form* of his plays will be seen to have an active existence and a psychological depth. *Form,* in connection with art, is more than shape. In the artistic sense, *form* is a structure or an articulation; that is, it is an entity resulting from the relationship of mutually dependent factors. It is art created by a human intellectual act. The form becomes apparent when the conditions of the expression and the principles whereby to relate them are uncovered. Then it can be perceived that the connection between the form and the content is so vital that they may be said to be identical. Form is so important in a consideration of a work of art that the implication is that if the form is not apparent, either the work is imperfectly designed or the critic has not seen the design.

Organic unity as a completeness in itself is not a new concept in Western thought; it originated with Socrates who likened a literary conception to a living being. Socrates in Plato's *Phaedrus* demands of a discourse that it *be* a living thing. Although the totality of such a conception was demonstrated by Plato through philosophical activity, it was not until Aristotle that drama as a coherent conception of art

---

* the Moment

was codified. For centuries, Aristotle has been cited in one guise or another in connection with dramatic art. Frequently, the criteria are applied to any genre with dramatic qualities. Unlike the rigidity with which the *Poetics* was adhered to in earlier theatrical periods, contemporary critics tend to select an aspect of it as the basis for their commentary. For instance, Francis Fergusson has isolated "the tragic rhythm of action" as the constant in tragedy with which to discuss such playwrights as Sophocles, Shakespeare, Racine, Ibsen and Wagner's opera. Robert Corrigan, on the other hand, considers "the tragic sense of life" an appropriate approach to discuss drama. Not all critics are Aristotelian and few concentrate solely on Ibsen. Erich Auerbach, who is oriented to the literary nature of diverse genres, one of which is medieval drama, presents a "figural" interpretation. What he terms a "figural reality" prefigures something beyond itself and this concept is indicative of his interest in discerning a universal pattern that is cohesive.[3]

One recent study of Ibsen has been written by James Hurt. In *Catiline's Dream,* he has devised a formula that has its rationale in a mythic-psychological base.* Another writer, Brian Johnston (*The Ibsen Cycle*), views Ibsen's work from a Hegelian point of view. Other studies select a specific quality to develop. For instance, Herman J. Weigand explores the psychological relationship in the social plays. Under the provocative title *Ibsen's Feminine Mystique,* Vincent J. Balice writes an interpretation that interprets Ibsen women as surrogates for Jesus Christ.

Norwegian studies also tend in their treatment of Ibsen to direct their interest toward one particular facet of the work or to an overall view. *Symbolikken i Henrik Ibsens skuespil (Symbolism in Henry Ibsen's Plays)* by Arne Duve concentrates on symbols; in *Ibsens rimeteknikk (Ibsen's Rhymetechnique)*, Leif Maehle analyzes the poetic language. *Ibsen paa scenen (Ibsen on the Stage)* is a study of productions Gunnar Heiberg has viewed. Psychology receives the attention in

---

* An earlier study — O. Holtan: *Mythic Patterns in Ibsen's Last Plays.* U. of Minnesota Press, 1970.

6

Ibsen og den moderne psykologi (*Ibsen and Modern Psychol-ogy*) with Ingjald Nissen; these are individual essays.

Even though a direction is indicated in these interpre-tations, what is missing in the results is an expression of the totality of the work in all its ramifications, one that is related to a central core, *and* the consideration of drama as "live" theatre.[4] It is rather like sewing without knotting the thread (see Chapter III). Applying the same criteria to dissimilar writers is justified by Fergusson by analogy — the selected works are analogous in that they are *imitations of an action*.[5] However, generalizing from an isolated focus is limiting and the uniqueness of the individual creation can be obscured. Perhaps the tendency to provide a single focus stems from the Scribean emphasis in the 19th century which placed stress on one aspect, on playwriting as a craft with a special for-mula. Although the difference in *quality* is one in kind, it may be that the original well-made play as immortalized by Aristotle in the *Poetics* set a precedent for this kind of delineation. However, Sophocles' *Oedipus* was an atypical example of Greek drama. In any event, the critics tend to be devoted to one consideration whether it be theme, character, structure, language, ideology, psychology, mythology, or some other criteria. For the most part, the critics are divided in another important way. Either they regard drama as a liter-ary genre sans performance or they write reviews of perfor-mances which are judgmental rather than illuminating.[6]

Studies of Ibsen which take cognizance of Kierkegaard differ in their approach and vary in degree. Some scholars merely mention him; others extend their remarks to specific and obvious examples but without consideration of the theatrical reality.

While most approaches to Ibsen are often interesting and informative, they are less than satisfying because they stray from the totality of the work or lose sight of the work as a separate entity, and they do *not* knot the thread in the material so that the stitching will hold; there is no center.

7

The aesthetics of the poetic impulse is not sustained in either content or artistic intent, or from an objective point of view. The creative intuition as a "product of the practical intellect"[7] receives scant attention.

Because, in this study of Henrik Ibsen's drama, the Kierke-gaardian interpretative premise is a part of the Northern ethos, there is an added validity to the proposal that other approaches have not wholly considered. An "Other" dimension is also brought into play through the metaphysical tenets of Kierkegaard's beliefs. This latter dimension is not incompatible with art. The contention is that the frame of reference which is being presented here will reveal the organic unity of each of Ibsen's dramas without sacrificing the relationship of the work to the corpus of the authorship and without losing the principle that each play is a work of art with its own laws. This is a heuristic approach in that the text (including the silence) and the theatre space are the script.

The interpretation will be partially assisted by reference to those 19th century theatrical currents in Norway that are supportive to a study that considers the drama and the occasion as integral. A contrasting view will be afforded with a consideration of Bjørnstjerne Bjørnson, an important Norwegian playwright, a contemporary of Ibsen's, who had a significantly different view and who was infinitely more popular in Norway. Their place in the spectrum of the 19th century Norwegian theatre is necessary to the efforts of this work which recognizes the Northern background as an integral consideration.

Finally, a cognizance will be given to how Ibsen has been interpreted and the *nature* of the reaction to his work which is sharply contrasted by the movement described as "Ibsenism in America," and will touch upon the theatrical currents of the 1890's as well as the 1920's to the present. A further consideration will be an indication of how Ibsen's seed has been nurtured and changed in the work of later dramatists.

8

It is believed that the dominant aesthetic articulated will make a contribution to Ibsen scholarship, modern drama, and theatrical presentations that strive for artistic truth. It is thought that the Kierkegaard perspective will cast a double reflection upon Henrik Ibsen, one that will illuminate his dramatic idiom, point up the essence of the work, and reveal the poetic consciousness of the man, yet recognize the individuality of his art. It is my conviction that what is partially responsible for the moribund condition of the theatre is that in theatrical performance the integrity of the dramatic work has been violated — most often by misinterpretation or failure to recognize the controlling consciousness and the conditions of the art form.

The Essence

As the progenitor of modern drama, Henrik Ibsen has generated activity in dramatic interpretation, theatrical production and dramatic authorship. He accomplished the task of giving style to the serious bourgeois drama, a problem which had existed since the *comedie larmoyante* of the 18th century. That an awareness of the artistic *consciousness* of Norway's foremost dramatist is tantamount to understanding his work and the subsequent dramatic and theatrical movement he initiated is the premise of this study. Since Søren Kierkegaard's existential view — a way of life based on decision — is the frame of reference by which the dramatic art of Henrik Ibsen is being considered, some of the terminology used in this study has its essence in Kierkegaard's philosophy and requires qualification.

Within the title of this work, *HENRIK IBSEN'S THEATRE AESTHETIC AND DRAMATIC ART: A Reflection of Kierkegaardian Consciousness — Its Significance for Modern Dramatic Interpretation and the American Theatre*, two words, *reflection* and *consciousness*, have a special significance that recurs throughout the study.

The word *reflection* refers to a Kierkegaardian idea which presupposes more than the mirror image that the word suggests. Georg Brandes describes it as the mirror chamber

11

which has repeated reflections psychologically applied. Reflection goes beyond a persuasion that Henrik Ibsen's dramatic work simply parallels Kierkegaardian categories and concepts. Rather, the correspondence indicated is an expression of the inward,[8] that something is hidden. Although there is a correspondence in the authorship that indicates perfect understanding, there is endless difference. A further consideration is that Kierkegaard conceived of reflection as an active entity which involved the awakening and the sharpening of thought. The nature of reflection is that its time is before action, and it sets all the elements in motion. In referring to reflection as a "gadfly" and saying of reflections that they must turn the comfortable way of thinking topsy-turvy in the dialectic of the truth, Kierkegaard brings into focus a significant feature of his own work and that of Ibsen when he claims that in the sphere of reflection everything is done inversely.

Consciousness refers to a property of the soul, the imagination, which Kierkegaard considered to be *instar omnium*.* With Kierkegaard, consciousness is a movement of becoming;[9] the movement is reflected in the metamorphosis of the individual, the movement Ibsen highlights in moments of personal confrontation when the individual can come face to face with himself. Broader than thought, consciousness suggests an awareness of one's own existence, of the inmost part of the human soul. It is not a romantic idea but has its manifestation in reality. There are two facets to the Kierkegaardian consciousness, the finite and the infinite. For this reason consciousness is opposition, the opposition between the finite and infinite. It is a trinity because of the "I" presence. Going beyond thought, consciousness has an energy which when released generates change, the change occurring when the sum-total of the concentration is maximal.

Whereas the intention of this interpretation is to focus on

---

* worth all of them

12

Henrik Ibsen's work so as to reveal the nature of his art as a reflection of a special kind of inner consciousness, it is the category of *Øieblikket,* that moment of actuality when man is "in and out of time," that is to be the apex of the study. *Øieblikket* is the Archimedean point from which all is possible, the point from which he could lift the whole world, the point which for that very reason must lie outside the world, outside the limitation of time and space. Related to that moment of being are two essential and related categories: *den Enkelte* and *Ofringen.** They are categories which lend themselves to theatrical expression, the singular nature of each category projecting a stage image that is definitive and alien because of its individuality; the images disturb the audience. Each of Ibsen's plays center on the effort to awaken the individual to a sense of self, to the importance of the individual in contrast to the public, a thought Kierkegaard felt contained an entire philosophy of life and the world, and this awakened individual is hated by all; "at slaae ham ihjel ansees for en Gudsdyrkelse."** The nature of the sacrifice he says does not interest the world, changes with Ibsen from a naive symbol to an explicit act that has a more sophisticated intention. It also becomes the link through which one achieves a sense of contemporaneity with the past.

Other categories essential to this study are *Existents-Sphaerer, Valget, Springet, Metamorfose, Gjentagelsen,* and *Øieblikket,** and such concepts as truth, faith, love, hypocrisy, doubt, dread, despair, illusion, delusion, and absurd — the concepts will be demonstrated in connection with the how and the why of their relationship to *Øieblikket.* In addition, the relationship of specific vocabulary as is introduced

---

* the Individual and the Sacrifice
** "To put him to death is regarded as a divine service."
* Spheres of existence, the Choice, the Leap, Metamorphosis, Repetition, the Moment.

13

in connection with maieutic communication — the masses, paganism, Christianity, Christendom, existentialism, Socrates, the eternal — will be articulated. However, it is from the category of *Øieblikket* that transition will be effected to the American, Scandinavian and European dramatic scene.

Biographical Sketch

Søren Aabye Kierkegaard — *Henrik Johann Ibsen*

Søren Kierkegaard was born in 1813 and died in 1855; Henrik Ibsen was born in 1828 and died in 1906. Their existence overlapped briefly. But, by the time Ibsen had published his first play, *Catilina*, in 1850, the major portion of Kierkegaard's work had been written. By 1855, most of Kierkegaard's authorship had been published. The exceptions: *Synspunktet for min Forfatter — Virksomhed*, which was published in 1859 (posthumously); *Dømmer Selv!* in 1876; *Papirer*, eight volumes of his writings, were published between 1869 and 1881. Letters and documents were not printed until 1953 and there are even more papers and letters in the Royal Library.[10]

Gerhard Gran observes in his study of Ibsen that, in 1866, at the time *Brand* was published, *Staadier paa Livets Vei* (1845), *Enten-Eller* (1843), and *Øieblikket* (1855) had impregnated the intellectual atmosphere, not only in Denmark, but in Norway also. He writes that no author was cited, discussed, and made to appear foolish as was Kierkegaard.[11]

Ibsen was to remain firm in his assertion that he had read little of Kierkegaard and understood less. Yet, his poem

15

"Paa Vidderne" (1859) and his plays: *Kjaerlighedens Komedie* (1862), *Brand* (1866), *Peer Gynt* (1867), and *Kejser og Galilaeer* (1873), *Gengangere* (1881), *En Folkefiende* (1882), *Fruen fra Havet* (1888), *Bygmester Solness* (1892), are overtly Kierkegaardian.

Although it is not the intention in this study of Henrik Ibsen's dramatic art to determine if Ibsen was influenced by Kierkegaard, it is of interest that his friend, Georg Brandes, a Danish critic, who wrote the first book about Kierkegaard in 1877, believed that Ibsen followed in Kierkegaard's footsteps.[12] Magdalene Thoresen, a prominent woman in literary circles, closely associated with Ibsen through his marriage to her step-daughter, was an avid reader of Kierkegaard. In a letter to Miss Wiehe in 1877, she wrote that she "laeser ingen hellere end ham (Kierkegaard)."*[13] She also compares Ibsen's personal idiosyncrasies to Kierkegaard's. Before Ibsen was celebrated, Magdalene Thoresen did not regard him highly, confiding to Brandes that his writing was as flat as a drawing. She thought that he ought to be more than a collaborator of Kierkegaard.[14]

Other connections indicate that Ibsen was aware of Kierkegaardian ideas — Pastor Lammers of Skien who may have been a model for Brand had close contact with Ibsen's mother and sister; Christopher Brun, a theological student with whom Ibsen spent some time in Rome (the winter of 1864-65), held views similar to Kierkegaard.[15] In Grimstad, Ibsen read *Enten-Eller* (and other writings by Kierkegaard). In it there is a critique of Scribe's *Les Premières Amours (Den Første Kjaerlighed — The First Love)*[16] and an important essay on *Don Giovanni,* an opera Ibsen was to attend during his Copenhagen theatre-study tour in 1852. Most persuasive of these secondary references is a letter written by Edvard Grieg to Ibsen concerning *Brand.* In it, he writes,

---

* "prefers to read nothing but him"

17

Det er underligt med Sandheden, givet i Poesi kan
Folk taale den, den gaar En ikke naermere ind paa
Livet end at man kan nyde den, i ren Prosa derimod,
som Kierkegaard har sagt den, er den for skarp,
for naesevis.*¹⁷

Ibsen's views on the borrowing of sources, or of others
pointing out such borrowings, he has expressed in the second
edition of *Gildet paa Solhoug* (written in 1856, preface 1883);
"Det, der gør et kunstvaerk til sin ophavsmands åndelige
ejendom, det er, at han har påtrykt vaerket sin egen personligheds stempel."** A letter from Ibsen to Frederik Hegel in
1866, rejects the assumption that it was Søren Kierkegaard
that he had in mind when he wrote *Brand*. As he expresses it,
the presentation of ideas will always possess certain points of
resemblance to the story of Kierkegaard.¹⁸

In that Ibsen's aesthetic sensibility bears the weight of this
study, it is Ibsen and Kierkegaard's "personligheds stempel"
that has interest. The author's personality is the factor that is
added in great works of art according to Frithiof Brandt in his
writing about the young Søren Kierkegaard in 1892. For
Kierkegaard, the personality exhibits itself in the form and the
content of a work of art. It is the residue that remains when
the rest has been filtered off.¹⁹ Consequently, to understand
something of what gave birth to each man's personal scenario
and to understand a little of the problems they had as mature
men, it is to their formative years that attention will be given.
These are the years that Ibsen contrasted so vividly in the
characterizations of Brand and Peer Gynt.

W. H. Auden writes in his introduction to *Brand* (and he
credits his observation to Ibsen) that the condition of child-

---

* "Isn't it a strange thing about the truth — when presented in poetic
form, we can endure it; it does not come too close to prevent enjoyment;
on the other hand, in prose, such as Kierkegaard uses it, it is hard and
aggressive."
** "What makes a work of art its creator's spiritual property is the
fact that he has impressed upon it his own personality." (Fortale til
Anden Udgave, 1883)

hood that most poets experience is isolation from the social group and a playmate, the nature of the condition Ibsen was to dramatize with many of his characters: Brand, Peer, Hedvig, Lille Eyolf, and to suggest in others.[20]

Kierkegaard's and Ibsen's childhood were also to remain outside their peer group, and like the children in Ibsen's plays, they were often taunted by their contemporaries. The way in which Kierkegaard and Ibsen were to respond to the insensitivity directed at them was to develop their inner resources. Differences between Kierkegaard's and Ibsen's childhood were not as radical as those that separated the stoic Brand and the irrepressible Peer, who in some ways are caricatures of states of existence Kierkegaard and Ibsen claimed they had experienced or had "gjennemlevede."*[21] It is in terms of mental stimulation and economics that the most significant distinction in their childhood lies.

Kierkegaard's father was fifty-seven years old when Søren Kierkegaard, the youngest of seven children, was born, and according to his own notes, he was not a robust child.[22] Brought up in a Christianity which emphasized the sufferings of Christ, living with a parent who was self-willed, well-read and preoccupied with spiritual matters and a somber view of life had its effect. In *Synspunktet,* he speaks of having been richly endowed mentally and living in comfortable circumstances but that melancholia was always with him, "Imidlertid maa dette dog forstaaes saaledes, at jeg meget tidlig var indviet i den Tanke, at det at seire er at seire i uendelig Forstand, hvilket i endelig Forstand er at lide."** His mother was Michael Pedersen Kierkegaard's second wife, forty-five years old when Kierkegaard was born. Prior to her marriage, Ane Sørensdatter Lund had been the housekeeper in the Kierke-

---

* "lived through"

** "This (melancholy) however, must be understood in connection with the fact that I was very early initiated into the thought that to conquer means to conquer in an infinite sense, which in a finite sense means to suffer."

19

gaard household; little is written about her by Kierkegaard or by biographers. During his childhood, Kierkegaard's father kept a tight rein on him, imposing a discipline that Kierkegaard was later to regard as fortunate in that it gave him the habit of self-control, a habit he regarded as necessary to writing. He writes in *Synspunktet* that his childhood predisposed him step by step to become the kind of author he did become. In regard to school, his father expected him to work hard and to produce superior work.

Although personal freedom was restricted, in that he was not even permitted to go for a walk alone, Kierkegaard enjoyed a freedom of another sort. He and his father went on make-believe walks in the study, during which time they discussed philosophy. But, even more stimulating than their discussions was the father's imagination which was boundless; he would fantasize in minute detail the imaginary journeys the two would take. The stratagem recalls Lars Forsell's play of the 1960's, *Söndagspromenaden*.* However, Justus' imaginary trips

---

* *Sunday Promenade.*

20

21

with his family around the dining-room table every Sunday reflect a 20th century current, the plight of the disengaged man,[23] rather than the individualist.

An unfinished metaphysical essay written by Kierkegaard in 1842-43 "De omnibus dubitandum est"* contains a description of Johannes Climacus which is considered by George T. Flom to be autobiographical.[24] Johannes describes how his father's sense of the dramatic overwhelmed him, "Hvad før foregik episk, det skete nu dramatisk; de samtalede paa Touren."** It seemed to Johannes that he was witnessing a world coming into being. In his maturity, Kierkegaard was to continue to see pictures in his imagination, not in reality; it was as if pictorial presentation of itself lacked substance. Something was needed to stimulate his interest. That other quality he expresses in reference to the nature of the difference between a drawing rendered by an artist and one rendered by a non-artist, the difference lying in the perspective. The same idea was presented by Ibsen in his poem "Paa Vidderne." For an art work to have reality, Kierkegaard had to see it poetically and from a perspective in which the mind and the eye are one, in existence, as on a stage.

The all-powerful imagination of the father engaged itself in dialectics of a kind that was impressive. Kierkegaard's pseudonym, Johannes of the essay, narrates one instance wherein the father's procedure is presented. In an argument, he would give his opponent every opportunity to speak, then he would ask his adversary if there was anything more that he wished to add. When he was absolutely certain that nothing further was to be added, "i Haandevending var Alt anderledes"*** — everything would be changed. With the father's

---

* "Everything must be doubted" from Descartes' *Principles of Philosophy*.

** "A dramatic representation supplanted for the former epic narrative; for they conversed on the way."

*** "In a twinkling of the eye all was different" (idiomatic expression meaning "before you could say knife").

22

response, everything became clear: the things that had seemed positive no longer were, and those that were doubtful became certain. Johannes, reflecting upon the imaginative/mental stimulus his father gave him, recognized that what other children possessed in the enchantment of poetry and the surprise of adventure, he had in the calm of a vivid intuition and the swiftly changing perspectives of a dialectic.

Kierkegaard's attraction to drama and theatre was not impeded by his propensity to see "in the mind's eye." Rather, the curious combination of the imaginative and the dialectic heightened his enjoyment and enabled him to give conceptual significance to his writings on the mimetic art. Further, the simultaneous presentation of the aesthetic and the religious was to become a significant aspect of his authorship.

Ibsen's childhood was not as strictly controlled as was Kierkegaard's, and although a religious tradition was upheld, it was not rigidly practiced. Henry Jaeger speaks of the imposing church in the square and the religious nature of the community that Ibsen lived in as a child; the house where he was born, "Stockmansgaard" was located opposite the church. Unlike Kierkegaard, Ibsen was the second child in the family, assuming the role of the eldest upon his brother's death three weeks after Ibsen was born. Jaeger writes that Ibsen felt himself to be an outsider from an early age. In the first years of his life, Ibsen had enjoyed advantages but when he was eight years old, his father who had been a well-to-do merchant (as Kierkegaard's father also had been) over-extended himself and lost his assets. The family moved to a decrepit farm property outside of Skien (Venstøp) where they lived in comparative seclusion. After the 1835 economic setback, the father changed from a charming extrovert (who enjoyed storytelling) to an embittered individual with whom Ibsen had little in common, while the mother, said to have had an artistic nature and a talent for painting, led a lonely existence. Writing to Hedvig after his mother's death, Ibsen expressed tenderness for her.

23

Hans Heiberg points out that events in Ibsen's life which occurred between the ages of seven and fifteen are little known, but he does refer to Ibsen's puppet theatre, his silence, his bribing farm boys not to walk with him, and his ability to verbally subdue his tormenters when the necessity presented itself — the latter talent Kierkegaard also possessed. Other instances of Ibsen's childhood interests are mentioned by Jaeger; the long hours alone reading, with special attention directed to Harrison's *History of London,* a book which was

to find its way into the set of *Vildanden;* the practicing of magic, actually giving performances; constructing characters and sets; building a fort; painting.[25] Clare Thue Ebbell points out that Ibsen read the Bible and the King's sagas, his favorite refuge a little room off the kitchen.[26]

Instead of the stimulating companion that Kierkegaard had in his father, Ibsen had to rely on himself, creating his own private world, even though he found some companionship with his sister, Hedvig. The school he attended was a private secondary school which had been started by Johan Hansen and W. F. Stockfleth. [27] He was not to follow the bourgeois route of the traditional schooling and preparation for the university as Kierkegaard had.[28] At the age of sixteen, Ibsen left school, becoming an apprentice to a Grimstad apothecary. During the Grimstad period, he studied for the University

24

examinations, wrote poems (some sonnets about the war between Germany and Denmark), drew caricatures of the locals,
painted, and it was in Grimstad that the seed of his first play,
Catilina, was born (the result of his reading Sallust's *Catiline*
and Cicero's orations against Catiline).

Unlike Kierkegaard, Ibsen was not to attend the University
(did not pass his examinations in the required way) and his
career took a more practical, yet artistic bent — as writer,
theatre director, designer and amateur painter. The object (or
purpose) in referring to Kierkegaard's and Ibsen's formative
years as a prelude to presenting the Chronology that follows,
is to show the direction that their careers were to take. Even

25

though Ibsen was deterred by the financial aspect of his family's situation, his interest and Kierkegaard's were in a similar direction, though in a different form.

During his lifetime, Kierkegaard was an inveterate patron of Det Kongelige Teater in København, enjoying the company of the most significant names in the "golden age" at the royal theatre, some of the people Ibsen was later to have contact with under other circumstances. Theatre was an important part of Kierkegaard's life, with attendance not simply confined to the theatre in København. Through the voice of Constantine Constantius, his alter ego in *Gjentagelsen*, Kierkegaard reveals his acquaintance with Berlin's three theatres: the Opera House, the Dramatic Theatre and the Konigstadter Theatre, the latter receiving artistic and conceptual emphasis in his writings.[29]

Theatrical troupes visited the scenes of Ibsen's youth, but it was not until he came to Kristiania that he was to become immersed in the theatre. In 1850, after his first play was staged, *Kjaempehøien*, he was issued a seasonal pass to the Kristiania theatre. Later he was to become part of Det norske Theater in Bergen and in Kristiania, and as director, he was involved in selecting the repertoire. During his study tour in København in 1852, Ibsen responded enthusiastically to the same theatrical milieu that Kierkegaard had earlier, meeting the actress Johanne Luise Heiberg and her husband, Johan Ludvig; she was later to be instrumental in seeing Ibsen's plays staged in Denmark and it was he who introduced Ibsen to some of the more sophisticated techniques of theatre.[30] The interest that Kierkegaard and Ibsen shared in the theatre extended to written criticism of the mimetic art.

At one point in his lifetime, Georg Brandes wrote to Ibsen that he considered Ibsen to be the Master, and himself the Squire, an analogy that is not inappropriate in connection with Kierkegaard and Ibsen. It is Kierkegaard who is the Master in reference to philosophical concepts, existentially conceived, those concepts that Ibsen articulates in dramatic

26

form, but, happily, with a difference. Kierkegaard would want everyone to be free in relationship to himself, "befrygtende at blive til Latter ved Repetenterne; et eftersnakkende Ecchos saedvanlige Gjengivelse af det sagte."* Sometimes Ibsen, as the Master dramatist, gives a Kierkegaardian idea a deeper dimension by dramatizing a unique point of view, "et nyt Hvorledes af det gamle Hvad."**[31]

Kierkegaard, in his Master's dissertation, *Om Begrebet Ironi*,*** uses the expression "Opfattelsens Virkeliggjørelse"**** referring to philosophy as activity opposed to theory. Intermittently in his works, Kierkegaard has expressed a wish for a poet who could present his existential view, a poet who might resolve to prefer such situations, rather than stuff and nonsense[32] (the situational reference being the Divine command that Abraham sacrifice Isaac), asking himself where could a poet be found who would be able to relate what the two talked about on the way to Mount Moriah, concluding his thought with the lament that in his age the probability of encountering a poet with a presentiment of such collisions would be unlikely. An early play in 1838,[33] written the year of his father's death, did not lead Kierkegaard to use the dramatic *genre* to present his existential vision, although he did use dialogue frequently in his exposition.

But Kierkegaard drew heavily upon the theatre and drama in his authorship (and even jested about joining a company of traveling players in *Enten-Eller*),[34] which might suggest the supreme paradox, since he considered most art to be in the aesthetic sphere, the sphere of existence he rejected; however, the simultaneous presentation of aesthetic and religious works constitutes a vital part of his stratagem. To captivate a reader

---

* "fearing to be made ridiculous through repetitioners who produce what is said like a prattling Echo."
** "a new how of an old what"
*** *The concept of Irony*
**** "the conception made actual"

28

with the aesthetic and then introduce the religious swiftly compelled him to take notice. With the ethical stance Kierkegaard had introduced choice, the basis of conflict, and with the religious, the absurd, "to be or not to be." Through the theatre, the honesty of the art form, and the "imitation of an action" he had a natural deception with which to articulate the truth. Kierkegaard had objected to Goethe as a poet, finding in him a representative of the characterlessness of the age (the hypocrisy of men). He is described as a poet who used the ethical idea for his own profit. Ibsen, like Pascal, whom Kierkegaard admired, wore the hair shirt of humility. A glance at the Chronology confirms the fact that he was subject to one humility after another. Although Ibsen may not be the poet that Kierkegaard hoped for, he is the dramatist who dramatized an existential view which presented "such situations rather than stuff and nonsense."

In one sense Kierkegaard and Ibsen are an inverse image of one another, each using the other's calling or vocation for his own design, each corroborating the aesthetics that Jacques Maritain posits when he voices the idea of creative intuition as a product of the practical intellect. Maritain differentiates between the speculative and the practical intellect, the first knows only for the sake of knowledge to be grasped while the object of the second is human activity and human tasks to be achieved, not Being to be grasped. The practical intellect immerses itself in creativity and molds intellectually that which will be brought into being.[35]

The Chronology points out the relative security of Kierkegaard's early years as opposed to the economical upheaval that made it necessary for Ibsen to become an apprentice in his adolescence. Kierkegaard admits to the economical advantage he enjoyed, realizing that his freedom from care and trouble enabled him to concentrate upon his work. However, he considered it a misunderstanding to take that to mean he was insensible to suffering that was not self-imposed.

In addition, the Chronology indicates the ceaseless activity

29

each author engaged in, with Ibsen's constant need of sustenance juxtaposed against his creative productivity. In terms of quantity, his authorship is considerably less than Kierkegaard's, especially startling when it is taken into account that Kierkegaard died at the age of forty-two, the age when Ibsen was beginning to get a foothold in his profession. While Ibsen was to travel to various countries, and to live abroad for many years, Kierkegaard was to have three trips to Germany, living the rest of his time in Denmark. Yet, there is a comparable sophistication in their authorship. The total dedication to work that Kierkegaard imposed upon himself is expressed by the exclusion of personal ties and the renunciation of the girl he loved, Regine Olsen, which does not correspond to Ibsen's marriage and parenthood, and a family life that was to be supportive of his work, if not personally fulfilling.

The effects of emotional upheavals, the disappointments and the sorrows each man lived through can only be surmised. In their authorship, however, a consonance of thought and an individuality of vision is reflected that has a significance to the interpretative focus which will be used in the consideration of Henrik Ibsen's drama.

Chronology

Søren Aabye Kierkegaard 1813-1855

I. The Beginnings — 1813-1840

1813	May 5	Søren Aabye Kierkegaard is born; Nytorv, Copenhagen.
1821		School in Copenhagen, Borgerdydskole.
1828	April 20	Confirmed by J. P. Mynster, who becomes subject of attack. Upon his death in 1854, Kierkegaard became incensed with Professor Martensen's eulogy to Mynster in which he called him a witness for the truth.
1830	Oct. 30	Student at the University of Copenhagen.
	Nov. 1	Enters Royal Life Guards (drafted).
	Nov. 4	Discharged as unfit for service.
1831	April 25	Completes the first part of the second examination (Latin, Greek, *magna cum laude;* mathematics, *summa cum laude*).
1834	July 31	Mother dies.
	Dec. 17	First article published in *Kjøbenhavns Flyvende Post.*

| | | 29 | Sister, Petrea, dies. |

1837   May   Meets Regine Olsen (age fourteen years).

1837-38   Begins teaching Latin at the Borger-dydskole — 1 semester.

1838   Writes play *Striden mellem den gamle og den Saebekielder*, a satirical play; the hero, Willibald, is thought to be Søren Kierkegaard.

1838   May 19   "The Great Earthquake" was a traumatic event, concerns his father's boyhood curse, hurled at God. Kierkegaard's dissipation prior to his father's death is attributed to this knowledge; he was also disturbed by his father's belief that God's curse lay on the family.

       Aug. 9   Father dies (Michael Pedersen Kierkegaard). It had sobering effects on him.

       Sept. 7   *Af en endnu Levendes Papirer* (*From the Papers of One Still Living*) is published against his will (criticism of H. C. Andersen's novel *Kun En Spillemand* [*Only a Fiddler*]). The novel describes a genius and his development. Kierkegaard writes that the hero is a weakling because genius is not something that can be blown out by a wind; rather it is a raging fire which the storm fans.
Kierkegaard uses his own name as author.

1839   Aug.   Inherits Rd. 31,000.

1840   July 3   Completes his theology examination (for degree) *magna cum laude*.

   July 19-Aug. 6   Journey to Jutland.

       Sept. 10   Engagement to Regine Olsen.

II. The Fullness of Time — 1841-1855

1841   Jan. 12   Preaches his first sermon.

July 16   Dissertation for Master of Arts Degree accepted. Title *Om Begrebet Ironi med stadigt Hensyn til Socrates* (*The Concept of Irony with Constant Reference to Socrates*). Degree is equivalent to Doctoral degree.

Sept. 16   Dissertation printed; Sept. 29 defends it (written in Danish, defended in Latin).

1841   Oct. 11   Breaks engagement with Regine, returns ring.

Oct. 25   Leaves for Berlin — attends Schelling's lectures and theatre. (Schelling engaged in demolishing Hegelian system.) He writes about the theatre in *Gjentagelsen*.

1842   Mar. 6   Returns to Copenhagen.

Nov. 11   Brother, Peter, ordained.

1843   Feb. 20   *Enten-Eller* (*Either-Or*), ed. by Victor Eremita, published. First use of pseudonym in published work. The book established him as a powerful and an original writer. In *Papirer* (*Journals*) 1852, he writes that the *Either* means the enjoyment of life in the unbridled sense. Whereas he showed marriage as *Or*, but it was not his life's *Or*.

May 8   Leaves for Berlin for a short visit.

16   *To opbyggelige Taler* (*Two Edifying Discourses*) by S. Kierkegaard, published. *Opbyggelige Taler* are edifying or uplifting discourses. They are unpreached sermons, written for men and women to speak aloud to themselves; they are directed to an audience who read and pondered what they read.

Oct. 16		*Gjentagelsen (Repetition)* by Constantine Constantius also referred to as an experiment in experimental psychology. It concerns the category of repetition. *Frygt og Baeven (Fear and Trembling)* by Johannes de Silentio. It contains four versions of Abraham's trial. *Tre opbyggelige Taler (Three Edifying Discourses)* by S. Kierkegaard published.
Dec. 6		*Fire opbyggelige Taler (Four Edifying Discourses)* by S. Kierkegaard, published.
1844	Feb. 24	Preaches terminal sermon in Trinitatis Church.
	Mar. 5	*To opbyggelige Taler (Two Edifying Discourses)* by S. Kierkegaard, published.
	June 8-13	*Tre opbyggelige Taler (Three Edifying Discourses)* by S. Kierkegaard, published. *Philosophiske Smuler (Philosophical Fragments)* by Johannes Climacus, published. He says that he hoped to show that contemporaneity was of no avail because in all eternity there can be no direct transition from the historical to the eternal.
	17	*Begrebet Angest (The Concept of Dread)* by Vigilius Haufniensis defines the idea of *angest* and analyzes his spiritual attitude with reference to sin and sexuality. Despair is theme.
	Aug. 31	*Fire opbyggelige Taler (Four Edifying Discourses)* by S. Kierkegaard, published.
	Oct. 16	Moves from Nørregade 230 to his house on Nytorv 2.

1845	Apr. 29	*Tre Taler ved taenkte Leiligheder* (*Three Discourses on Imagined Occasions*) by S. Kierkegaard.
		Staadier paa Livets Vei (*Stages on Life's Way*) edited by Hilarius Bogbinder, published. Presents aesthetic, ethical and religious spheres of existence.
	May	*Atten opbyggelige Taler* (*Eighteen Edifying Discourses*) (1842-43) by S. Kierkegaard, published.
	Dec. 27	*Corsaren* (*The Corsair*) by Frater Taciturnus, published in *Faedrelandet* (newspaper managed by Goldschmidt which ridiculed distinguished men of Denmark).
1846	Jan. 2	First attack on S.K. in *Corsaren*.
	10	S.K.'s reply as Frater Taciturnus in *Faedrelandet*.
	Feb. 7	Considers qualifying himself for ordination.
1846	Feb. 27	*Afsluttende uvidenskabelig Efterskrift* (*Concluding Unscientific Postcript*) by Johannes Climacus and edited by S. Kierkegaard, published — "the problem of his authorship" is presented.
	Mar. 30	*En literair Anmeldelse* (*A Literary Review*) by S. Kierkegaard, published, contains "Nutiden" ("The Present Age").
	May 2-16	Visit to Berlin.
1847	Jan. 24	*Bogen om Adler* (*Book on Adler*) in its first form.
	Dec. 1	*Bogen om Adler* completed in its third form. Kierkegaard was reluctant to publish it because it dealt with a priest against whom he felt no animosity.

The longest part of the book was published in 1849 as one of the *Tvende ethisk-religeuse Smaa Afhandlinger* by H.H. (*Two Minor Ethics — Religious Essays*).

Mar. 13   *Opbyggelige Taler i forskjellig Aand (Edifying Discourses of Varied Tenor)* by S. Kierkegaard, published.

Sept. 29   *Kjerlighedens Gjerninger (Works of Love)* by S. Kierkegaard, published. In "Forord," he says that these are Christian reflections; therefore, they are not about love, but are about *works* of love.

Nov. 3   Regine Olsen marries Johan Frederik Schlegel. K. considered her marriage as the repetition for him in that he again received everything double, that he recovered himself again in a way that made him realize the significance of it (not a religious repetition).

Dec. 24   Sells house, 2 Nytorv.

1848   Jan. 28   Leaves apartment.

April 26   *Christelige Taler (Christian Discourses)* by S. Kierkegaard, published. He says his aim is for the hearer to test his life, to be observant of where he is.

1848   July 24-27   *Krisen og en Krise i en Skuespillerindes Liv (The Crisis and a Crisis in the Life of an Actress)* by Inter et Inter, published (his last aesthetic work). It is a tribute to Fru Heiberg although her name is not mentioned.

Sept. 1   Preaches in Vor Frue Kirke.

Nov.   *Synspunktet for min Forfatter — Virksomhed (The Point of View for My Work as an Author)* by S. Kierkegaard considered finished, published by his brother in 1859. (Explanation of his authorship.) *Den bevaebnede Neutralitet (Armed Neutrality)* by S. Kierkegaard, written toward the end of 1848 and the beginning of 1849, but not published. (His position as a Christian author in Christendom.) Preserved in *Papirer.*)

1849   May 14   Second edition of *Enten-Eller* published. *Lilien paa Marken og Fuglen under Himlen (The Lilies in the Field and the Birds in the Air)* by S. Kierkegaard, published.

       May 19   *Tvende ethisk-religieuse Smaa Afhandlinger (Two Minor Ethics — Religious Essays)* by H.H., published.

       July 30   *Sygdommen til Døden (Sickness Unto Death)* by Anti-Climacus, published by S. Kierkegaard. (A Christian psychological exposition for edification or awakening. The sickness unto death is despair.)

       Nov. 13   *Ypperstepraesten (The High Priest) — Tolderen (The Publican) — Synderinden (The Woman Who Was a Sinner)* by S. Kierkegaard, published. Three discourses at the Communion on Fridays.

1850   April 18   Moves to Nørregarde 43 (now 35), Copenhagen.

       Sept. 10   *Til Selvprøvelse (For Self-Examination),* by S. Kierkegaard.

       Sept. 27   *Indøvelse i Christendom (Training in Christianity)* by Anti-Climacus, S. Kierkegaard, ed.

       Dec. 20   *En opbyggelige Tale (An Edifying Discourse)* by S. Kierkegaard, published.

1851	Jan. 31	*Brev til . . . Dr. Rudelbach (Letter to Dr. Rudelbach)* by S. Kierkegaard, published. Constitutes the beginning of a direct critique of the establishment.
	Aug. 7	*Om min Forfatter — Virksomhed (On My Work as an Author)* by S. Kierkegaard, published. (A statement on his work.) *To Taler ved Altergangen om Fredagen (Two Discourses at Communion on Friday)* by S. Kierkegaard, published.
	Sept. 10	*Til Selvprøvelse* by S. Kierkegaard, published. The book is commended to this age; in the preface he asks reader to read the book aloud. In 1847 in *Papirer* he wrote something about his punctuation, admits to a special feeling for rhetoric and his practice of reading aloud. He points out that punctuation has to consider irony, epigram, subtlety, as well as the rhythm of the sentence.
1851-52		*Dømmer selv (Judge for Yourself)* by S. Kierkegaard, published posthumously, 1876. (The second part of *Til Selvprøvelse.*)
1854	Jan. 30	Death of Bishop Mynster.
	April 15	H. H. Martensen named Bishop.
	Dec. 18	The article against Martensen published. "Var Biskop Mynster et Sandhedsvidne?" (Was Bishop Mynster a Witness for the Truth?) *Faedrelandet (The Fatherland)*, Mandag d.18 Dec. 1854, published.
1855	Jan.-May	Articles generated by attack on Martensen.
	May 24	*Øieblikket* 1-9.

June 16	*Hvad Christus dømmer om* (*What Christ's Judgment is About*) by S. Kierkegaard, published.
Sept. 13	*Guds Uforanderlighed* (*The Unchangeableness of God*) by S. Kierkegaard, published.
Sept. 25	(Issue 10 published posthumously.)
Nov. 11	Dies.[36]

Chronology

Henrik Johann Ibsen 1828-1906

I. The Beginnings — 1828-1850

1828	March 20	Henrik Johann Ibsen is born in Skien (a small town sixty miles southwest of Kristiania).
1832-3		Family moves from Stockmansgaard (the Stockman's Building) to a more expensive home (also in Skien), the Hundevad estate.
1834		Father, Knud Ibsen, has financial difficulties.
1835		Knud loses assets, economically wiped out. The family moves to a farm property, Venstøp, outside of Skien. Danish theatrical troupes visit the community — plays by Eugene Scribe, Johan L. Heiberg, Adam Øehlenschläger presented.
1843		End of formal education, leaves secondary school (studied German, Humanities, and Bible).
	Oct. 1	He is confirmed in Gjerpen church in Venstöp parish.

		Family (mother nee Marichen Altenburg, father, five children) returns to Skien to live in Knud's half-brother's house.
	Dec. 27	Henrik leaves for Grimstad to become apothecary apprentice (small town on the south coast of Norway).
1844	Jan. 3	Ibsen arrives at Grimstad; apothecary is owned by a man named Reimann.
1846		Shop is sold. New owner moves apothecary to a better location; Ibsen promoted to assistant.
1846		Also studies for university exams. Reads Kierkegaard's *Enten-Eller* which contains analysis of Scribe's play, *Les Premières Amours* (*Den Første Kjaerlighed-The First Love*). Reads other works by Kierkegaard, and writers — Holberg, Øehlenschläger, Wergeland.
	Oct. 9	Illegitimate son is born to Ibsen by Else Sofie Borkedalen, housemaid, ten years older than Ibsen. Child's name is Hans Jacob Henriksen. Ibsen contributes to his support for the next fifteen years.
1847		"Resignation, his earliest extant poem, is written.[37]
1848		Visits family at Skien during vacation.
1849		Writes *Catilina*, 1st play — uses pseudonym of Brynjolf Bjarme (historical/psychological approach). Writes sonnet urging defense of Denmark (Germans marched into Denmark) "Vaagner Skandinaver" — manifesto to Norwegian and Swedish Brothers to wake up.
	Sept. 28	"I Høsten" ("In the Autumn"), his first poem to be published in *Kristiania-*

41

Posten under the same pseudonym he used with *Catilina.* Poetry said to be inspired by his love for Clara Ebell.

An oil painting of the pilot, Svend Hansen Haaø, gazing at the sea, is from this time. Ibsen was to acknowledge this work in 1894 as a painting he did during the Grimstad apprenticeship.

Also painted during this period is the religious painting discussed in Chapter IV, "Propheten Elias under en gyvelbusk i ørkenen" (The Prophet Elias under the juniper tree in the desert).

Writes verse play, *Normannerne* (paganism and Christianity), and starts a novel, *Fangen på Akershuus (The Prisoner of Akershuus),* to deal with Christian Lofthuus, Norwegian Leader of peasant rebellion.

Two years later, Ibsen was to write a poem "Paa Akershuus" ("At Akershuus").

Dec. 24   Management of Christiania Theater rejects *Catilina.*[38]

1850   Jan. 2   Official opening of the Bergen theatre with a performance of one of Holberg's comedies, *Den vaegelsindede (The Weathercock).* See: *Det Første Norske Teater* Bernt Lorentzen, s. 39.

April   Leaves Grimstad for Kristiania, visits his family for the last time.
Last poem in Grimstad — "Maaneskinsvandring efter et Bal" (Moonlight Promenade after a Ball).

12   *Catilina* published privately (250 copies), cost paid by friend he met in Grimstad, Ole Schulerud.

	28	Arrives in Kristiania, to prepare for University examinations at Heltberg's "Factory" — meets Bjørnstjerne Bjørnson there.

28   Arrives in Kristiania, to prepare for University examinations at Heltberg's "Factory" — meets Bjørnstjerne Bjørnson there.

Re-writes *Normannerne* as *Kjaempehøien* (*The Burial Mound*).

May 19   Completes a part of *Rypen i Justedal* (*The Ptarmigan in Justedal*).

August   Leaving school examination (Artium Examination).

Sept. 3   Results of matriculation Examinations — grades in Greek and Arithmetic unacceptable for university entrance. Attends lectures in literature and philosophy (some lectures given by Welhaven on Holberg).

Sept. 26   *Kjaempehøien* is staged at the Christiania Theater— his first play to be staged.

Sept.-Nov.   Free-lance writer.

Dec. 9   He is granted a free pass for the season — Christiania Theater.

Winter of 1850-51   Teaches at Thranite Movement's Sunday School — with friend Theodor Abildgaard.

II. The Fullness of Time 1851-1906

1851   Poems printed — "Ederfuglen" (The Eider Bird) and "Bergmanden" (The Miner). Journalistic activities: satirical newspaper *Andhrimner* (first known as *Manden*); Andhrimner was the name of the cook in Valhalla and the name given to the satirical periodical published by Ibsen and others. Also theatre articles for *Samfundsbladet* (hand-written periodical of Student's Union). Writes for *Arbeider-Forenin-*

43

gernes *Blad* (*The Journal of the Workingman's Societies*) whose purpose it was to shift aim of the labor movement from a revolutionary to a parliamentary one.

June 8   Writes *Norma eller en Politikers Kjaerlighed* (*Norma* or *A Politician's Love*), musik-tragedie, tre Akter, a parody of Storting members, inspired by Bellini opera — not intended for performance.

July   Poem "Helge Hundingsbane" (Helges Ungdom, Helge og Sigrun, Helges Død) (Helge's Youth, Helge and Sigrun, Helge's Death) appears in *Andhrimner*, uses pseudonym for last time.

Sept. 15   Free pass to theatre renewed.

Oct. 15   Concert by Student's Union — purpose to support Det norske Theater in Bergen. Ibsen wrote a prologue in verse.

Oct. 21   Arrives in Bergen to take up position at the Bergen theatre. (Engaged by Ole Bull)

Nov. 6   Begins assignment (resident dramatist).

1852   Jan. 2   Writes prologue for Foundation Day, Bergen Theatre (in verse).

April 15   Grant to study theatre conditions in Copenhagen, Berlin, Hamburg and Dresden. Goes to Hamburg first.

ca. 22   Copenhagen. Meets significant people in the theatre: Johan L. Heiberg, Director of Det Kongelige Teater; Th. Overskou, stage instructor at DKT; Johannes Luise Heiberg, leading actress; Michael Wiehe, great tragedian; Frederik Hoedt (founded new school of acting); Han Christian Andersen.

Attends the theatre: Sees Shakespeare

44

for the first time — *Hamlet, King Lear, Romeo and Juliet, As You Like It;* Holberg's Comedies — *Barselstuen (The Lying — In Room); Den Vegelsindede (Lucretia); Jacob von Tyboe; Pernilles Korte Frøkenstand (Pernilla's Brief Mistress-ship); Mester Geert Westphaler eller Den meget talende Barbeer (Master Geert Westphaler or the very talkative barber).* Also sees Øehlenschläger's tragedy, *Håkon Jarl (Earl Håkon);* Mozart's opera *Don Giovanni;* Heiberg's vaudeville *Nej (No);* a play by Henrik Hertz and one by Jens Christian Hostrup at the Casino Theatre on Amaliegade; also goes to Det Kongelige Hofteater at Kristiansborg. The repertoire included a play by Scribe and Legouve, *La Bataille des Dames,* a vaudeville by Fru Heiberg, and one by Henrietta Nielsen.

Possibly Ibsen read Hermann Hettner's *Das Moderne Drama* (written in 1851) at this time. Hettner turned against the drama of his day, favoring the Shakespearean model. He believed that the historical model should mask modern concerns and deal with psychological problems and he viewed the fairy tale play as a form that permitted truth and reality to exist alongside one another.

June 6 Dresden — more theatre activity. Money runs out.

August Returns to Bergen — is made stage manager.

Oct. 6 New season opens with Ibsen's production of Enevold de Falsen's *Drage-dukken.*

1853 Jan. 2 *Sancthansnatten (St. John's Eve),* fairy tale comedy that is in satirical, ballad style. Foreshadows *Kjaerlighedens Komedie* (*Love's Comedy*); has Kierkegaardian overtones, recalls *Midsummer Night's Dream* (Shakespeare). Published posthumously in *Efterladte Skrifter* (*Posthumous Writings*, 1909) because it was disowned by Ibsen.

	Spring	Romantic friendship with Rikke (Henrikke) Holst; writes poems for her: "Markblomster og Potteplanter" (Earth Flowers and Pot Plants), "Toget Til Ulrikken" (Trip to Uulrikken on 15 May 1853), "Til R:H!" (To R: H!)
1853		Revises *Kjaempehøien.*
1854	Jan. 2	First performance of the revised version performed — Foundation Day program.
1855	Jan. 2	*Fru Inger til Østeradd* (*Lady Inger*) play on 16th century Norway — titled historical play; removes "historisk" from title page of second edition — Foundation Day program.
	Nov. 27	Reads a paper on Shakespeare for Bergen literary Society. (Shakespeare's influence on Scandinavian Society.)
1856	Jan. 2	*Gildet paa Solhoug* — at Bergen — Foundation Day program.
	Jan. 7	Meets Suzannah Thoresen at home of her step-mother, Magdalene Thoresen.
	Mar. 2	Makes brief theatre visit with his company to Trondheim.
	April	Returns to Bergen; company remains to finish tour.
	Spring	Engagement to Suzannah.
	Summer	Walking tour with C. J. Anker in Western Norway (from Bergen to Hardanger back through Voss).

1857	Jan. 2	*Olaf Liljekrans* (rewritten from *Rypen i Justedal,* i.e., *The Ptarmigan in Justedal*) ballad play Bergen — Foundation Day.
	Feb. 2	Reads paper to literary society on the heroic ballad and its significance for modern poetry, subsequently published in *Illustreret Nyhedsblad* (*The Illustrated News Paper,* "Om Kjaempevisen og dens Betydning for Kunstpoesien."
	April	Contract is renewed, seeks leave in July.
	July	Appointed director of the Norwegian theatre Møllergaten, Kristiania.
	Sept. 3	Assumes duties as artistic director.
1858	June	Marries Suzannah Thoresen. Det Laerde Holland society formed (The Learned Holland) with friends.
	March 5	Det Kongelige Teater in Copenhagen rejects *Haermaendene paa Helgeland* — considers it crude.
	Nov. 24	Produces *Haermanendene* at Kristiania Norwegian theatre.
1859	Jan.	Publishes poems: "Paa Vidderne" ("On the Heights") is published in New Year Supplement to *Illustreret Nyhedsblad,* reflects Kierkegaardian pattern. Also published "I Billedgalleriet" (In the Picture Gallery).
	Dec. 23	Son, Sigurd is born.
	Nov.	He and Bjørnson form a Norwegian society. Principle aim was to combat Danish dramatic art in Norway.
1860		Starts writing *Svanhild* (a short prose version), later revised as *Kjaerlighedens Komedie.*

47

	Aug. 6	Applies for and is refused a travelling scholarship — six month study tour to London, Paris, larger German cities, Copenhagen and Stockholm.
1860-61		Winter. Attacked in the press, and by the Theatre Board for his lack of enterprise. He remains silent.
1861	Mar.-April	Publishes four articles in *Morgenbladet* (*The Morning Paper*) concerning the two theatres in Kristiania. Ibsen defends the policies of the Norwegian theatre and says that a national dramatic art is the goal.
	July 18	Sends opening scenes of opera libretto, *Fjeldfuglen* (*The Mountain Bird*), based on *Olaf Liljekrans,* to composer M. A. Udbye.
1862		Writes poem "Terje Vigen" (set during Napoleonic Wars, Norway blockaded). It is a poem about a sea captain who after much trepidation conquers his thirst for vengeance and even attains peace. There are forty-three stanzas, nine lines each. See entry of 1849 regarding an earlier painting on a similar subject. Ibsen's parentage can be traced back to a Danish sea-captain, Peter Ibsen. Ibsen's grandfather, also named Henrik, went down with his ship in 1798, near Grimstad, the scene of "Terje Vigen."
1862	Feb.	Poem is published in the New Year supplement to the *Illustreret Nyhedsblad.*
	Mar. 14	Applies for grant to study folklore in Western Norway (Hardanger, Sognfjord, Molde, Ronsdal).
	June 1	Norwegian theatre forced to close, financial reasons.

	June 24	Starts off on study tour — collects folktales, not published until 1936.
	Dec. 31	*Kjaerlighedens Komedie* published as a New Year supplement to *Illustreret Nyhedsblad.*
1863	Jan. 1	Appointed as artistic consultant to reorganize Christiania theatre, temporary appointment.
	Mar. 6	Applies for travel grant to tour districts north of Trondhjem for folktales, songs. Granted an award; uses money for support while working on *Kongs=Emnerne.*
	Mar. 10	Applies to Storting for annual grant; is refused.
	May 27	Applies for another grant — for a year's study in Rome and Paris (art history and literature). Awarded a grant.
	July 19	First biographical article on Ibsen is published in *Illustreret Nyhedsblad,* written by Paul Botten-Hansen.
	July-Aug.	Intense work on *Kongs=Emnerne.*
	Oct.	*Kongs=Emnerne* published.
	Dec. 13	Poem published, "'Til Norge," *Illustreret Nyhedsblad,* (under title "En Broder Nød!" — "A Brother in Need").
1864	Jan. 17	*Kongs=Emnerne* performed in Kristiania, produced by Ibsen.
		Dano-Prussian War — Germans invade Denmark. Failure of Sweden and Norway to come to Denmark's aid against Germany.
1864	April 5	Leaves Norway for Italy, settles in Rome around May 9. (En route stops at Copenhagen, goes to Lubeck and Berlin where he sees German victory parade; Vienna.)

49

	Summer	In Rome until the end of June, goes to the mountains for summer.
	Aug.	Is joined in Rome by Suzannah and Sigurd. He is impressed with classical art.
1865	Mar. 25	Applies for and receives another grant to complete work on *Brand*.
	Nov. 14	Enters publishing contract with Frederik Hegel, Gyldendal publishing house.
1866	Mar. 15	*Brand* published in Copenhagen by Gyldendal, as are all his later plays. *Brand* is his first popular success. (strong Kierkegaardian focus.)
	Apr. 30	Awarded a small grant by Royal Norwegian Scientific Association.
	May 12	Awarded an annual grant from the Norwegian Parliament.
	June-Sept.	In Frascati for summer.
	June 28	Receives a travel grant.
1867	Nov. 14	*Peer Gynt* published (considered [but is not] the antithesis of *Brand*).
	Oct.-Nov.	Returns to Rome from Sorrento by way of Pompeii and Naples.
1868	Summer	Middle of May — travels for five weeks (Florence, Bologna, Venice, Bolzano). Settles in Berchtesgaden for summer.
	Sept.	Munich.
	Oct.	Goes to live in Dresden.
1869		Works on *Kejser og Galilaeer*.
	June 3	Mother dies.
	July 3	Receives travel grant for the study of art and literature in Sweden.

	July 27-30	Attends Orthographic Convention. Is decorated by Carl XV with the Vasa Order in Stockholm.
	Sept.	Receives invitation to represent Norway at the opening of the Suez Canal.
	Sept. 30	*De unges forbund* is published, the last play with two different spellings.
	Oct.-Dec.	Sails from Marseilles, travels in Egypt, sails through Suez Canal.
	Mid. Dec.	Returns to Dresden via Paris.
1870	July 19	Leaves Dresden for Copenhagen. Franco-Prussian war breaks out. Remains in Copenhagen until October.
	Oct.	Returns to Dresden.
1871	Jan. 24	Receives Order of Dannebrog from Denmark.
	May 3	*Digte* — selected poems published.
1872		Working on *Kejser og Galilaeer*. Goes to Berchtesgaden for the summer.
	Sept.	Returns to Dresden.
1873		June-July — serves as judge at International Art exhibition in Vienna.
	July	Decorated — at the coronation of King Oskar II of Sweden and Norway. Made a Knight of St. Olaf.
	Oct. 16	*Kejser og Galilaeer* published.
	Nov. 24	*Kjaerlighedens Komedie* — first performance at Kristiania Theater.
1874	July 19	Arrives in Kristiania for a two and one half month visit.
	Aug.	Archeological convention in Stockholm.

51

	Sept. 10	Torchlight parade in his honor — by Kristiania students. Performance of *De unges forbund.*
1875	April	Moves to Munich — for son's education.
	Aug.	Summer in Tyrol.
	Oct.	Munich.
1876	Feb.	*Kejser og Galilaeer* translated into English by Catherine Ray — his first play into English.
	Feb. 24	*Peer Gynt* performed at Kristiania teater, music by Edvard Grieg.
	April 10	First play to be produced outside of Scandinavia (*Haermaendene paa Helgeland*), Court Theatre, Munich.
	June 3	Meiningen players perform *Kongs= Emnerne.* Guest at the Duke of Saxe-Meiningen's Court, decorated by Duke. (Bjørnstjerne Bjørnson had recommended the play.) The play is a vehicle for the Meiningen specialty — grouping and moving the crowds.
	Aug. 5	Summer in the Tyrol.
1877		Father dies.
	May	Associates with the Society of Crocodiles, Munich literary society.
	Sept. 6	Receives honorary doctoral degree from the University of Uppsala, Sweden. Back in Munich by end of month.
	Oct. 11	*Samfundets Støtter* published. Performed in September.
1878	Aug.	Moves to Rome for one year. Sigurd enters the university. (Some notes on modern tragedy written.)

52

1879	Dec. 4	*Et Dukkehjem* published.
	Dec. 21	Première, København.
1880	June 2	*Et Dukkehjem* adapted by Ibsen — 1880 — for German performance — forced on him because German actress would not perform the last act as written. Spends summer at Berchtesgaden.
	Nov.	Returns to Rome for the winter. Starts his memoirs. Son completes law degree.
	Dec. 15	*Samfundets Støtter* performed in London. First performance on an English stage.
1881	June 28	Summer in Sorrento. Works on *Gengangere*.
	Dec. 12	*Gengangere* published.
1882	May 20	World première *Gengangere* in Chicago.
	July	Son receives degree — Doctor of Law from The University of Rome.
	Nov. 28	*En Folkefiende* published. Summer in Gossensass and Tyroll.
1883	Aug. 28	First European performance of *Gengangere* produced by August Lindberg — Helsingsborg, Sweden.
1884	Nov. 11	*Vildanden* published.
1885	Jan. 9	*Vildanden* 1st performance in Bergen.
	June-Sept.	Visit to Norway: Kristiania, Trondhjem, Molde, Bergen.
	June 14	Speech to workers in Trondhjem.
	Oct.	Takes up residency in Munich (lives there 1885-91).

1886	Nov. 23	*Rosmersholm* published.
	Dec. 22	Guest of Duke Georg II of Meiningen for production of *Gengangere;* directed by the Duke; successful.[39] Receives decoration from the Duke — the Great Commander of the Saxon-Ernestine Order.
1887	Jan. 17	*Rosmersholm* produced by Bergen theatre — first performance.
	July.-Oct.	Visits Denmark and Sweden.
	Dec.	His publisher, Frederik Hegel, dies.
1888	Nov. 28	*Fruen fra Havet* published.
1889	Feb. 12	Première in Bergen of *Fruen fra Havet.*
	Mar. 3-15	Goes to Berlin and Weimer, is honored. Summer in Gossensass, meets Emile Bardach and Helene Raff.
	Oct.	Returns to Munich.
1890	July 18	George Bernard Shaw reads a paper before the Fabian Society in London on Ibsen.
	Dec. 16	*Hedda Gabler* published.
1891		Shaw lecture — *The Quintessence of Ibsenism* (i.e. expansion of 1890 paper) published.
	July-Oct.	Vacation in Norway. Decides to live in Norway again.
	Aug.	Meets pianist, Hildur Anderson.
	Oct. 9	Attends Knut Hamsun lectures in Kristiania. Hamsun attacks Ibsen for over-simplification of characters and using them for his polemics.
1892	Oct. 11	Son Sigurd marries Bjørnson's daughter.

54

	Dec. 12	*Bygmester Solness* published.
1893	Jan. 19	Première *Bygmester Solness* in Trond-hjem.
	July 11	Grandchild born.
1894	Jan. 12	*Lille Eyolf* published.
1895	Jan. 12	*Lille Eyolf* première at Deutsche Theater in Berlin.
	July	Moves for last time to 1 Arbin Street, Kristiania.
1896	Dec. 12	*John Gabriel Borkman* published.
1897		*John Gabriel Borkman* simultaneous première at the Swedish and the Finnish theatres in Helsinki.
	April 29	Son is refused professorship at The University of Kristiania.
1898		*Samlede Verker* appears in Denmark and Germany (first volume of his collected works).
	Mar. 20-	Seventieth birthday celebrated.
	April 16	Receives the Grand Cross of the Danneborg Order in Denmark and the Order of the North Star in Sweden. — Other honors and world wide recognition.
1899	July 14	Son appointed head of Foreign Office in Norway.
	Sept.	Attends the opening of Norway's first modern theatre — the National Theatre in Oslo.
	Dec. 19	*Når Vi Døde Vågner* published.

1900	Jan. 26	The first full production of *Når Vi Døde Vågner* — Stuttgart Court Theatre.
		Illness — erysipelas.
		Summer spent at sea resort.
1901		Suffers first stroke in Kristiania.
1903		Another stroke — unable to write or walk.
1906		May 23 dies.

Korrespondanceafbryder*

The Creative Consciousness

The Paradox:

Kierkegaard and the poet

In writing about Søren Kierkegaard, it is not inconsistent to speak of him as a poet and as a philosopher, and possibly a theologian is more appropriate in view of the corpus of his work and his stated intention. That the *New Testament* was the source of his life's work was an admission he was firm about. Kierkegaard's concern was with the misstatement of truth and he longed for a poet who would give dramatic form to his existential view — a way of life based on decision. It is also true that he regarded his work as a learning process.[40] One can detect the poetic proclivity in his work as well as the conscious determination to use the poetic to communicate to his audience, an audience who would otherwise not listen to direct discourse. The use of the poetic is almost a metamorphic correspondence to his own inner changes, the climax of his

* two-way switch

57

personal metamorphosis occurring mid-way in his career, or more appropriately when his moment of commitment was affirmed and clear to him. At that time he decided to write religious works under his name.

He could understand poetry because he was reflecting the Creator and when his religious conversion was definite, he could no longer use poetry in the same sense. It seemed pretentious to him. That the battle not to compete with God was difficult for him is verifiable simply by observing his natural inclinations which are expressed overtly in the pseudonymous works and less obviously in the direct works.[41] Kierkegaard could understand the phenomenology of the image and that the image precedes thought. He could understand that poetry is a phenomenon of the soul, of the dreaming consciousness. He understood that art awakens new depths in an individual and, thus, can bring about an awakening. And, in his works, not only those consciously aesthetic, but those in the ethical/ religious category too, there is a sensibility which reflects the body and soul of the work. In *Efterskrifter* Kierkegaard concedes that the poet is able to interpret death in a diversity of moods, even to the limit of the comical, and he pledges himself to the same diversity of effects in prose.

Ibsen and the poet

In 1874, Ibsen spoke to the Norwegian students about the task of the poet. He told them that they had the same problem as the poet, which was to make clear to themselves, and thereby to others, the temporal and eternal questions which are astir in the age and in the community to which they belong. For himself, he had been inspired by that which, so to speak, stood higher than his everyday self. The reason that he had been inspired by this illusive but beautiful element was that he wanted to confront it and make it part of his self. He had also been inspired by the opposite, by what appeared on introspection to be the dregs and sediment of one's own nature. It was his belief that no one could picture poetically that for which he had not to a certain degree served as a model, that is, "gjennemlevede."*

In the epic *Brand* (*Utkast i Episk Form*)** he writes about entering the misty world of the present and in a verse that echoes the boy on the mountain in "Paa Vidderne," he says that his poem is like a heathergrown hill that rises steadily aslant above the peasant farm. But beyond the hill, if you

stand free, you can glimpse a ring of white peaks. His lute is tuned to play a muted song, but deeper strings lend color to the chords. Consequently, a poem is thus concealed within the poem and he who is able to fathom this will grasp the song.

* "lived through"
** a fragment in epic form

The Speculative/Practical Intellect and Creative Intuition

In that Kierkegaard laid the foundations of an existential philosophy, the dynamics of which are under consideration in reference to the aesthetic consciousness as reflected in the dramatic art of Henrik Ibsen, it is pertinent to delineate the nature of the intellect that is involved, "For the entire dynamism of the intellect and its typical approach to its object depends on this very object and they are basically different when the object is knowledge and when the object is action."[42]

Jacques Maritain, in writing about creative intuition and the intellectual basis of poetry distinguishes between the speculative intellect and the practical intellect[43] as two basically different ways in which the same power of the soul, the intellect, exercises its activity.

The speculative intellect has its identity in knowledge and it longs to see Truth, to grasp that which is its only goal and life, whereas the practical intellect has its being in action. From the beginning, the object of the practical intellect is not Being to be grasped, but human activity and human tasks to be achieved. To immerse itself in creativity, to mold intellectually that which will be brought into being, "to judge about ends and means, and to direct or even command its own powers of execution, these are its very life."[44]

If the purpose of Søren Kierkegaard's authorship was simply knowledge of a theoretical nature, it would be appropriate to consider him solely as a speculative intellect, and certainly, philosophy is dominant in his writing. But he did not believe that transcendent existence could be attained through thought alone. He did not ascribe to "I think, therefore, I am," but he did believe "I am, therefore, I think." Therefore, the seething activity that the existential nature of his vision generates is directed to Truth, but a Truth that is always in flux. Within one phase of his work, the poetic impulse asserts itself and finds pleasure in imitation; in the other phase the impulse is

60

subdued and direct. Henrik Ibsen, on the other hand, is a dramatist who is a thinker. His art is not art for beauty's sake, although the poetic element is dominant, but, rather, it is art that is at one with a human need, resolving the people's longing, clothing in words their secret urges as he has said in the epic *Brand*. Arnulf Strømme views Ibsen's drama as an objectification of the *tensions* in the poet's mind, which is a society *in nuce**; the individual possibilities of the poet's mind become in the drama, the individual's (i.e. character's) possibility.[45] The idea of psychological expression that is suggested by Strømme has some validity in connection with Kierkegaard, in that the objectification of the subjective, the "possibility made actual" supports his existential view. Nevertheless, with Ibsen and with Kierkegaard, there are dimensions other than psychological self-consciousness.

It is not a digression at this point to consider Ibsen's response to "det moderne gennembrud"** because it is an indication of his spectral[46] or visionary thinking and his response is an assistance in clarifying the aesthetic operating within him. "Det moderne gennembrud," a movement initiated by the Danish literary critic Georg Brandes in the 1870's called for a literature that would show that it was alive by taking a contemporary problem for discussion. The impact on Norwegian writers: Ibsen, Bjørnstjerne Bjørnson, Jonas Lie, Alexander Kielland and Amalie Skram quickly followed and is reflected in their work.[47] The Norwegian attitude was art for life's sake so that the period is centrically-centered on self in the sense of making a better life and refining the sensibilities. Ibsen's plays of this period are cloaked in a social situation, appearing to be entirely of that situation, but actually, they are very much more. The paradox of an inverted dialectic is suggested in a line from *Kejser og Galilaeer*, "Det som er, det er ikke; og det som ikke er, det er."*** — so it is

---

* in a nutshell
** "the modern breakthrough" (Danish term)
*** "That which is, is not; and that which is not, is."

61

when one attempts to make an assessment about Ibsen's immediate focus. His reaction to Brandes' dictum transcends realism; the ability to be of a literary movement and yet transcend it is a characteristic which asserts itself throughout his work, whether the movement is romanticism, naturalism, neoromanticism or expressionism. The point is that the *core* of Ibsen's thinking is the same regardless of the literary movement of the day.

The need for the artist to maintain a distance from the social scene Ibsen expressed in "Paa Vidderne" in 1869; the sentiment of the boy on the heights is stated ten years later by Nora, "Jeg må stå ganske alene, hvis jeg skal få rede på mig selv og på alting udenfor."*

It is probable that the individualism of the early Viking literature with which Ibsen was so deeply engrossed during the Nationalistic Romantic Period[48] (seven plays within the period 1850-63, an unfinished play, an opera fragment, and poetry)[49] simply coalesced with the Brandes enlightenment of the 70's and the Kierkegaardian perspective. The neoromanticism in the 90's only reaffirmed the nature of the path Ibsen traveled from the beginning. He acknowledges as much in the 1883 Preface to *Gildet paa Solhoug,* a play he wrote in 1855.

In the 1883 Preface to *Gildet,* he writes that the work he had been doing on *Fru Inger til Østeraad* in 1854 led him, of necessity, to immerse himself in the literature of the Middle Ages in Norway. So far as it was possible, he tried to live himself into the ways and customs of the period, into the emotional life of the people, into their patterns and thoughts. He continues in this vein, speaking about the individualized, distinctive, and fully formed men and women, with their changing fortunes and the encounters between men and women, and between individuals generally (see Chapter V).

---

* "I must stand quite alone, if I am to find out about myself and everything around me."

What Ibsen wrote about Dr. Stockman in *En Folkefiende* was true of his own situation. In a letter to Georg Brandes in 1883 he writes that in ten years the majority might possibly reach the point where Dr. Stockman stood at, but during those years, Stockman has not been standing still. With the modern breakthrough, the boy "paa Vidderne"* has changed and assumed another shape; he has "gaar in Nuets Taage-verden ind."** With the social plays the milieu is in tune with the contemporary, but there is a symbiotic connection to the inner life of the personae, the center which emanates from the author's primordial base, what Maritain calls "the soul."[50] The Ibsen protagonist, as does the Kierkegaardian pseudo-nym, changes his mask according to the existential situation he or she is in, responding to life, instead of initiating it. The tragic can become comic as sometimes is the case in *Vildanden* and the comic can combine with the tragic and even become absurd (*En Folkefiende, Lille Eyolf*). The distorted image, chameleonlike, then takes on other colors and reflects itself inversely, poetically. Yet, before the curtain falls, an individual may come face to face with himself.

---

* boy on the heights
** entered the misty world of the present

To further the concept of *object* (i.e. the object as knowledge or the object as action) as a differentiating feature in terms of the intellect (which is a singular concern in a study that considers the acknowledged initiator of existentialism[51] and the progenitor of modern drama) Maritain treats another point, *appetite*. In the case of *appetite* or will — not in terms of decision but as it is conceived of in the larger sense of man's energy of desire and love directed toward some existential good — the relation of it to the intellect and truth is different. In connection with the speculative intellect, the will or appetite is involved only to activate the intellect, to exercise its own power; when that occurs, the appetite's function ceases and reason is the practice. The situation is different with the practical intellect because the will as activity is an essential aspect of the work. Reason in this case operates with the *energizing force* of the appetite in a *movement* towards its own ends, *not simply* with *Being to be grasped,* as it is with the speculative intellect where there is truth's

64

conformity of the intellect with Being. In practical or creative knowledge, there is no previous existing thing which the intellect can be at one with. The practical intellect must make itself consonant with that which is not yet existing, that which must be brought into being. Truth in this instance is the conformity of the intellect with the straight appetite, an appetite directed to the ends that are to be created. In reference to Kierkegaard, he is consonant with the *truth,* but it is not static truth; it exists in the sense that it is undercover (an idea Kierkegaard considers in his treatment of repetition). Kierkegaard's purpose is to reveal this truth in connection with the *New Testament* and Christianity to *hiin Enkelte.** He believed that what was called Christianity — and which he designates as Christendom — was not the Christianity of the New Testament. His was a mission which was intended to demonstrate the nature of Christianity as existence — *Christenhed* — instead of viewing it as historical phenomenon or speculative thought. While Ibsen presents existential truth poetically, he also demonstrates at one and the same time how far his character's world is from the Christianity of the New Testament.

One of the correspondences (and the term has Swedenborgian connotations)[52] in the work of Kierkegaard and Ibsen has been referred to, that is, that both authors are objective about the subjective. It is a persuasive indication of how their work is analogous, even though the *nature* of their subjectivity is somewhat different. The difference between *poetry* and *art* contributes to an understanding of this subjective link. Poetry is *subjective,* the word being applied generically to various fields of creative knowledge.[53] Maritain considers poetry as process, an "intercommunication between the inner being of things and the inner being of the human self," a different concept than art which is the creative or work-making activity of the human mind. The subjective link has sig-

---

* "that individual" for whom he writes

65

nificance because that was the only way that Kierkegaard could conceive of Christianity and it was a subjective experience for the individual; it was poetry to him. Because God was the only creator, he (Kierkegaard) could not presume to be on the same level. As frequently as he refers to himself as a poet, he is equally emphatic in rejecting that designation insisting that he is not a poet, but is a dialectician. In *Papirer*, he states that normally the dialectic is foreign to poets. He regarded maieutic communication (Christianity) wherein the subjective is essential as *art*, seeing in indirect communication a dialectic that the elasticity of dialectics duplicates.

The paradox that is suggested in calling Christianity art is less a contradiction than a distinction that becomes clearer with reference to Maritain who refers to *art* as a *virtue* of the practical (i.e. creative) intellect, a virtue in the philosophical sense, an inner strength developed in man. Art is an *intellectual* essence; which is in the realm of making, "an intrinsic perfection of the intellect"[54] or a perfection of the soul which accounts for the degree to which art is great.[55] Therefore, whether the referential point is the art of Søren Kierkegaard, the art of Henrik Ibsen, or the art of a lesser dramatist such as Eugene Scribe (to whom Ibsen is frequently compared) the reference is valid since the art is correspondent to the intellect producing it. This would not necessarily mean that the work is poetry. That is, the essence in the preconscious life of the intellect producing it is a qualification that is discriminatory in respect to the work that is produced.

Maritain's view of poetry is that it is a kind of knowledge making known something that cannot be known in any other way but through the spiritual world of an individual subjective experience. Such a view poses another thought — the moral responsibility of the artist. Oscar Wilde has said that the fact of a man being a poisoner is nothing against his prose.[56] In terms of technique and sophistic pragmatism the point is not disputable. But Maritain believes that such an artist is so directed to the good of the work that he loses sight of the soul, thus warping the relationship of the senses and the intellect to reality which is the prerequisite of the activity of art that is poetry. There are exceptions in which the artist sacrifices himself and the result is a work of art, a sacrifice to that "all-devouring glory of art," (but here again the balance is off-center) and, says Maritain, it is not for us to judge such a person, but leave him to God. He is expressing the Platonic suspicion of the artist-poet in a Christian context. It is also Kierkegaard's contention that the authorship ought to be a serious calling, one that implies an appropriate mode of existence.[57] The disregard for this truth is dramatized in *Bygmester Solness* and *Når Vi Døde Vågner*. Notwithstanding a certain amount of professional recognition, neither Solness nor Rubeck live in such a way as to realize their potential. In terms of the degree to which one is an artist or a poet, Ibsen has treated in *Vildanden* and *Lille Eyolf*; Hjalmar and Allmers are not artists of any significance. Ibsen is showing that there is poetry in a human being but that this is rarely considered in the proper perspective. It is a thought that he expressed in speaking of Bjørnson whose life Ibsen felt was a work of art.[58] Some aspect of the poet-artist is articulated in each Ibsen play, but in the guise of another profession. Ibsen was also concerned with the daemonic side of poetry and was constantly at war with the trolls as he termed the demands of poetry. Ibsen and Kierkegaard would agree with Maritain that the authorship of the age lacked the perfection of the intellect.

The points that Maritain has made about the intellect, subjectivity and the poet-artist,[59] are cogent to this discussion. Kierkegaard's existentialism was not a result of speculative thought and Ibsen's drama, though tending toward the Platonic (as does modern drama), was a product of the practical intellect. Secondly, subjectivity is central to the authorship of Kierkegaard and Ibsen. Kierkegaard has said that all essential decisiveness is rooted in subjectivity, and it is this feature which removes Kierkegaard from the realm of the speculative intellect. The third issue — that the artist is not necessarily a poet is a consideration that Kierkegaard was positive about. In his opinion there were only two or three poets in a generation. The poet is divinely gifted and understands intuitively.

Creative intuition is important to the aesthetic of Kierkegaard and Ibsen. The nature of the useful and the fine arts clarifies its significance.

Even in the useful arts, the rules are not ready-made recipes, but are vital ways of operating discovered by the creative eyes of the intellect in the labor of invention. The craftsman's first need is to be satisfied. What the appetite demands is a satisfaction by means of the rules discovered by the intellect. Maritain cautions that when the ways of operating become rules, they become obstacles. In the fine arts, what the appetite demands is the release of pure creativity of the spirit in its longing for beauty. And the straightness of the appetite means that it tends to this aim by rules discovered by the practical intellect, the first of which is the *creative intuition* from which the whole work originates.

Creativity is the spirit of engendering and does not belong exclusively to material organisms, "it is a mark and privilege of life in spiritual things also."[60] Creativity of the spirit is the first ontological root of the artistic activity. In the fine arts, it is pure, the intellect striving to produce beauty. The need is different; it goes further than the useful. The *need* is not extraneous to the intellect. It is this idea of something more, something universal and eternal, that the work of Kierkegaard reflects; it is here that Ibsen's creativity goes further. The essential thing in the fine arts is the need of the intellect to manifest externally what is grasped within itself in creative intuition — as it was with Ibsen. Creative intuition is the primary rule if there is a rule, because it deals with the very conception "in the bosom of the spirit of the work to be engendered in beauty." A work can be perfectly made but if creative intuition is lacking, the work is nothing; the artist has nothing to say (i.e. Scribe). On the other hand, if creative intuition is present, and passes to some extent into the work, the work exists and speaks to us, "even if it is imperfectly made and proceeds from a man who has the habit of art and a hand which shakes." If there is a rule of the perfect artist, it would be, writes Maritain, that she/he[61] should cling to creative intuition and do what she/he wants. This is not then simply an esoteric view; it is practical as there is intuitive reason in the obscure and high regions close to the soul that dictates the act of creation. It is in this way that the fine arts are transcendent, and it is in this way that Kierkegaard and Ibsen are compatible even though one wrote expository non-fiction of an extraordinary kind and the other "imitates an action" in a genre I have designated[62] as drama/ theatre to indicate its completeness.

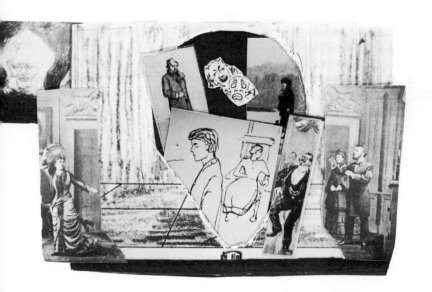

Den Enkelte
i.e.
The Individual
*"en Enkelte" er eensom**

Kierkegaard viewed the individual as a category of spirit and more frequently he conceived of the individual in terms of spiritual awakening. In developing this idea, he qualifies 'individual' in a way that points to the spiritual sense of the category in its pure form. The religious individual is the one who has been awakened spiritually; he has experienced *angestens skrig*** and he has come to a recognition of his solitary state in the finite world. He is the knight of faith who renounces the universal to become the individual as does Nora in *Et Dukkehjem* and as did Thea in *Hedda Gabler*. A seemingly awakened individual is not necessarily the religious or conscious individual, but rather, he may be the expression of a worldly title in that he *thinks* he is religious, not unlike Brand. He is a pseudo-individual who is "mouthing the words" although with Brand it can be said that he was sincere, if misguided. With so many of Ibsen's characters, while

---

* an individual is solitary
** scream of dread

there is anguish there are also impediments that prevent them from experiencing life fully.

Awareness of ideality has been the purpose of Kierkegaard's interest in the individual. To be conscious of self and eternal responsibility, is to live in such a way that consciousness and liberty of action does not constitute a withdrawal from life. On the contrary this consciousness would sustain and clarify and illuminate all that had to be done with one's relations to life. King Haakon (*Kongs=Emnerne*) is the ideal representation of such an individual, the knight of faith. It is Thea (*Hedda Gabler*) who is perhaps the most human portrayal of the fully realized individual in Ibsen's plays.

The individual is to be found in the midst of *Vrøvlehovder*.* It is there, here and there, that an individual may be lurking and to be able to reach this person is Kierkegaard's desire. In each play of Ibsen's there is such a character, one who has potential or possibility, but one whose possibility does not always materialize. Kierkegaard emphasized the difference between understanding something in possibility and understanding the same thing in actuality. In possibility, the understanding does not mean change. One can use imagination yet remain in the old ways. When it comes to actuality, there is change, and with the change comes the question of self-preservation.

For Kierkegaard the real problem was to awaken the individual. He was convinced that all the external institutions — ecclesiastical, social, and political — glossed over or overlooked this essential necessity. However, it was not with the government that he felt the protest should be directed. It was his belief that in the future each effort at reformation, if its leader is a true reformer, will direct itself against the mass as such and not against the government. He reiterates his stance that he, as an individual, does not in the remotest degree infringe upon any civil institution whatsoever, and indeed a

---

* Twaddlers

71

man who stands alone never becomes a physical power, the same sentiment, i.e., but with a difference that Ibsen expresses in *En Folkefiende*.

In a speech to the workmen at Trondhjem in 1885 Ibsen said that the most indispensible individual rights are not as yet safeguarded. He did not look to any institution for these rights because a ruling majority does not grant the individual either faith or liberty of expression beyond an arbitrary fixed limit. Nobility of will and mind were lacking. It was his belief that there were in the whole of Norway not more than twenty-five free and independent individuals.

Ibsen was adamant in asserting his separation from the political. In a letter written in 1890 to H. L. Braekstad, he states that he never belonged to a political party. Rather, he felt the necessity of independence in order to work and shape his own course, his life-task being to depict human characters and human destinies.

The individual as essential to his work is affirmed in a discussion of the primacy of character in his plays. Before he puts down one word, he has the character in mind through and through. He must penetrate into the last wrinkle of his soul so he always proceeds from the individual. As soon as he is certain of the individual in every aspect of humanity, the stage setting and the dramatic ensemble all come naturally. But he must have his character's exterior in mind — how he stands, walks, talks, conducts himself. Then, he lets him or her go until his or her fate has been fulfilled.

The importance of the individual to Kierkegaard and Ibsen is a dominant feature in their personal lives and in the purpose and development of their authorship. The individual is their audience and Kierkegaard wrote in *Papirer* that if he had to carve an inscription on his grave it would be none other than "den enkelte."*

---

* "the individual"

72

The Inversion

"Det, der gør et kunstvaerk til sin ophavsmand's
åndelige ejendom, det er, at han har påtrykt vaerket
sin egen personligheds stempel."*
—Henrik Johann Ibsen, 1883

Søren Kierkegaard and Henrik Ibsen describe similar but
different situations in life, playing the same music and dancing
the same dance over and over with new partners and in a different context. Some instances reflect this empathy and show
the compatibility of their vision as well as the divergences.
Consider the following examples:

Fru Inger til Østeraad (1855)

Kierkegaard describes a painting in a church — angels
holding out to Christ the cup of Suffering. Eventually, there
will occur a moment when the picture will blessedly turn itself
around. That is, it will not seem so very long before a reversal will take place. It recalls the Agnes and the Merman
story wherein the pictures of the saints turn their faces to the
wall when the guilty Agnes enters the church.

---

* "What makes a work of art its creator's spiritual property is the
fact that he has impressed upon it his own personality." (Fortale til
Anden Udgave, 1883)

In Ibsen's drama, Lady Inger feels that her actions, which have been for Norway, have been misunderstood. She turns the picture of her ancestors to the wall as a sign of the guilt and anxiety she is feeling. Her dedication to the Norwegian cause has resulted in her sacrificing one of her daughters, and later, unwittingly, a son.

The possibility never made actual

—the man who became a merchant would have preferred to have been an artist—Hjalmar *Vildanden*.
—the man who married a girl but her sister is the one he loved—*John Gabriel Borkman*.
—a conception of a Herculean work that is never finished— Allmer's book *Lille Eyolf*, also *Bygmester Solness, Når Vi Døde Vågner*.
Also the ironic, inverse situation in *Hedda Gabler*.
—the shipwrecked man who has saved himself by holding on to a plank and is tossed by the waves between life and death. He gazes at the land; the answer is uncertain—*Peer Gynt*.

Jealousy — love — hate

Spontaneous love can become jealousy, and it can become a torment because spontaneity is a fermenting element that has not yet undergone change. The fermenting element is a poison and if love kindles itself in poison, jealousy appears —Rita Allmers *Lille Eyolf*. Spontaneous love can also be changed to its opposite, hate. Hate is a ruined love and Hjørdis displays hate when she is willing for her husband to kill Sigurd; Hedda is doing the same thing when she burns the manuscript. Spontaneous love can change into something else — *habit*. A way to avoid habit is to keep a slave as an Eastern emperor does, and a friend. Peer's *(Peer Gynt)* slave is Anitra; his friends, his mother and Solveig. Nora *(Et Duk-*

74

kehjem) has Dr. Rank for her friend; she has been the slave. Her husband, Torvald, has had her for his slave and Dr. Rank for a friend.

Strength

He is strongest of all at the time when he seems overcome. It is a question of trust, if one does not have trust, one does not receive strength. Such a man although in opposition does not get the worst of the battle in this life or in eternity. However, a man who literally stands alone never becomes a physical power. Consider the bittersweet response of Dr. Stockman in *En Folkefiende*.

Introversion

Introversion is the direct opposite of immediacy. Such a person is in despair, sits in despair, behind him a door which is a nothing, but it is a real door— albeit a locked door. Behind it sits, as it were, the self, and watches itself employed, in filling up time with not willing to be itself and yet is self enough to love itself — John Gabriel Borkman.

Another phase of the idea suggests *Hedda Gabler*. If introversion is absolutely maintained, then suicide will be the danger. If the person talks to someone, the impulse may be dissipated. If despair was a hero, the confidant could be put to death. It would be the task of the poet to represent this agonizing self-contradiction in a daemoniac character who is not able to get along with a confidant, and not able to have a confidant, and then resolve it in such a way — suicide.

The way

Kierkegaard quotes the New Testament concerning the way. "Veien, som forer til Livet, er trang, Porten anever — Faal de som finde den."* He gives an example of two men and two paths. The man on one path is there because he willed the Good in truth, and humbly and gladly followed its becoming; the other man is on a different road because fear drove him there. A double-minded person would stand at the parting of the way — *Peer Gynt.*

NOTES TO PROLOGUE

1 "Drama is essentially an experience, the result of combining the written words of the play with the living speech and actions of the performer in the theatre before an audience."
2 Elizabeth Barrett Browning "How do I love thee" from *Sonnets to the Portuguese.*

* "The way that leadeth into life is straitened, the gate narrow— few be they that find it."

76

3 In considering what usually is referred to as Ibsen's symbolism, the idea Erich Auerbach presents in the *figura* is a more appropriate designation because it is a connection between events or persons that signifies not only itself but the Other, a higher reality in concrete terms. The figural representation differs from symbolism by being a comparison in which both parts are real in actual history, for instance Abraham's sacrifice of Isaac relates to Jesus and God, and in the plays the sacrifice is repeated over and over in contemporary terms.

4 The diversity of Ibsen criticism is treated elsewhere in the dissertation.

5 And surely this is the one constant in the *Poetics*, which Aristotle limited to tragedy.

6 Walter Kerr of *The New York Times* is an exception. He is one of the more astute critics of living theatre. Ibsen scholarship is brought into focus in Chapter III which treats the dialectic.

7 Jacques Maritain.

8 The Danish word *Indesluttehed* refers to the truly Kierkegaardian *inwardness* that is indicated.

9 The Danish word for becoming in this sense is *vordelse*, i.e. giving birth to.

10 *Søren Kierkegaard's Journals and Papers*, Volume I. Howard V. Hong and Edna H. Hong.

11 *Staadier, Enten-Eller, Øieblikket* hadde impregnert aandsatmosfaeren i denne tid, ikke bare i Danmark, man ogsaa i Norge, ingen forfatter blev y den grad citeret, diskuteret og bevrøvlet som Kierkegaard, in *Henrik Ibsen-Liv og Verker*, Gerhard Gran.

12 *Henrik Ibsen, Critical Study*, Georg Brandes.

13 "Brev fra Magdalene Thoresen" *Memoir og Breve*, Bind XXX.

14 She was on familiar terms with Bjørnson and Ibsen.

15 Koht writes that Ibsen had many talks with Brun the first winter that he was in Rome (1864).

16 *Henrik Ibsen og Skien*. Oskar Mosfjeld, s. 149.

17 *De Tre*. Bergliot Ibsen.

18 Frascati, June 9, 1866. *Samlede Verker*.

19 *Søren Kierkegaard*, Frithiof Brandt.

20 Humanistic psychology recognizes Auden's (i.e. Ibsen's) requisite for the creative person. Elizabeth Monroe Drew writes in *The Higher Levels of Human Growth* that the one recurrent factor in the lives of creative people is the presence of a supportive influence such as Auden's "playmate"—whether that influence be an adult, a child, books, a place, or some other "companion".

21 Note to "gjennemlevede." Ibsen reference in speech to Norwegian students, September 10, 1874; Kierkegaard reference in *Faedrelandet*, XIX, 52.

22 *Kierkegaard the Cripple*, Theodor Haecker.

23 *The New Theatre of Europe*, edited with an Introduction by Robert W. Corrigan.

24 "Søren Kierkegaard" George T. Flom. *Scandinavian Studies and Notes*, Vol. VI. Feb. 1920.

25 See *Henrik Ibsen Som Maler*, Otto Lous Mohr (in reference to Ibsen's painting).

26 *I Ungdomsbyen med Henrik Ibsen*, s. 27.

27 *op cit.* Oskar Mosfjeld, s. 98.

28 Kierkegaard was at the university for ten years (1830-40) during which time he was the affuent young man about town.

29 See Chapter I—Kierkegaard and the Theatre "med et sideblik til" Henrik Ibsen wherein the content of this paragraph is developed and conceptually related.

30 See Chapter I for more on the Heibergs.

31 *Søren Kierkegaard's Papirer*, s. 388, entry 593.

32 *Frygt og Baeven*, s. 29.

33 *Striden mellem den gamle og den Saebekielder (Søren Kierkegaard's Papirer*, s. 285, Bind II). See Chronology, p. 1.

34 Appreciation to Howard V. Hong for sending me the information concerning Kierkegaard's jesting about joining a company of travelling players. The pseudonym is thought to be Kierkegaard.

35 *Creative Intuition and the Practical Intellect.* Jacques Maritain, p. 33.

36 Referred to charts of Alexander Dru, 1958; and Howard V. Hong and other sources; see biographies, *et al.* in Bibliography.

37 Ibsen wrote over three hundred poems.

38 The spelling of the titles used is in accordance with that of the original.

39 Earlier, Bjørnstjerne Bjørnson had brought Ibsen to Meiningen's attention and he is credited with introducing Ibsen to the German theatre. The Duke was to become known for his adherence to the ensemble principle in performance and for the way his company (The Meiningers) handled crowds, realistic battle scenes, off stage sounds. When Meiningen produced *Kongs=Emnerne* in 1876 [See Chronology entry June 3, 1876.], it was not well received. According to Karl Frenzel, critic, the play's construction and the foreign temper of the action could not be naturalized on the German stage.

40 Kierkegaard did not consider himself a teacher.

41 See Chapters I and III.

42 At that time he decided to write religious works under his name.

43 Jacques Maritain, p. 34. His study *Creative Intuition and the Practical Intellect* basis of discusion of speculative and practical intellect.

44 By practical intellect Maritain means creative intellect but with qualification.

45 *Structuren i Ibsens Dramaer* av Arnulf Marcellus Strømme, 1951. Dramaet er en objectivering av det spente diktersinn, som er et samfunn in nuce. Diktersinnets individuelle mulighter blir i dramaet til mulige individer.

46 The word was used by a woman who had been a girl during the

time that Ibsen lived in Grimstad. She said none of the girls liked him because he was "spectral." Edmund Gosse, p. 18.

47 Camilla Collett anticipated Brandes, wrote *Amtmandens Døttre* (*The Sheriff's Daughters*) in 1855. It concerns the problems of a middle-class marriage where love is given little consideration. Whereas Ibsen's interest was the individual, Bjørnson's concern was with the masses; Jonas Lie wrote social history on a high artistic level; Alexander Kielland's concern was with the social and moral evils of his day; Amalie Skram was a naturalist whose concern was with women.

48 National Romanticism (1840-60) was always latent in Norway and achieved preponderance in the nation's artistic life, *Scandinavian Literature* (Bredsdorf, Mortensen, Popperwell).

49 *Kjampehøien* (*Burial Mound*); *Sancthansnatten* (*St. John's Eve*); *Fru Inger til Østeraad* (*Fru Inger*); *Gildet paa Solhoug* (*The Feast at Solhoug*); *Olaf Liljekrans; Haermaendene paa Helgeland* (*Vikings in Helgeland*); opera fragment, *Fjeldfuglen* (*The Mountain Bird*); *Rypen in Justedal* (*Rypen in Justedal*) part of a play; Svanhild.

50 The word *ånd* in Norwegian has meanings which are associated with the consciousness of life and the intellectual side of consciousness, "intellektuelle siden av bevissthets livet."

51 As a noun, the word *existentialism* never occurred in Kierkegaard's own writings. It is an expression that was used by Johan Sebastian Welhaven (1807-1873).

52 Emanuel Swedenborg (1688-1772) scientist and theologian. His philosophy claims direct mystical communication between the world and the spiritual realm and affirms Christ as the true God.

53 I.e., Music, painting verse, drama/theatre.

54 Maritain.

55 I.e., whether it is poetry.

56 Oscar Wilde is cited by Maritain.

57 Kierkegaard shared this view with Socrates.

58 It could have also been an ironical remark as Ibsen was frequently ambivalent about Bjørnson.

59 NOTE: That the artist is not necessarily a poet (Maritain) is an important point and is connected to Kierkegaard's spheres of existence as will be shown. With Ibsen's drama the distinction has concern in regard to the individual's self-fulfillment.

60 Maritain.

61 *She/he* is being used to replace the generic *he*.

62 See page 1 of the Proposal.

63 The individual is an essential Kierkegaardian category — see Chapter III.

Kierkegaard and
the Theatre
with *et sideblik til* Ibsen

I

"kunde komme bag alt dette Formummede"*
                    — Søren Kierkegaard
"den dramatiske Kunst . . . har i højere Grad end
nogen anden Kunstart. . . . i denne Kunsts inderligere
og langt mere umiddelbare Forhold til Virke-
ligheden."**

                              — Henrik Ibsen

* to "get in behind the scenes of all this mummery"
                    Øieblikket 7
** "drama . . . more than any other art . . . the more intimate and
direct relation . . . to reality"
          brev (letter) to the King 6 August 1860

82

Kierkegaard and the Theatre

with *et sideblik til* Ibsen

The intention in considering Kierkegaard in connection with the theatrical focus is not to view him as a man of the theatre or a dramatist in the sense that Norway's Henrik Ibsen was, but to view him as a man whose innate sense of the theatre and drama extended to a complete understanding of the artistic principles inherent in the mimetic form and his genius in reflecting those principles within the scope of expository non-fiction and relating them to a particular vision. While his treatment of character and situation presents the limitations of the aesthetical-speculative stance, it also illuminates the existential. That he considers the theatre as a viable communicative force is reflected in the dramatic-theatrical nature of his literature and in the unique way he treats the innumerable analogies he makes to theatre and drama.

In 1848, Søren Kierkegaard wrote an article entitled *Krisen og en Krise i en Skuespillerindes Liv* in which he says "i Danmark er der kun een By og eet Theatre,"*[2] that theatre, the Det Kongelige Teater (Royal Theatre) in Copenhagen. It is part of the irony and the paradox of life that the theatre

---

* "there is in Denmark but one city and one Theatre"

and the church were two significant communal forces that existed side by side, and the incongruency was not lost on Kierkegaard, who utilized the reality to support his "attack on Christendom." In Øieblikket 6,[3] he writes that the difference between the theatre and the church is essentially that the theatre honestly and honorably acknowledges itself to be what it is; on the other hand, the church is a theatre which dishonestly tries in every way to hide what it is. The theatre says openly what the church says secretly; therefore, it is a good thing that the Church had the Theatre alongside of it for the church is a joke. Notwithstanding the dichotomy that the close proximity of the theatre and the church suggested to Kierkegaard, the Royal Theatre was considered to be one of the foremost playhouses in mid-nineteenth century Scandinavia. Hans Christian Andersen refers to it in his biography *Mit Liv Eventyr* as being one of the finest theatres in Europe.[4] That this theatre, located on Kongens Nytorv, was a center of cultural and social significance for Kierkegaard is evident in his writings, wherein one cannot only discern the nature of the Royal Theatre's repertoire and some of the stage conventions, but it also becomes clear that Kierkegaard was a patron of the arts and that he was on familiar terms with most of the prominent figures of that milieu. He refers to actors Peter Frydendahl, Johan Stage, N. P. Nielsen, C. N. Rosenkilde, and Ludvig Phister, whose role as Captain in the comic opera *Ludovic* is the subject of a sensitive critical essay.[5] Johan Ludvig Heiberg, playwright, director, critic, man of letters and his wife, Johannes Luise Heiberg (nee Pätges), the actress commemorated in *Krisen,* were intimates whose company he valued. He attended the soirées presided over by Fru Heiberg, which by the 1840's were considered the apogée of Danish cultural life. She later became a director and was influential in getting Ibsen staged in Denmark. Kierkegaard was often in the audience of the Royal Theatre as noted by Frederick Marker in a reference to Hans Christian Andersen, "On most evenings, he [Andersen] could be found in the stalls

84

together with the foremost figures of the Danish Age: Øehlenschläger, Thorvaldsen, Heiberg, Kierkegaard."[6]

The enthusiasm that the theatre generated for Kierkegaard
is reflected in his theatrical and dramatic references which are
always in a context that has a significance in relation to a
concept he is exploring. Lest the image of Kierkegaard be
distorted, it is appropriate to add that in his youth, Kierkegaard was considered and considered himself an aesthete,
frequenting the theatre and seeking entertainment; not only
was he a devotee of drama but also of opera. It was one of the
unique features of the Royal Theatre that it could accom-
modate drama, opera, and ballet. Even though the ballet, reflecting the unique talent of choreographer August Bournon-
ville, was a significant art form, it is inconspicuous in Kierkegaard's writing. In *Enten-Eller* I, Kierkegaard discusses
Mozart's *The Magic Flute* and he compares Molière's and
Mozart's *Don Juan*.[7] Later, in an effort to dispel a more
serious image, he consciously cultivated a cultural and social
life, one that would suggest a gregarious nature while, in
reality, he often limited his participation to a brief appearance. It was part of his stratagem to disconcert and disarm
his associates whose ideas he was in conflict with. Further,
he gave himself out to be a poet. Under this guise, he had
the freedom of throwing out a number of ideas and not being
taken too seriously. Then, when he was secure from the pressure of his adversaries, he would go bluntly about his real
concern. Each move Kierkegaard made was carefully calculated
as to what the possible effect would be. In point of fact,
Krisen caused him considerable consternation for by this time
(1848), he had established himself as a religious author. He
debated the wisdom of publishing the article, wondering how
his public would react, "men nu en Artikel om en Skuespil-
lerinde."* Finally, his decision was that it would serve as a
reminder to his audience that it was the aesthetic work with

---

* "but now an article about an actress."

85

which he began. Consequently, *Krisen* was published under the pseudonym Inter et Inter,[8] a double entendre meaning between and between, suggesting an intermission in a theatrical sense but also indicative of the place *Krisen* had in his work.

Throughout his writings, Kierkegaard displays an awareness of audience relationships and he articulates a familiarity with dramatic literature and theatrical art that is extensive. His oneness with both would seem paradoxical to the author of *Opbyggelige Taler i forskjellig Aand*[9]* in which he states that *purity of heart is to will one thing*, i.e., the religious, if it were not that he did believe there were exceptional people endowed with special gifts. In making a distinction between the religious and the secular poets, he writes that it is the latter which most people are familiar with and of whom he is suspicious. *The* poet he would acknowledge has something "religious" in him although he hastens to say that the existence of three such individuals in a century would be unusual since the attainment of the needed requisites requires discipline, an attitude of receptivity, and an independent mind to which few people could aspire. It is for this reason that he would be against poets being subsidized by the State; the comfort of the support would end the call and fill the land with bad poetry. He recognizes that the poet is listened to, although he reflects "hvor nøiagtigt og hvor laenge husker man ikke hvad Digteren har sagt, isaer hvad han har sagt ved Hjaelp af Skuespilleren"!**

In this discussion of Kierkegaard and the theatre, two aspects are dominant: his mimetic sensibility and his response to theatrical and dramatic art.

---

* *Edifying Discourses of Varied Tenor*
** "how long and how accurately does one remember what the poet has said, especially what he has said with the help of the actor." *Kjerlighedens Gjerninger.*

Mimetic Sensibility

Although Kierkegaard's literary work is written in expository prose, it does express a histrionic sensibility not unlike the criteria he would require of the poet. The expression is one that Francis Fergusson uses specifically in reference to grasping the stage-life of a play "in the mind's eye" whether that be achieved vicariously through reading or through activity. Histrionic sensibility is the direct-mimetic response of the reader or the interpreter to the *action* of the work. Despite Fergusson's emphasis on dramatic art, he does acknowledge histrionic sensibility as a direct awareness applicable to other more general situations where such perception is sought. Such a sensibility is akin to possessing an ear for music; the individual having this quality is attuned to the nuances and subtleties of expression, the essence of the expression. It is also an important awareness for a writer in terms of communicating his vision. Fergusson views histrionic sensibility as something that can be cultivated and he cites the Moscow Art Theatre's system of training an actor as a prime example. In learning to free his emotions, cultivate his perceptions and discipline himself, the actor is able to respond mimetically with his whole being to the playwright.[10] Kierkegaard and Ibsen are natural exponents of the histrionic impulse that Fergusson describes.

87

Israel Levin, Kierkegaard's copyist, describes Kierkegaard's powers of imagination as daemonic, saying that he could poeticize himself into any existence; on one occasion he lived only to think and feel like a miser. Enthusiasm for a particular play, one he felt should be seen several times to be fully appreciated, prompted Kierkegaard to express how one should experience the performance. He suggested observation of the actor, then turning away of the eyes, shutting them and letting the image materialize; finally, the eyes should be opened again and the actor looked at. With an actress like Fru Heiberg, one should cast down the eyes lest the attraction be dangerous, in terms of being a distraction. The eyes should be opened again and these movements repeated so swiftly that a conception of what is being presented is gained.[11] Kierkegaard is presupposing a familiarity with the play, and in this case a particular play, *Den Første Kjaerlighed* by Eugene Scribe, translated by J. L. Heiberg. And, in discussing ancient tragedy, Kierkegaard writes that, in order for him to understand the deep sorrow of the Greek tragedy, he must live himself into the Greek consciousness.[12]

This specialized sensitivity was shared by Ibsen; he and Kierkegaard, by virtue of their genius and their vocation, had developed their histrionic sense to a high level of refinement. In a letter to Christian Hostrup, Ibsen describes how he experiences vicariously the recreating of what Fergusson terms "the stage-life" of a play. Responding to Hostrup's play *Under Snefog,*[*][13] he writes to him:

> Det har vaeret mig en sand hjertens glaede og nydelse
> at laese og leve med i denne elskvaerdige digtning."

and he writes that Jutland where the play takes place —

> —blev under laesningen så forunderlig naervaerende
> i min forestilling, skjønt jeg jo aldrig har vaeret der
> ved vintertid.

---

* In the Snowstorm

88

I teatret går jeg her naesten aldrig, men jeg laeser gerne et skuespil en gang imellem om aftenen, og da jeg har en sterk indbildningskraft for det dramatiske, så kan jeg se alt det der er rigtig sandt, trovaerdigt og pålideligt, lys levende for mig; laesninger virker naesten som en opførelse.*

It is this kind of sensitivity to the reading of a work that Kierkegaard consciously endeavored to evoke. His ability to insinuate himself into a character or a situation tends to generate a reciprocal response in *den enkelte*** who constitutes his audience, often referred to as tilhøreren.*** Kierkegaard indicates that he does not expect all of his readers to respond similarly since they are not all at the same level of awareness.

Kierkegaard's predisposition for the direct-mimetic response is strongly reflected in his mode of articulation. Not only are there vivid scenes and characterizations in his work which reflect existential activity but the approach to language is histrionic. Kierkegaard recommends that his listener read the discourses aloud, giving as his reason that reading aloud helps, the individual to realize that he does not have primarily an author to consider, but himself, merely prompted in reflection by the author. To heighten the sense of immediacy, within an organic framework, Kierkegaard plays on the oral values of language: repetition, alliteration, consonance, assonance,

---

* "It has been a real joy to read the beautiful work and actually to live in and with it."
Of Jutland where the play takes place—
"—was marvelously present in my mind as I was reading although I never have seen it in the winter."
"I hardly ever go to the theatre here, but I enjoy reading a play now and then in the evening, and as I have a powerful imagination where anything dramatic is concerned, I can see everything that is really natural, authentic, and credible actually happening before my eyes. Reading a play produces in me almost the same effect as seeing a performance."
** the individual
*** the hearer

rhythm. His punctuation is also geared to the ear as well as to the mind with the exclamation point, the question mark, the lack of commas, the dash — often creating a subtext. Their use frequently creates movements or causes one to *pause,* which for Kierkegaard was the same thing, "Standsningen er ogsaa Bevaegelse."*[14] One sometimes has to stand still in order to come to himself. (He referred to Socrates as "en Tanke-streg"** — a thought mark in world history, and between *Enten-Eller* there is also "en Tankestreg" which has a signifi-cance in that there is a pause when the individual is b̃e-tween spheres of existence.)

Another way in which Kierkegaard's language has an added dimension is in the play on words. The repetitive technique recalls Falstaff's play on the word *courage* in Shakespeare's *Henry IV* and Falk's perusal of the word *love* in Ibsen's *Kjaerlighedens Komedie.* In a similar way, and with a similar intent, Kierkegaard will choose a concept and view it from every possible angle for to view the context of a concept was not to dethrone it, but to enrich it.[15] Repetition of the word has an echoic effect in addition to reinforcing the significance of the concept. Within the focus there is also a back and forth movement that reveals the dichotomy involved, indicates the *way,* and implies the choice. *Udødelighed,**** for example, is the Judgment; *udødelighed* is not a life indefinitely pro-longed; *udødelighed* is the eternal separation between the just and the unjust; *udødelighed* does not follow as a matter of course; it is a separation which follows as a consequense of the past. Then Kierkegaard questions what *udødelighed* re-quires of him (mit uhyre Ansvar) **** and the significance of *udødelighed* to the way he lives so that what emerges is the essence rather than the definition of a word.

---

* "Pausing is also movement."
** a dash, literally a thought mark.
*** immortality
**** "my immense responsibility"

Examining a concept from diverse angles is central to the authorship of Kierkegaard and Ibsen. Each work of Ibsen's is a *variation* of a central theme, reflected from a different point of view. The essence of their concern is: What does it mean to be *den enkelte*.* Closely aligned to this idea is that only through the God or love can possibility become actuality.

---

* that *single* individual

Theatrical and Dramatic Art

For Kierkegaard, the worldly art of the theatre was a means he could use to clarify the spiritual relationship to man. He speaks of the prompter, the actor, and the audience in connection with the understanding of man's relationship to God.

The prompter was an important adjunct to the 19th century theatre, often to the chagrin of the audience, for there was a tendency for the actors to keep their eyes on him; missing a cue or forgetting a line was not an infrequent occurrence.

In discussing the interaction of the prompter and the actor, Kierkegaard does not voice annoyance at the distraction; rather, he mentions the stage convention in a conceptual context. He describes the prompter in *Opbyggelige Taler* as *af hiin Skjulte,** he who sits on a stage and prompts by whisper. The other one strides out and draws every eye to himself; he impersonates a distinct individual. Because theatre is an illusionary art, each word becomes true when embodied in the actor. The words become true through him and yet he is told by *af hiin Skjulte* who sits and whispers. Thus, says Kierkegaard, the speaker is not really the actor as most people think. Kierkegaard then transfers the analogy to the religious scene where God is the critical theatregoer who looks on to see how the lines are spoken and how they are listened

---

* the hidden one

92

to, something Kierkegaard adds, that the customary audience does not do. Digressions are frequent or seem to be, but what these asides do is create an intimacy with the audience which brings the discussion back to the present. Kierkegaard then makes his point, that the speaker or *the word* spoken is the prompter, and the listener stands openly before God. The listener is the actor who in all truth acts before God.

In discussing the idea of living one day at a time, Kierkegaard again focuses on the actor, this time in an effort to dispel fear of the future. He indicates a familiarity with the actor's art, a familiarity he assumes his readers share. It is well known, he says, that in front of the actor, blinded as he is by the footlights, there is darkness "den sorteste Nat."*[16] But this condition does not upset the actor. If you ask him, he will say that it is the darkness that gives him support and calms him. To be able to see any single individual would decompose him, "Saaledes med den naeste Dag."**[17]

Another instance where the actor is brought into play is in reference to suffering. To perish in suffering is an illusion. It is as when one actor in a play kills another. It seems as though he killed him but it is known by all that he was not hurt.

The necessity of contrast to achieve a recollection prompted Kierkegaard to observe that this can sometimes be best achieved in a theatre. Consider an erotic situation in which the smug aloofness of country life is the essential point. Presented in the theatre, the environment and the noise force the contrast into evidence.[18]

Exasperation with the idea of people being satisfied with mediocrity and compromise, their committing themselves to a way of life "til en vis grad"*** engendered a theatrical comparison. As it is on the stage, Kierkegaard says, no matter how

---

* "the blackest night"
** "So it is with the next day."
*** "to a certain degree"

tenderly the actor and the actress embrace one another, this is nevertheless a theatrical union, so also is it in relation to the unconditional, all this thing of "til en vis grad" is theatrical, it grasps an illusion. Only *enten-eller* is the embrace that grasps the unconditional.[19]

The insights that Kierkegaard reveals in his discussion of theatrical and dramatic art are more penetrating because of the unique context in which he places them. *Schattenspiel an der Wand,* a play of shadows on the wall which was a parlor game of the period, is compared to the Sophists, the grotesque figures who perform in such plays. This image was used to emphasize that their exertions did not relate to the Idea.[20]

Kierkegaard expresses the Socratic view of comedy and tragedy, that they are in some sense one. He, too, has fused comedy and tragedy: "Jeg siger Vittigheder, Folk leer — jeg graeder."*[21] In exploring the nature of the comic, he makes

* "I make jokes, people laugh — I weep."

94

a distinction between the comical which occurs by accident, and that which is comic from the contradiction of the infinite and the finite. The true form of the comic is, that the infinite may move within a man, and no one is able to discover it through anything that appears outwardly.[22] It is the contradiction which is implicit to the comical stance that makes the person comical. A person does not become comical because of his subjectivity but because of the objectivity around him which is incommensurable with his interest. Such Ibsen characters as Stockman in *Folkefiende,* Pastor Manders — *Gengangere,* Hjalmar — *Vildanden* — reflect variations of the comic sense as Kierkegaard views it. What lies at the root of both the comic and the tragic is this connection, the contradiction, which is one that is between the infinite and the finite, the external and that which becomes. Consequently, the subjective existing thinker is as bifrontal as existence itself because if one has the pathos of the infinite, one has at the same time, the comic.[23]

Some of the dramatists which Kierkegaard most frequently refers to are Sophocles, Aristophanes, Shakespeare, Holberg, Goethe, Molière, Øehlenschläger, Scribe, Heiberg. All but the first two dramatists had plays on the Danish stage in Copenhagen between 1829 and 1849.[24]

A *Papirer* entry in reference to Antigone and Greek tragedy reflects on the predicament of Antigone and what she had to contend with as daughter of an ill-fated marriage, engaged to Kreon's son, and subject to the anger of the Gods who were pursuing her family.[25] Kierkegaard sees the implications possible in a contemporary approach to the play, not as a means of revitalizing the past but to present a new point of view. The play could become a romantic tragedy if Antigone would fall passionately in love but be unwilling to marry because she belonged to the family of Oedipus, and would not leave a family which might be persecuted by the Gods. Though not his explicit intention in this entry, Kierkegaard is indicating how dramatic form changes in response to the way the dramatist looks at experience. Reflecting on tragedy, Kierkegaard asserts that the age of tragedy is past; it remains mired in ethical difficulty; though the idea triumphs, the hero is destroyed.[26] Another thought that he posits in connection with Antigone is the consequence of making her into a man, because then as a hero, she could fall in a duel.[27] Kierkegaard is voicing an important consideration in the treatment of dramatic action: the role of woman. For instance, Shakespeare's Lady Macbeth expresses her frustration in the cry "unsex me" while Ibsen's Hedda burns the manuscript and Shaw's Joan asks to be treated as a man; and, more recently, Genet in an effort to avoid a sexual stereotype wanted men to perform the female roles in *The Maids* (*Les Bonnes*), the effort directed to conveying an asexual image. Dramatists have found it difficult to portray the woman as an individual, disassociated from the role society has written for her. Although Kierkegaard has conceded that the order of knighthood proves its immortality by the fact that it makes no distinction between man and woman, it was an effort for him to envision a woman experiencing masculine despair.[28] More often, his interest is in showing that the feminine figure could show immediacy and sorrow more

96

than the masculine form could. Not only does Kierkegaard dwell on the feminine sensibility in "Skyggerids,"* his sketches on reflective grief, but it is a concern in his writing about the ancient and the tragic motif in the modern, and in his criticisms of the actress.[29] Kierkegaard's consideration of the woman in different contexts reflects, not so much an ambivalence on his part, as it does a pondering of an idea. Ibsen's handling of the female character was to show her functioning within society as her role dictated and to have her situation serve as an analogy of an individual problem that had a deeper significance, as opposed to her simply reflecting a "woman" problem; in his later plays, the lines of demarcation between the topical and the universal become less self-conscious, his women characters remaining among the greatest roles in theatrical history.

The reference to Aristophanes' play *Clouds*[30] are numerous, and, as usual, they are connected with some concept that is being delineated. In this instance, the dramatic analysis is in connection with possibility. Kierkegaard remarks upon the symbolism and the irony of the *title* of Aristophanes' play; the stratagem was an integral aspect of his own work as it was in Ibsen's. *Clouds* illustrates the empty activity that goes into the Thoughtery. It is, therefore, with deep irony that Aristophanes, in the scene when Strepsiades is to be initiated into this wisdom, allows Socrates to call upon the clouds, the airy reflection of his own hollow interior. *Clouds* describes perfectly the directionless movement of thought which incessant fluctuation configures in every way as do clouds, which in the play represent in turn: a mortal woman, a centaur, a leopard, a wolf, a bull. Kierkegaard emphasizes the fact that the clouds resemble, but are *not* these creatures, for all this is vapor or the obscure, self-moving, infinite possibility of becoming, yet the vapor is too barren to allow anything to become estab-

---

* Shadowgraphs

lished. It is full of possibility but no content, a theme Ibsen was to express in *Vildanden*.

In his Master's dissertation, *Begrebet Ironi,* Aristophanes is treated in connection with possibility, and also with actuality.[31] He observes that the essence of the Greek comedy lies in apprehending actuality ideally, in bringing an actual personality on the stage in such a way that he is representative of the Idea.[32]

Some quotations from Shakespeare's plays are written in German from A. W. Schlegel's translations; others are cited in Danish. Kierkegaard's obvious appreciation of Shakespeare is reflected in the succinct and original comparisons he makes. In speaking about the Apostles and the idea of fish who eat the fishermen, "det er jo naesten ligesom Hamlets Vanvid, naar han siger om Polonius at han er til Gjestebud, dog ikke der, hvor han spiser, men der, hvor han bliver spiist."*[33] Another comparison is in reference to the *New Testament.* The Christian battalions which "Christendom" places in the field no more resemble what the *New Testament* understands by Christians than did the recruits that Falstaff enlisted resemble able-bodied, well-trained soldiers eager for battle.[34]

Hamlet made an impression on Kierkegaard. Within "Skyldig?" — "Ikke Skyldig?",** there are a few pages titled "Et Sideblik til Shakespeare's Hamlet"*** within which he ponders the words of a critic, Ludvig Börne, who called it a Christian drama. Kierkegaard would call it a Christian drama too, but then he would have to criticize it for not remaining consistent. He points out that Hamlet should have had religious postulates which conspired against him so as to produce religious doubt. Since Shakespeare did not do this, Hamlet is a victim of morbid reserve and the aesthetic demands a comic

---

* "It's almost like Hamlet's madness when he says of Polonius that he is at supper, not where he eats, but where he is eaten."
** "Guilty "—"Not Guilty?"
*** "A side-glance at Shakespeare's *Hamlet.*"

interpretation.[35] He concludes his "side-blik" at Hamlet by saying that one can learn from him, and learn the more one reads him.

Molière's *Don Juan* is discussed in reference to Mozart's opera *Don Giovanni* with Molière's play suffering by the comparison.[36] The seducer is significant to Kierkegaard, and in viewing Don Juan in the play and in the opera he distinguishes between two kinds of seducers, the comical and the psychological. To differentiate between the two seducers, he remarks that with the first, attention is directed to the relationship of the seducer to the environment and is comic because the dramatic effect will come largely from the incongruity between the aspirations of desire and the pettiness of the frustrations it encounters. The second kind of seducer is the reflective seducer, the Johannes of "Forførerens Dagbog,"*[37] who will assume a psychological stance and the result will be *interesting* rather than comic.

Kierkegaard claims that Molière relied upon the comic rather than the psychological in his Don Juan although he admits psychology is not lacking in the characterization. However, Molière has not revealed Don Juan's attributes in action, and, Kierkegaard observes, he does not present him as a great seducer. In not having Don Juan live up to his reputation, Moliere created a ridiculous figure. Although there are many scenes which are excellent comedy, the failing is that dramatically, the audience does not see Don Juan as he is supposed to be, that is, as a sensuous character; instead, what has been effected is a discordant character. It might seem, Kierkegaard suggests, that the sensuousness of Don Juan would be best interpreted in ballet, but this is not so for the ballet, at most, can only represent the pangs of despair; the expression in pantomime is not individualized. Kierkegaard recognizes that the operatic form relies for its effect upon musical evocation, that it is inseparately joined to the content so that

---

* "The Diary of a Seducer"

sexual desire in the immediate is called forth. For this reason, Mozart's *Don Giovanni* (*Don Juan*) is unique as a seducer. He goes through life like a god with such charm and energy that he invests his self-indulgence with beauty. For Kierkegaard, Mozart's seducer demonstrates the fact that when passion is separated from moral will and the rule of the spirit, it degenerates into lust.

Kierkegaard's criticism of Molière has limitations because of the perspective from which it is viewed. It is not valid to consider the dramatic form in connection with pure music or dance (each art form has its own laws) and Kierkegaard was aware of the discrepancy. Secondly, Molière's characterization of Don Juan should not be judged from the point of view of psychological credibility but from the aesthetic of its creator. Kierkegaard does, however, admire Heiberg's adaptation of Molière's work, saying that it was more correct and more successful as a comedy, being more unalloyed, but he concludes the opera is the ideal interpretation.

The Norwegian-born "Danish" dramatist of the 18th century, Ludvig Holberg, is mentioned frequently by Kierkegaard. Mester Geert Westphaler, the main character in a play of the same name, is related to the idea of *lunacy*. Geert is a chatty man who talks continually about himself and his bit of a journey which is a kind of lunacy, but then, it is also lunacy when one is asked about faith and talks about the whole world, with the exception of one's self. Ibsen also had an interest in Mester Geert Westphaler. When he was a member of the Holland group,[38] a critical literary circle in Kristiania, whose members revered Holberg, he became known as Geert Westphaler, with no apparent derision intended. In writing about Christenhed,* Kierkegaard cites *Ulysses von Ithacia,* a mock-heroic parody. A line from the play describes an empty book, "Dette skal vaere Troy."** Kierkegaard retorts that so it is with all this about Christendom. Many of Kierkegaard's

---

* Christenhed = Christianity; Christendom = pseudo Christianity
** "This is supposed to be Troy."

dramatic references go into detail about an aspect of the play, and then in the last line, he makes his point. For instance, in *Den ellefte Juni*,* he deliberates about the character, Stundenstrup, who is clearly in the right about the Town Hall, that it is a very handsome building, and that it is for a song that these honest men are willing to sell it. It is the most brilliant transaction that can be imagined. This must be conceded by his paternal uncle at the town of Thy, by all the kindred in Salling, and by all shrewd men wherever they are. *But,* what Stundenstrup neglected to consider was whether these honest men stood in such a relation to the Town Hall that they were able to dispose of it. If not, the price, no matter how low, is dear. "Saaledes med Christendommen."**[39]

* *The Eleventh of June*
** "So it is with Christianity."

101

Goethe's *Faust* is alluded to in a reference to the Sophists who entice youth to know everything in a broad culture. Kierkegaard indicates the resemblance to the Mephistophelian counsel given the student. He was advised not to enroll in any of the several faculties where he would become a man of culture and learn the appropriate instruction for becoming an accomplished statesman and skilled in private affairs. Kierkegaard was incensed with the hypocrisy of the clergy whom he viewed as more concerned with the proper credentials and their careers than they were with Christianity. He describes the priest as a half worldly half Churchly civil servant who is a person of rank, a man who hopes to receive a knightly order and assure himself of a living. He quotes a Danish jingle, "hvem kan bedst, det kan vor Praest."*[40] In *Kjaerlighedens Komedie,* Ibsen dramatizes the hypocrisy of religion and marriage, suggesting a comic condition which is not without pathos.

In his play, *Aladdin,* Adam Øehlenschläger contrasts Aladdin, the heroic dreamer, to Noureddin, the representative of darkness. Kierkegaard uses the contrast to explain a proverb which he thought inappropriate to this world: "kun den, der arbeider, faaer Brødet."**[41] Rather, in the outward world everything is made payable to the bearer. This world is in bondage to the law of indifference, and to him who has the ring. The spirit of the ring is obedient, whether it be Aladdin or Noureddin. But, in the world of the spirit, its is quite different, "kun den, der stiger ned i Underverdenen, frelser den Elskede, kun den, der drager Kniven, faaer Isaak."***

After 1830, Eugene Scribe surpassed other playwrights in popularity on the Danish stage. The impact of this lesser dramatist on Kierkegaard continued until the last year of his life, although not in the same way. The relationship has an

---

* "He who knows best, that is our priest."
** "Only the man who works gets the bread."
*** "Only he who descends into the underworld rescues the beloved, only he who draws the knife gets Isaac."

102

interest in connection with Ibsen, as, so frequently his technique is said to reflect Scribean technical skill. In *Enten-Eller I*, Scribe's play *Den Første Kjaerlighed** is discussed and praised; the opposite point of view is presented in the second volume.

Ronald Grimsley, in his study on Kierkegaard and French literature, points out that Kierkegaard's knowledge of French culture was wider than is supposed.[42] Kierkegaard studied French and it was one of the subjects he took for the University of Copenhagen's entrance examination. It was not from Dumas, Hugo, or Musset, but chiefly from Scribe that the Danish theatre took its impulse.[43] The popularity of Scribe with the Danish public was, in part, a result of the social attitude which encouraged French culture. Private performances were given in French by French troupes. When the plays were presented for the popular audience they were given in translation. On the title page of Kierkegaard's study is written *Den Første Kjaerlighed, Lystspil i een Akt af Scribe, oversat af J. L. Heiberg.***[44]

In the essay, Kierkegaard pays homage to the literary merits of the play, treats the author as a typical representative of modern comedy, of the well-made play in which the dramatic action is commensurable with the situation, the point he criticized Molière as being deficient in. The play for Kierkegaard is without fault and the poet is revealed in the way the characters are presented in speech and situation. Peter Hansen, in his work on Danish theatre history, refers to Kierkegaard's *analysis of Den Første Kjaerlighed* as "en aandfuld panegyrik."****[45]

For Kierkegaard, *the performance of the play is the play*, unlike other critics who mention the play, then the perfor-

---

* *The First Love*
** *The First Love* A Comedy in One Act by Scribe, translated by J. L. Heiberg.
*** "a soulful panegyric"

103

mance. He is profuse in his admiration of the Scribean play which he claims to have seen in French, Danish, and German. If he were to show the theatre in its full glory, he would say go and see *Den Første Kjaerlighed*. To understand Kierkegaards' response, it must be realized that he had his own inimitable way of interpreting phenomena and that he had the pleasure of seeing this play performed at the Royal Theatre with star performers. He says that the Danish stage has in Madame Heiberg, Frydendahl, Phister, and Stage a four-leaf clover which appears in all its beauty in Scribe's play, "Frydendahl som Derviere, Jfr. Pätges som Emmeline, Stage som Rinvild, Phister som Charles."*

In terms of production, Kierkegaard regards *Anledningen*** as of the greatest importance. It is this condition which decides the play's aesthetic value. A creation is a product from nothing, and *Anledningen* is the nothing from which everything comes, yet *Anledningen* is the essential category from the sphere of the idea to actuality, and represents a oneness to the nature that understands it. Unawareness of *Anledningen* is the reason reviews are so bungling. If he had not experienced a connaturality with the play, he could not have written about it. *Anledningen* had a significance in another more personal context for Kierkegaard, and also for Ibsen. They have lived through the experiences expressed in their writing, an under-current which heightens the immediacy of their art.

Den Første Kjaerlighed is about youthful love and the romantic attitude toward life. The ironical treatment of the romantic and the contradiction between appearance and reality attracted Kierkegaard. It is a play that shows how the aesthetic and the romantic attitude toward love leads to its downfall.

---

* Frydendahl played Derviere, the father, Jfr. Påtges (Fru Heiberg) played the young girl, Emmeline, Stage was the new suitor, Rinville and Phister was the "first" love.

** *Anledningen* = *the occasion*

A sixteen-year old girl, Emmeline, a spoilt only child, refuses to meet the young man, Rinville, whom her father wants her to marry. She insists on remaining faithful to her childhood sweetheart and cousin, Charles, to whom she swore eternal love eight years earlier. The father finally agrees to cancel Rinville's visit, but in the interim, Rinville has arrived at the house and intercepted the letter. Charles arrives, married and in debt. Rinville persuades Charles to change identities with him and when Emmeline sees them, she immediately falls in love with Rinville who is pretending to be Charles. This love vanishes when Emmeline discovers that he no longer has the ring which she gave him, but she is revived when he presents the ring which he has managed to obtain from the real Charles. Eventually, Emmeline discovers the truth, learns that Charles is married and she agrees to marry Rinville, consoling herself with the thought that she had mistaken the past for the future.

There are cogent ideas in this well-constructed, seemingly banal one-actor which had interest for Kierkegaard. Emmeline had lived in the world of illusion; the ring, a physical object, had sealed her love. Although Charles was freed from this naiveté, he still clung to his love of mystification, thus, the concealment of his marriage. Kierkegaard sees a similarity in these two attitudes, since, in illusion, the individual is concealed from himself, while in mystification, he seeks to conceal himself from others.

In *Enten-Eller* II, Kierkegaard, through Judge Williams, gives his response to *Den Første Kjaerlighed* as an ethical judgment. He does not praise Charles and Emmeline as dramatic characters in the way the author of Part One did. The Judge criticizes Charles' moral depravity which he says is not what one should learn from a poet, and he considers Emmeline too shrewd. In focusing on the aesthetic and ethical attitudes by means of contrast, Kierkegaard illustrates the characteristic of the aesthetic and the ethical attitudes,

105

thereby presenting a life-view, "love is comic," the cynical view expressed by Ibsen in *Kjaerlighedens Komedie.*

Besides the conceptual interest that Scribe engendered in Kierkegaard, he also liked the same characteristics of Scribean drama that the Danish audience enjoyed: well-constructed comic plots and situations which had dramatic appeal; lively dialogue; the mingling of sentiment and emotion, comedy and pathos; the social comedies which generated thinking about problems previously ignored; the enthusiastic response of the actors who felt they were provided with an opportunity to demonstrate their art.[46] Kierkegaard believed that the audience should be able to enjoy the dramatic unfolding of a play; this enjoyment Scribe provided.[47] However, Kierkegaard recognizes that if things move too easily, it is easy to miss a great deal; a point to be considered in contemplating his and Ibsen's maieutic focus.

There are references to Scribe throughout Kierkegaard's works. By 1849, he renounces Scribe as a secret accomplice to the very devices he so skillfully describes.

Heiberg's play *Alferne** is called a little masterpiece by Kierkegaard. The occasion for the acclaim was a reference to a situation that particularly irked him, Bishop Martinsen and his royal commission. In Scene 2 of the play, the schoolmaster, inadvertently plunges below the surface of the earth and finds himself surrounded by gnomes. The schoolmaster says, "Hvilket Nonsens, der er ikke Bjergtrolde — og her er min Bestalling."** His observation is that the gnomes do not care about a royal commission, which is the same value it had for Kierkegaard. *Kong Salomon og Jorgen Hattemager,**** Scene 26, is brought into focus regarding the Christian paradox, which is not this or that, something wonderful and yet not so wonderful. Its truth is not like Salomon Goldfarb's opinion,

_____

* *The Fairies*
** "What nonsense — there are no gnomes, and here is my commission [to prove it]."
*** *King Salomon and Jorgen the Hatter*

106

much before and behind, and yes and no at the same time. In another instance, a play is simply identified as that of State Counselor Heiberg's, the implication is that the play is so popular that the characters are immediately recognizable. Kierkegaard comments that Herr Zierlich, a character in the play, possesses a sense of decency to such a degree that he finds it indecent for men's and women's garments to be hung in the same closet. The play is *Aprilsnarrene,** a vaudeville in which Fru Heiberg, then Anna Pätges, appeared when she was thirteen years old. Actually, it was Madam who thought it unseemly that Miss Trummeir was shut in the closet with Herr Zierlich's coat. The reference is used as an opening to the idea of the difference of living for something which the age "har faaet i Skab sammen."**

Other dramatists from whom Kierkegaard drew illustrations were Johan Hermann Wessel, Henrik Hertz, Christian Hostrup, Richard Cumberland, Thomas Overskou, Ephraim Gotthold Lessing.[48] Their plays occupied a place in the repertoire of the Royal Theatre during Kierkegaard's lifetime.

His dialectic is especially stimulating when he considers a play in the theatrical context and extends its content by relating it to another essence. The sense of immediacy is intensified when a particular actor is focussed upon as he is in the critique of Phister's role as Captain Scipio in the comic opera *Ludovic*.

The art of acting and its relation to the comic are astutely conjoined in Kierkegaard's critique of Phister, whom he regards as a reflective artist, diligent in every detail. He titles the article "Her Phister som Captain Scipio,"*** using the pseudonym Procul which is Latin for "at a distance," suggesting the distance between the reflective critic and the reflective artist. In using pseudonyms, Kierkegaard is accentuating a position, creating a poetic personality. Within this criticism

---

* *April Fools*
** "has put together in a closet"
*** "Herr Phister as Captain Scipio"

Kierkegaard voices some of his opinions concerning critics. Their roles should be interpreters, disclosing something in the performance that the artist is not conscious of. He recognizes that there are few critics able to respond to a reflective performance where everything is consciousness. Ordinarily, reviewers prefer only to admire the immediate but the immediate performance is lacking in self-consciousness. At the end of his critique, Kierkegaard criticizes critics who make a judgment after having seen but one performance. With his writing about the theatre, he hopes to pay back a little of the debt that is owed great artists.

Phister is considered an apt subject for a critique because the richness of his repertoire is masterful. He is a diligent actor who studies his part and gives reflective attention to every detail. Admiration of Phister's art is requisite for writing about it because to admire is to be able to understand the whole. In attempting to understand Phister's masterful portrayal, Kierkegaard associates his need to understand with infatuation, or self-love, since he wants to approximate what the artist has experienced.

Scipio, Captain of the Papal Police, reflects Kierkegaard's view of the comic as contradiction with the environment, and he credits Phister with having insights that accentuate the contradiction.

In Act I, Scipio is inebriated, not drunk. He is the kind of man who constantly drinks but never seems to be really drunk. It might even be that he cannot get drunk. Phister has insisted upon being clad in a brilliant uniform which is exactly the contradiction that is needed because the more brilliant the outside of the uniform is, the more shocking is the perfunctory side of him that clashes with it (an example of the double reflection on a small scale that Kierkegaard and Ibsen express in their artistic communication), and both sides can be seen at once. Kierkegaard discusses Phister's posturing and mannerisms as indicative of an ambiguity within Scipio, an uncertainty between the military and the civilian stance. For instance, Scipio comes in late, lagging behind his men, exhibiting a sidewise gait, bustling, an incomparable way to indicate civilian busyness — arriving in the greatest haste, late.

Whereas it is not difficult to play a drunk, Phister must portray a man who is drunk, yet is not drunk. The comic subtlety consists in portraying his singular state of inebriation telegraphically, that is surreptitiously — with the fluttering hand, the cough, the hand to the mouth, a suggestion of a stagger.

As Kierkegaard discusses each phase of Scipio's characterization, he comments upon the strength of Phister's art. For example, in the second act Scipio is sober, but in terms of acting he looks more like a drunken man, which is quite right, a natural reaction to giving up drink. This is an instance where Phister's art is fully revealed. Ibsen's awareness of the actor's art was as astute as Kierkegaard's.[49] In his letters to directors and performers, and notes to his plays, insights are recorded that reflect his mimetic sensibility and his professional experience. Ibsen indicates, often in detail, how a particular role should be played; sometimes he will suggest a particular actress or actor for a part, relating his choice to the performer's talents.

Subtlety of expression, the mimetic sensibility, the sense of occasion, dialectics, indirect communication, irony, were Kierkegaard's forte. It is not surprising that he was perceptive about histrionic art. A lengthy footnote in *Staadier paa Livets Vei* describes Fru Nielsen, an actress he refers to as "det vaesentlig Qvindelige."* The footnote is in conjunction with an observation about marriage in which he says that woman's beauty increases with the years. He prefaces his remarks with the admission that examples of histrionic art might be misleading because everything there is concentrated upon the instant; consequently, everything has to be essential. Yet, in theatrical life, he does find collaboration for his view, particu-

---

* "the essential feminine"

109

larly in the person of Madame Nielsen. She has been able to express the essential in all the feminine characters she has portrayed regardless of the variation in roles. Time has no power over her. She represents pure femininity to him and her art is durable; it is seeing the beautiful in truth.

The idea of feminine youthfulness as something that is embodied in a mature woman is developed in *Krisen og Krise i en Skuespillerindes Liv,* a short essay in praise of Fru Heiberg. The actress is granted an immunity to time, of a kind that is achieved in art. In her youth, the actress can only express herself in an unconscious way with potentiality for the transparent expression of self. The interest for Kierke-gaard is in the *metamorphosis* of the artist. It is in the idea

that maturity as the time when one has definition that brings Ibsen's characters into focus; considering them prior to this does not have the same significance.

As the metamorphosis unfolds in connection with the actress

110

(Fru Heiberg), it is a return to the first condition, and it is a repetition in this sense, not in the religious sense of being received back again to be reconstructed as a new condition.[50] As the actress moves from the immediate to a more reflective mode, clarity of conscious thought is uncontrived and intuitively expressed, a mode of art that Kierkegaard did not subscribe to.

Kierkegaard also attacks the aesthetic cultivation of the masses, the audience that senses and responds to the beauty of the young actress although she is as yet not defined. For them, art-appreciation is her damnable prettiness and her devilish liveliness. When the metamorphosis of the actress comes into its own and is revealed, the masses lose interest. Because of her age, the actress is regarded as passé. The irony is that it is only in the later years that admiration is justified.

The actress who does not have the natural gifts is lucky in some respects because she can enact her metamorphosis quietly; the public does not ruin the process by its inquisitiveness or by misunderstanding what is happening. Restlessness distinguishes the possibility of someone becoming an actress in the real sense, while possessing the quality of soulfulness means the actress is attuned to thought and idea, that she can relate to the playwright's words and to herself even more. Such a condition indicates that she is in the right rapport with the tension of the stage. (Tension was a condition Kierkegaard expressed in his study of Phister; its necessity to dramatic art Kierkegaard could understand.) Although the actress must have grace and training, Kierkegaard sees a potential danger in these two attributes, in that the actress may deceive herself with habit and remain unchanged. Her metamorphosis would become more difficult, yet it is only with her metamorphosis that her time begins (as with Ibsen's Nora).

Time is the dialectic which comes from without and destroys some of the natural youthfulness, but it makes the genius more manifest in the aesthetic relation to the idea. In the sense of ideality, the actress will become younger and younger. The

111

most demanding role such an actress could be assigned would be Juliet in *Romeo and Juliet*. Distance from age is required for an actress to re-create the role. As she gets older, however, and if she assumes older roles, she will do so with the same perfectibility of her earlier roles, thus there is a metamorphosis of continuity that will extend over the years.

Kierkegaard was not alone in commemorating Fru Heiberg; Ibsen wrote a poem to her, "Rimbrev til Fru Heiberg,"*⁵¹ in which he expresses a thought in regard to her art that Kierkegaard has expressed about love (and which Ibsen dramatizes in *Kjaerlighedens Komedie*), that it will live in memory and that is what life truly means:

> Og se det er livet just,
> liv i mindet. . . .

A Recapitulation

On theatre, Kierkegaard is sophisticated in regarding performance as the play, reiterating in this insight his view of form and matter as integral. He sees that the tendency of the age is in the direction of the comic. He believes that the critic's functions is to illuminate the work of art. He understands consciousness as coming to itself, not only in reference to the average individual, but in reference to the dramatist and the actress, that is, the artist. He does not disregard technique, but he stresses the external appearance and the inner life resting in the double reflection; it is the inner essence that has more significance for him. The categories of repetition and metamorphosis, the inartistic masses, the paradox of youth and age find expression in his writings on theatre, particularly in *Krisen*. As with artistic communication, his theatrical and dramatic references are immediate; he has an awareness that art forms — theatre, drama, music, dance — have their own

---

* "Rhymed letter to Fru Heiberg."

112

laws; his conceptual references have an existential point in relation to the idea.

"En sideblik til" Ibsen is an appropriate adjunct to the substance of this chapter. The correspondence of his and Kierkegaard's dialectic and aesthetic sensibility suggests, if not a double reflection, an indication of a compatible consciousness.

NOTES TO CHAPTER I

[1] The expression used in *Staadier paa Livets Vei* in reference to Shakespeare.

[2] *Samlede Vaerker XIV*, p. 118.

[3] *Øieblikket* Nr. 6, s. 212. "Det er derfor Lykke, at Kirken har Theatret paa Siden af sig; thi Theatret er en Skalk. . ."

[4] *Mit Livs Eventyr* I, s. 215, "den kongelige danske Skueplads kunde da vistnok ogsaa henrignes til een af de første i Europa."

[5] Ludvig Phister was also a well-known Holberg actor. The article referred to is *Hr. Phister som Captain Scipio (Papirer IX)*. *Ludovic* is a comic opera in two acts, originally in French by J. H. Vernoyde Saint-Georges, translated into Danish by Th. Overskou, a playwright, theatre manager, historian.

[6] *Hans Christian Andersen and the Romantic Theatre* by Frederik Marker, University of Toronto Press, 1971, p. 30. (Adam Øehlenschläger was a significant Danish playwright; Bertel Thorvaldsen was a famous sculptor.)

[7] *Don Giovanni* — Mozart opera in two acts (libretto — da Ponte).

[8] References to it are in *Om min Forfatter-Virksomhed; Synspunktet for min Forfatter Virksomhed*.

[9] Interpreted as *Purity of Heart* by Douglas Steere, 1948.

[10] Francis Fergusson, *The Idea of a Theatre*, p. 252. New York.

[11] *Enten-Eller* I, s. 256-57, Bind 2.

113

[12] *Enten-Eller* I, s. 137 (*Samlede Vaerker* Bind 2) "maa leve mig ind i den graeke Bevidsthed."

[13] "Breve til Christian Hostrup," Munchen, den 2 April, 1888. *Samlede Verker*, s. 162, Bind XVIII.

[14] *Opbyggelige Taler i forskjellig Aand*, Bind 11 *Samlede Vaerker*,'s. 139.

[15] *Enten-Eller* I, s. 129, "at Bebrebets Indhold ikke dethroniserede Begrebet, men berigede det."

[16] *Christelige Taler*, Bind 13, s. 74.

[17] Ibid.

[18] *Staadier*, s. 18-19, Bind 7, "i et Theatret hvor Omgivelsen og Larmen tvinger Modsaetningen frem."

[19] *Øieblikket* 1 (*Samlede Vaerker;* Bind 19, s. 94), "griber en Indbildning, kun *Enten-Eller* er Favnetaget, som griber det."

[20] *Ironi*, s. 156 (*Samlede Vaerker*, Bind 1).

[21] *Papirer* II A 132.

[22] *Efterskrifter*, s. 78, Bind 9. "Det sande Comiske er, at det Uendelige kan foregaa i et Menneske, og Ingen, Ingen opdage det paa ham."

[23] Ibid., s. 77. — "har jeg Uendelighedens Pathos har jeg ogsaa strax det Comiske."

[24] *Den Danske Skueplads* (1864), Thomas Overskou.

[25] *Papirer* III A 207, III C 37.

[26] *Staadier*, s. 234, Bind 8, "at vel Ideen seirer, men Helter gaaer under."

[27] *Papirer* — see footnote 23.

[28] *Sygdom*, s. 105, Bind 15. "Den ene Form er saa at sige Qvindelighedens Fortvivlelse, den anden Mandlighedens." "The one form is, so to speak, the despair of womanliness, the other of manliness."

[29] The reference is to Fru Nielsen and Fru Heiberg. Isak Dinesen has observed that the reason there are so few women artists is because art is an extension of a woman's being. She does not put art into objects. But, Dinesen adds, a woman can become a work of art, that is, an actress.

[30] Kierkegaard uses the Danish word for the title of Aristophanes' play, *Skyerne*, in *Ironi*.

[31] *Ironi*, s. 173, Bind I.

[32] *Ibid.*, s. 169.

[33] An example of Kierkegaard's juxtaposition of ideas within a contextual framework.

[34] *Øieblikket* 7, s. 217, Bind 19.

[35] *Staadier* II, s. 246, Bind 8, "saa er Hamlet vaesentligen en Ubesluttet, og det Aesthetiske fordrer en comisk Opfattelse."

[36] *Enten-Eller* I, s. 45, Bind 2. "De umiddelbare Erotiske Staadier eller Det Musikalsk-erotiske" (The Immediate Stages of the Erotic or the Musical Erotic).

[37] Contained in *Enten-Eller* I.

[38] Ibseu's membership in the Holland Group—see Chronology entry for 1858.

114

39 *Faedrelandet*, 10. Mai 1855. Nr. 107 s. 17 (*i Samlere Vaerker 19*).
40 *Faedrelandet*, 21. Mars 1856. Nr. 68 s. 36.
41 *Frygt og Baeven* (SV. s. 27).
42 *Søren Kierkegaard and French Literature* by Ronald Grimsley. Cardiff: University of Wales, 1966.
43 *Studier fra Sprog og Oltidsforskning* "Engang Den Mest Spillede-Studier i Eugene Scribe Teater i Frankrig og Danmark" by Erik Aschengren, København: G.E.C. Gads Forlag, 1969.
44 *Enten-Eller* I, *den Første Kjaerlighed* (*The First Love*) (*Les Premières Amours*).
45 *Den Danske Skuesplads*, Volume II, s, 534.
46 Grimsley, *op. cit.*; Thomas Overskou V, pp. 641-42, 740.
47 Erik Aschengren, *op. cit.* See note 31.
48 Wessel's *Kjaerligheden uden Strømper* (*Love Without Stockings*, 1772) contains reaction against French style.

Hertz wrote plays for Fru Heiberg. His play, *Svend Dyrings Hus* (*Svend Dyrings House*), 1837, is frequently discussed in reference to Ibsen's *Gildet paa Solhoug* (*Feast at Solhoug*, 1856) in similar use of ballad material.

Hostrup play *Under Snefog* (*In the Snowstodm*), referred to earlier.

Cumberland's play *The Jew* (1796) appeared many times on the Danish stage. The character (the Jew) was regarded as a miser; in actuality, he did works that were beneficial.

Overskou was a theatre historian, a dramatist and a stage manager from whom Ibsen learned something about staging during his 1852 study tour to Copenhagen. The play mentioned by Kierkegaard, *Capriciosa*, was about the inexplicableness of love.

Lessing's *Emilia Galotti* (1772) was referred to by Kierkegaard in reference to silence.

49 It is in his apprentice years at "det norske Theater" in Bergen and Kristiania that Ibsen acquired practical experience. At the Bergen theatre, he was first engaged as a dramatic poet and later as stage manager, while at the Kristiania theatre he was stage director. He also wrote theatre articles for the newspaper in his early years. See chronology. In his letters to the directors of his plays, Ibsen reveals a sensitivity and understanding of the histrionic art.
50 *Gjentagelsen* (repetition) a significant category for Kierkegaard. Stephen Crites (is in agreement with the nature of the repetition), p. 34 (*Crisis*).
51 "Rhymed Letter to Fru Heiberg" from Dresden, 1871, *Samlede Verker*, Bind 14, s. 43.

115

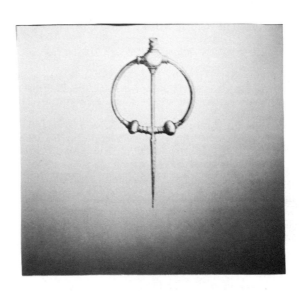

The Ancient
and the Modern

II

The Pagan / Christian Dichotomy

"The past is prologue" to the future

Modern aesthetics constantly goes back to Aristotle for the substantiation of its principles and whereas general premises are valid in connection with this criteria, there is the condition of the modern consciousness to be considered. In a fragmentary essay, "Det antike Tragiskes Reflex i det moderne Tragiske" which he dedicates to *Symparekromenoi*,* Kierkegaard expresses this viewpoint. He does not reject the ancient tragical motif but seeks to see how it is reflected in the modern.

From the point of view of the difference between the ancient and the modern, Kierkegaard's aesthetic and Ibsen's "poetics" become more visible. This chapter treats the pagan/Christian dichotomy and examines the nature of the comical-tragical mode that Kierkegaard believed in 1843 was the one appropriate to modern drama.

Kierkegaard's interest in paganism reflects his admiration for it and his rejection of it. He admitted that pagans had performed amazing exploits which had prompted the enthusiasm of poets and there were pagans who had lived rich lives enhanced by art and learning. But, lacking the God-relation-

---

* "The Ancient Tragical Motif as Reflected in the Modern" "the fellowship of buried lives"

119

ship, paganism lacked the spirit's definition of self. In *Øieblikket 5* he writes that one could not exist in the merely human life after having experienced Christianity. Furthermore, Christianity cannot be treated with the objectivity of paganism because eternal happiness did not arise with the pagan. Ibsen's earlier plays respond quite openly to this difference. In the first version of *Kjaempehøien* *[1] the Viking grave (a burial mound) and the cross decked with flowers articulate the existence of both cultures simultaneously; *Haermaendene paa Helgeland* sets the Viking code alongside the Christian; and, the pagan/Christian dichotomy is treated on a grand scale in *Kejser og Galilaeer*.

In his desire to illuminate the Christianity of the *New Testament*, Kierkegaard's repulsion for the hypocrite is unlimited; he associates him with the lowest form of pagan. It filled Kierkegaard with disgust to see people under the guise of Christianity living as pagans. In point of fact, they were worse than pagans because the pagan had never been exposed to Christianity. In its pure form, paganism was oriented in the direction of spirit while the paganism within Christianity not only lacked spirit, but was directed away from it.

The life around him he describes as paganism, refined by the thought that it is Christian.[2] For instance, the whorehouse which under Danish law could only be run by a Christian. In another instance, Kierkegaard refers to the adage that in business every man is a thief. He lists vainglories of titles, orders, and rank, that take the place of earnestness in living. (The hypocrisy associated with such outward signs of success are debunked by Ibsen in the banquet scene of *Vildanden*, where each guest displays his vacuity and his pettiness.)[3] The propagation of the race and the fact that the priest is paid for each child that he baptizes is pagan to Kierkegaard. He rejected the idea that parents thought producing children was pleasing to God. The bestowing of life on a child is paganism;

---

* *The Burial Mound*

120

it is anything but wellpleasing to God that one engages in the begetting of children. Rather, it is egoism in the highest degree that because a man and woman cannot control their lust, another must sigh for seventy years (the seriousness is dramatized in *Lille Eyolf* — Rita's and Allmer's relationship has been built upon sexual attraction — as a result of one such thoughtless instance, their son is crippled;[4] the ludicrousness of procreation is satirized in *Kjaerlighedens Komedie* by the proselytizing country priest, Straamand, his fat wife and their eight daughters). Kierkegaard did not see evidence of

responsible parenthood around him; Nora explains why in *Et Dukkehjem*, "Og jeg. — hvorledes er jeg forberedt til at opdrage børnene?"*

Kierkegaard considers the change from paganism to be that everything remained unchanged; and, as with so many of Ibsen's contemporary characters, he believed that people were living a life of refined paganism. Engstrand (*Gengangere*) displays cynicism and cunning that has ironic overtones. He would have the orphanage a home for seamen which would actually be a whorehouse. *Samfundets Støtter* exploits people for money. Bernick's greed almost ends with the unwitting

---

* "And what sort of qualifications have I to teach the children?"

121

sacrifice of his son.[5] Torvald's "honor"[6] cannot be sacrificed; Nora can be. *Kjaerlighedens Komedie* satirizes love and marriage and the denial of the human potential to a degree that is nauseating. In each of these plays, the human quotient is not present and in *Samfundets Støtter*, "the sacrifice" is not of a pagan or of a Christian kind.[7] Kierkegaard was concerned that the kind of paganism that existed in Christendom would be reflected in personal despair as it was with John Gabriel Borkman (paganism sans Christianity would be reflected in dread).

Kierkegaard viewed the difficulty with Christianity as emerging when it is about to be made present and actual. Becoming a Christian in the *New Testament* sense was a radical change. It involved a total transformation in a person to loosen him or her out of the cohesiveness to which he or she clung. Humanly speaking, it meant *separating* the individual from others, the action Nora had to take, the consequences Dr. Stockman had to accept. This separation from the group occurs in Ibsen's plays on two planes; sometimes it is the result of an enlightened consciousness but more often the action has its base in error, will or naiveté. Unlike the Christianity of the priests, family relations were not cemented with Christianity because all to which one clings must be relinquished.[8] The decisive thing is that the Christ position is a personal one as Sigurd demonstrated to Hjørdis in *Haermaendene paa Helgeland*. Sigurd is free of Hjørdis because he is a Christian and only in the hour of his death does he realize that, "Tak, Hjørdis; — nu er jeg så let og fri."* Her plan was to kill him and herself so that they could be together. Precisely at the moment that she mortally wounds him, she learns that he is a Christian and she throws herself off the cliff. Her bravado is similar but not as dramatic as that which Hedda Gabler displayed in her act of self-destruction.[9] Egil, Hjørdis' son, sees her riding away with the black horses to her pagan

---

* "Thank-you, Hjørdis. Now I am so light and free."

122

glory.[10] Nora (Et Dukkehjem), in a moment of truth about what her situation has been, frees herself by relinquishing her family. In the latter situation, the God idea is reflected in Nora's liberation.

It is appropriate to refer to what may have been Ancient Scandinavian drama[11] in this effort to bring into perspective the pagan and the Christian attitudes (and to see the nature of the ancient as reflected in the modern) in Ibsen's and Kierkegaard's dialectic for it is in the Northern ethos as reflected in this indigenous dramatic form that there is another link. That the Elder Edda was generally known is substantiated by Bjørnstjerne Bjørnson in the opening sentence of a paper he wrote in 1881 about the Norwegian Constitutional struggle. "It is now generally believed in Norway that the 'Elder Edda,' the mighty fragment of a fallen heathen temple, took its poetic form from Western Norway, or from people coming hence."[12] Although Ibsen does not refer to the "Elder Edda" directly in his writings in the way that he did with the saga and the ballad, his dramatic style reflects the classic, almost stark, simplicity of its structure, language and content more closely than that of the saga and the ballad. This is especially apparent at the point in his authorship when he abandoned rhyme and wrote in what he said would sometime be called poetry.[13] He writes that the moods, ideas, and thoughts of the material he had saturated himself with in the nationalistic romantic period had already been occupying him, that they were "eller i al fald mere eller mindre klart foresvaevede mig."*

Not only is the underlying ethos significant in the consideration of the Eddic material but the technique reflects that the past is prologue, and suggests that the pagan way may have been predisposed to Christianitiy. The subject matter of the Eddic lays in mythology and the heroic lore of the ancient North; they concentrate on the individual (as Kierkegaard

---

* "at least more or less vaguely conscious" to him.

123

and Ibsen do); generally limit themselves to one incident; are sparse and swift in the treatment of action; the sense of conflict is strong. There is an insistence in representing events indirectly through the speech of the characters; description is absent, yet there is succinct character delineation and the milieu is suggested, the cold mountainous land by the sea. With but little change this description of the Eddic lays could be a description of Ibsen's dramaturgical principles.

The lays that will be referred to are those considered to be indigenous to Norway: *Skirnismál, Lokasenna,* and *Helgakvida Hundingsbani* II.[14] They have been selected for the dominating feature peculiar to each; form, conflict, and the love/death theme respectively. The aspects to be treated are those that have significance to the Ibsen-Kierkegaard focus.

These lays are built up in a dialogic-dramatic form,[15] composed in simple measure with a pattern of alliterating sounds in unrhymed lines (unlike the ballad). The alliteration is borne by words of syntactical importance and the dialogue's dramatic power is enhanced through repetition related to contrasting conceptions and parenthetical phrases containing accompanying circumstances. Condensed metaphors appear to be independent of the situation until a deeper insight into their presence is comprehended. The tone of the lays is objective, with the feelings and the attitudes of the poets never betrayed. Furthermore, the Eddic lays reflect the stern fatalism, the ethical conceptions, the warrior spirit, characteristics which illuminate the Ibsen perspective, of which *Helgakvida Hundingsbani* II is a succinct example.

They are traditional in the sense that they were transmitted by oral performance. Internal evidence shows that the lays are in dialogue, contain what can be considered as stage directions, have a series of events arising from a conflict, include a change of scene, and present numerous characters, including supernumerary characters. Although the nature of the performance is not delineated, a hypothesis is possible through the surviving artifact and associative disciplines.

The form of *Skírnismál* is that of a love myth.[16] Its construction is impeccable — cyclic, conflict, crisis, denouement — and the psychology and dramatic intensity strong. There are instances in the lay that recall Ibsen's *Haermaendene paa Helgeland* and illuminate the pagan consciousness.

The lay is named after the character to whom the action is given, the servant, Skirnir, rather than to the god who motivates the action.[17] Skirnir is to woo Gerd, the goddess of the earth, for Frey, the sun-God.[18] One scene is a kind of foreshadowing of a similar account which is developed in the *Volsungasaga*, (a prose account of the heroic lays based on an earlier source). Ibsen wrote in the Preface to the second edition of *Gildet paa Solhoug* that he wanted to present the women of the *Volsungasaga* directly in dramatic form, the women who became Dagny and Hjørdis in *Haermaendene paa Helgeland*, the same women who earlier had appeared in the "Elder Edda" as Gudrun and Brynhild.[19]

The incident that reflects Skirnir's wooing of Gerd is more sophisticated in *Volsungasaga* than it is in the lay. Whereas Skirnir asks Frey for his horse[20] to lift him over the flame that is a barrier to Gerd's bower, *and* for his sword to fight the trolls, in the saga, Sigurd awakens the warrior maid, Brynhild, who has been put to sleep by Odin on a mountain, surrounded by fire. On his horse, Grani, he leaps over the flames. There is an echo of the situation in *Haermaendene* in a different context and dimension. Hjørdis will marry the

man who will slay the white polar bear that guards her door.[21] Gunnar, who loves her, places his trust in Sigurd (who unknown to Gunnar also loves her), Gunnar trusting Sigurd to perform the feat in his name. After slaying the bear, Sigurd spends the night with Hjørdis.[22] The intrigue takes on a kind of Scribean technical dexterity, but, in actuality, the duplicity has a deeper implication, evoking a tragic dimension which reflects a Kierkegaardian view of tragedy, that is, tragedy as based upon misunderstandings.[23] Gunnar's trust and Sigurd's loyalty also exemplifies the code of honor—similar to Skirnir's loyalty to Frey but lacking the complications of the class difference and the dual love motif—that took place over personal wishes. Fidelity to one's word was conceived of as the highest fidelity to one's self. Ibsen is interested in the emotional (internal) and the psychological conflicts which result when the individual is placed in an existential situation. With the supernatural elements, although subdued, a double reflection is presented that dramatizes two perspectives — the pagan and the Christian — and two different points of view — the finite and the infinite. In Ibsen's later plays, the double reflection is less pointed in that it takes place in the contemporary milieu. Even so, the contrast between the actual and the ideal is more poetic.

After Skirnir has accomplished his mission and Gerd has agreed to marry Frey, Skirnir tells Frey that she will meet him in three nights. The lay ends in an outburst from Frey. His longing is expressed in the closing scene which reflects the tension he has experienced and the frustration of more delay. Frey's earlier appearance at the beginning of the lay was a study in moodiness and sorrow. Its presence is felt as part of the background,[24] although all the action is given to his alter ego, Skirnir. It is sorrow which Kierkegaard considers to be the differentiation between the pagan and the Christian character. There is not in the pagan hero the acute pain that characterizes the modern hero — John Gabriel Borkman, for instance; rather, there is a melancholy brooding on the condition of life[25] that is hinted at with Frey and epitomized by Hamlet (Amled).[26]

The ending of *Skírnismál* brings together the anxiety of the past and the anticipation of the future, completing the cyclic structure that suggests a repetition in that the cycle will be repeated in another version or generation.[27] There is an open ending although the action is completed in that the mission is accomplished. It would be anticlimatic to more than suggest what earlier treatment appropriate to the fertility myth probably enacted. Gold plaquettes with corresponding pictorial renderings of Gerd and Frey's meeting in the grove Barri were found in Norway; other finds correspond in type.[28] Skírnismál is not, therefore, open-ended in the Ibsen or Kierkegaardian sense since it is obvious what the conclusion will be.

Lokasenna presents in its main character, Loki, a Scandinavian Mephistopheles.[29] Loki suggests the Kierkegaardian seducer and the Ibsen Gregers (*Vildanden*) or Hedda Gabler and Judge Brack (*Hedda Gabler*). Loki is attractive and clever, but not to be trusted. The plot is laid at the last banquet of the gods, just after Baldur's death.[30] The lay is called the "flyting" of Loki because he engages the assembly in a flyting or runnning dialogue of vituperation. In *Lokasenna*, it is the clash pattern that dominates, a pattern that is viewed by Humphrey Milness as a product of the period. He writes that everything indicates that the old northern world was a place where life was marginal, danger ever-present, violence everywhere, and . . . wit an absolute necessity in every engagement if a person was to stay alive . . . each clash carried out with as much flair as can be summoned (the kind of flair that makes Ibsen's Lokian figures fascinating;[31] Loki's intuition, the battle of the wits becomes an extension, in poetic terms, of mortal struggle).

Loki plays on the gods' and goddesses' human weaknesses, and upon human nature; they respond defensively, intimidated by negative suggestions. It matters little to Loki if his

127

accusations are true; he is always the cleverer, until he is ousted by Thor[32] — a proof, cited by Axel Olrik,[33] of the extent to which the ancient world of myths constituted an aesthetic tradition and not a religious one. In a similar way, Gregers, Hedda Gabler and Judge Brack are adept at locating the "Achilles heel" of an Ibsen character. So it is with Loki; he is deft in exposing his companions' points of vulnerability; his acts metaphorically reduplicate his killing of Baldur (see footnote 29). Hedda and Brack come closer to the Loki image than Gregers, in that their intentions are malicious.

Helgakvida Hundingsbani II stresses the love of Helgi and Sigrun. The parallels of technique and theme point to Ibsen's *Haermaendene paa Helgeland,* and to *Hedda Gabler* in particular, and also to the ending of *Når Vi Døde Vågner.* Hjørdis and Hedda express the same passion and strong will as the Valkyrie, Sigrun, in the Eddic lay. But, unlike Hjørdis and Hedda, Sigrun is not thinking of herself. Within the juxtaposition of the personal motive, Ibsen shows the lower pagan nature of Hjørdis and its contemporary counterpart in Hedda.

There are three Helgi lays; the plot is built around similar lines. A young hero, Helgi, wins the love and protection of a Valkyrie, Sigrun, marries her and dies at the height of his glory. She joins him in the grave and they go through their life-story again.[34] In the second lay, where the emphasis is placed more vividly on the love of Helgi and Sigrun than in the other two lays, the central idea revolves around Sigrun's absolute devotion, a devotion that not only includes the destruction of her own family but a devotion that continues beyond death. Her loyalty parallels Thea's devotion to Løvborg in *Hedda Gabler.* In the end of the Helgi lay, the youngest brother, Dag, becomes the avenger who kills Helgi.

The last strophes dramatize the return of the dead Helgi and Sigrun's visit to him in the burial mound. Her longing and love surmounts death. This lay contains the first appearance in literature of lovers meeting in a grave (as opposed to Ibsen's lovers going to the grave together — *Rosmersholm,*

John Gabriel Borkman, Når Vi Døde Vågner).[35] They sleep in each other's arms, but Helgi goes back to Valhalla before dawn and does not return again.

A tragic element is evoked in conjunction with fate. It derives from the belief that fate is strong and Sigrun is advised not to fight against it. However, it was believed in pre-Christian Norway that man still had a choice, and insofar as he wills and chooses, he is superior to his fate,[36] a concept Ibsen was to dramatize from a Kierkegaardian or an existential focus, inversely considered and extended. In point of fact, Ibsen articulates the idea of choice in diverse ways, considering or juxtapositing the pagan view within a contemporary perspective that included the advent of Christianity. The last strophe of *Helgakvida Hundingsbani* II is given to the maid. She expresses her fear of the dead and warns her mistress not to stay at the grave alone:

> verẞa olgari   allir á nottom
> dauẞir dolgar, maeri!   en um daga liósa.*

The ominous tone, in a different context, recalls Ibsen's fatalistic ending of *Rosmersholm*, his play ending with the housekeeper's words indicating that the dead mistress has taken Rebekka and Rosmer. The fatalism is different than in the pagan culture — the choice is apparent — and Rebekka concedes defeat. A pagan would not have relinquished the prize so long sought, or in the case of a Loki, there might have been Thor's intervention, or the Viking code in operation, although there might have been an overlapping of purpose when Paganism and Christianity were side by side. With Rebekka, Christianity had gotten hold of her, the Rosmer way. Kierkegaard discovered with Christianity that it teaches men to see death from the point of view of eternity and to fear judgment more than death. Christianity helped

---

* "All dead man's ghosts do grow more dread as daylight darkens the dimness of the night."

men to conquer their anxiety about death for only when there are worse things than death can death be conquered.[37]

Kierkegaard and Ibsen have taken into consideration the tenuous link between the pagan way of life and the aesthetical — and to some extent, the ethical way of life. Ibsen has shown the overlapping of the pagan/Christian worlds in his earlier plays, issues Kierkegaard has treated comparatively in reference to the Greek model (although he does consider paganism in general terms and has Scandinavian references). Kierkegaard's attack was also directed against philosophers and the Greek reference point gave him a platform in which to counter the sophistic arguments he encountered. (He had been deeply involved in Socrates' perspective through his Master's dissertation.) The Greek drama and *The Poetic Edda* offer a unique reference point in regard to Ibsen. In *Kejser og Galilaeer* he brings into play the pagan, the philosophical, and the Christian ways of life *and* places them in a setting where they exist simultaneously. His approach permits mobility of thought and action on a world-historic scale. It is in *Kejser og Galilaeer* that Ibsen reflects on the third way and leaves his audience to ponder just what he did mean. Is the third way the pagan way, is it a pagan/Christian synthesis — is it simply that the Christianity of the *New Testament* has not been expressed or that it cannot be???? Julian refers to the new life that one day will come, the leader who will come — the true Messiah, Baldur? Socrates? and/or Christ? — or the God in man? Is there to be another Ragnarok[38] or a new Jerusalem or an encounter of another kind as yet undesignated? It will be more appropriate to return to this "most philosophical" work of Ibsen's in connection with *Øieblikket* in a later section where it can be viewed in the light of the past and the future.

Ibsen is possibly articulating what Kierkegaard wrote in *Papirer* concerning Christendom, that is, Christendom is at the point where paganism ended, and man has in the place of one nut with a kernel, multitudes of empty shells.

The Tragic and the Modern

the comic-tragic

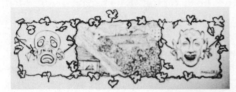

In his essay concerning the tragical motif and the modern, Kierkegaard's purpose is to show how the characteristic of ancient tragedy is embedded within the modern so that true tragedy may come to light.

He views the tendency of "nutiden"*[39] to be that existence has become undermined by doubt resulting in individual isolation. Isolation is shown by the way people are more and

---

* "the present age"

131

more immersed in multitudinous social exertions. Rather than counteracting isolation, the activities underscore the presence of it, "Det Isolerede ligger bestandigt i at gjøre sig gheldende som Numerus,"* whether the number is one or a thousand or an entire population. To feel their importance in comparison to a higher power, people count themselves. Kierkegaard considers David's need to savor his power resulted in his taking the census. Similarly, in Iceland, early settlers recorded their names in the *Landnámabók* or book of land-taking; in *Kejser og Galilaeer*, the Christians outnumber the pagans.

That many associations in a country contribute toward hastening that country's dissolution was an example of the negativity associated with the herd factor. Kierkegaard regarded the situation that prevailed in Greece when the state was in the process of dissolution to be the same. He considered the same state to be existing in his own age which he viewed as possessing a greater degree of melancholy and a more profound despair, the feeling Ibsen dramatized in his plays and that Edvard Munch painted in such subjects as: *Shriken, Angst, Aften på Karl Johan, Melankoli*.**

The reason for the situation in Denmark is attributed to the loss of the spiritual bond which held the state together politically. As a result, the sense of responsibility was missing, not only in government but in the opposition party (a condition Ibsen's *De Unges Forbund* projects). The effect is comic because the two powers are in opposition with one another but unable to come to grips with each other; one constantly vanishes from the other. With isolation, the effect is naturally comic and the comic lies in the fact that subjectivity as mere form asserts itself. So it is with every isolated individual who always becomes comic by stressing his own accidental individuality over and against necessary self-development.[40] Kierkegaard considers it comical for some individuals to be

---

* "The isolated idea is always in evidence where men assert themselves numerically."
** *The Scream, Anxiety, Evening on Karl Johan Street, Melancholy.*

132

imbued with the universal idea of wishing to be the savior of the world (a possible unconscious motive on a lower key with Brand, Dr. Stockman, Gregers). To equate oneself with Christ, a tragic figure who bore the sins of the world, is a ridiculous aspiration.

Kierkegaard's observations on the nature of modern drama are drawn from a comparison to Aristotle whom he felt the Danish critics and public held up as the model. The comparison brings out significant differences. The first divergence involves Aristotle's stress on thought and character as the source of action, yet his main thrust is that the plot is the thing. Kierkegaard observes that with Aristotle, individuals do not act in order to present characters, but the characters are included for the sake of the action or plot. (In modern tragedy, this is not the case.) Because the action does not issue exclusively from the character, the action does not find its sufficient explanation in subjective reflection and decision, although the action has an admixture of suffering. Ancient tragedy has not developed the dialogue to the point of exhaustive reflection, so that everything is absorbed into it. In the chorus and the monologue are the factors that supplement the dialogue and will not be absorbed in individuality or in action and situation.[41]

Ancient tragedy has an epic moment in it which makes it as much event as action. The explanation for this is that the ancient world did not have subjectivity fully self-conscious and reflective. Even with freedom of action, the individual still remained in the substantial categories of state, family, and destiny. This substantial category is pointed out by Kierkegaard as the fatalistic element in Greek tragedy (as it is also in Viking society) which is its peculiarity. Viewed in this way, the hero's destruction is not only a result of his own deeds but is also a suffering. Ibsen clings to the family base he found so supportive in the Icelandic family saga, but it gradually gives way to the fruitlessness of such a covenant.

134

Kierkegaard points out in *Kjerlighedens Gjerninger** that one must love one's neighbor and not slavishly be related to family.

In modern tragedy, the hero's destruction is really not suffering, but action. Therefore, in the modern context, situation and character are predominant. Considering the tragic hero as conscious of himself as a subject is fully reflective, and this reflection should have precipitated the severing of every immediate relation to state, race, and destiny, and even separated him from his own preceding existence. This subjective interest in the characterization is significant in considering Ibsen's drama because of his interest in the awakening of the individual. His work is also dedicated to the fellowship of buried lives. Kierkegaard claims that the interest in modern drama is in a definite moment in the hero's life, a moment considered as his own deed. For this reason, the tragedy can be exhaustively represented in situation and dialogue, since absolutely nothing of the immediate remains any longer. It is interesting that at the time Kierkegaard is writing about modern tragedy and wishing for such a poet as Ibsen, Ibsen was not yet writing. In any event, Kierkegaard regards modern drama as having no epic foreground and no epic heritage; the hero stands or falls on his own acts.[42]

Another point of difference between the ancient and the modern conception of tragedy is the nature of tragic guilt. Kierkegaard gives to it a prominence that also has significance for what he describes as the disposition of the age — the comic.

Aristotle requires the tragic hero to have tragic guilt. For Aristotle, the hero's guilt as well as the action of the play is intermediate between action and suffering, and this is where the tragic collision comes in. Therefore, Kierkegaard reasons, if the individual is guiltless, the tragic interest is nullified and the conflict is weakened as it would be if Solveig (*Peer*

---

* *Works of Love*

135

Gynt) were the central figure.[43] If the individual is absolutely guilty, then he is not of interest tragically. It is a misunderstanding of the tragic when the age strives to individualize the hero to such an extent that he is ethically responsible for his own guilt. This would mean that the hero is bad, and evil becomes the tragic subject which has no aesthetic interest — a play built around Bishop Nikolas (*Kongs= Emnerne*), for instance. (That is not to say such a play would not be interesting, but interesting is not the same as aesthetically satisfying.) Sin, Kierkegaard proposes, does not constitute an aesthetic element.

The error which Kierkegaard saw in the criticism of the period is attributed to the tendency of the age toward the comic. Because the comic lies in isolation, the effort to maintain the tragic in this isolation results in an evil in all its baseness, not the truly tragic guilt in its ambiguous innocence, an ambiguousness that Ibsen somehow managed not to wholly lose. Kierkegaard refers to *Faust* and *Don Juan,* which he does not consider to be isolated examples, as being constructed around evil; he regards them as being representative of the general consciousness of the age. Inasmuch as a modern hero is responsible for himself, Kierkegaard does not designate his downfall as tragic; it is bad. The despair of so many of Ibsen's characters indicates that the age has lost the tragic sense of life. Consequently, the healing power of the tragic is lost. The ironical occurs — the man who gains himself, loses himself — and becomes comical. Only when he acknowledges himself as a child of God, is he himself; when he tries to be absolute, he is ridiculous — Brand, Peer, Julian and others.

If the individual renounces the claim of the absolute, in order to become relative, he has the tragic within his consciousness and it is only then that he becomes happy. Such an individual has a gentleness not unlike Agnes (*Brand*), Thea (*Hedda Gabler*), Beata (*Rosmersholm*), and unlike Hedda.[44]

It is not that the age should not hold the individual responsible for everything — that Kierkegaard objects to; the

136

misfortune is that it does not do so deeply and inwardly enough. The age is too self-complacent in disdaining the tears of tragedy and dispensing with divine mercy. Kierkegaard's and Ibsen's purpose was to dispel that complacency with almost pre-Artaudian tactics, giving their audiences what they wanted doubly reflected *in concreto*. In place of catharsis, Kierkegaard suggests an emetic, "tag et Braek-Middel, kom up af denne Halvheds-Tilstand."*

What Kierkegaard has attempted to communicate is that if the hero is guilty, there is no destiny and the thought is transparent in the dialogue and the action in the situation. He viewed the guilt of the modern hero, however, as greater than that of earlier prototypes because of his subjectivity. As it is in ancient tragedy, the guilt is no longer passive, but active, and resides in the guilt of the individual character.[45] One of the facets of Ibsen's dramas is the degree to which this guilt is manifested in the character.

Kierkegaard's conclusion is that in ancient tragedy the sorrow is deeper, the pain less, while in modern tragedy, the pain is greater and the sorrow less. For the spectator to experience the appropriate emotion, he or she must live himself or herself into the prevailing consciousness of the play. (See histrionic sensibility, Chapter I.)

"Hvad om Alt i Verden var en Misforstaaelse, hvad om Latteren egentlig var Graad!"** The thought Kierkegaard posits in this sentence relates to his views on tragedy and comedy, and illuminates another aspect of the Kierkegaard-Ibsen consciousness. Tragedy and comedy occur from the contradiction that is inherent in existence; the tragic is the suffering contradiction; the comical the painless contradiction. When the aesthetical and the religious are brought together in the consciousness, he sees in them a unity of the tragic and the comic. Where the aesthetic sphere is in isolation, the comic

---

* "Take an emetic, come out of this lukewarmness."
** "What if everything in the world were a misunderstanding, what if laughter were real tears?"

137

is externalized and is purely comic. The existential consideration contains the essence of that which brings together Kierkegaard's view of tragedy as misunderstanding and the paradoxical nature of the comic-tragic.

Walter Kerr writes in his study of tragedy and comedy[46]
that they might crossbreed endlessly, but they do not give
birth to a third form. Therefore, it is most provocative to
contemplate Kierkegaard's articulation of the tragic and the
comic because he separates them in one sense as does Kerr,
but Kierkegaard brings them together in what he calls their
unity, which is misleading. It is not as a bastard form of
tragedy, the tragi-comedy, that is, a tragic story with an
element of comedy which might have a happy ending that
Kierkegaard unifies tragedy and comedy, but in existence.

In his consideration of comedy and tragedy as a unity,
Kierkegaard is in touch with the nature of tragedy as Walter
Kerr understands it — that tragedy precedes comedy and that
each is ever present in the other. If this is so, Kerr writes, the
two faces that the theatre shows "are the same face worn by
the same man."

To express the tragic and the comic in terms of misunderstanding, Kierkegaard proposes a simple situation in which
the girl is in the aesthetic sphere of existence and the boy is
in the ethical-religious sphere. They are united in loving each
other. If the passion is removed, the situation is ironical; if
the passion is posited, the situation is tragic. However, if the
man contemplates it, the situation is at once comic and tragic
while the heroine cannot see this is as she is too immediate.
The hero is conscious of the comic which saves him from
being comic. They express their passion differently, thus the
misunderstanding. The tragedy is that the two lovers do not
understand one another, the comedy is that two who do not
understand one another should love one another; this is the
paradox by virtue of the absurd. This situation is reversed in
Kjaerlighedens Komedie where Falk is in the aesthetic sphere

138

of existence and Svanhild is seen as entering the ethical sphere.

It is in the sense of misunderstanding, angest, the comic-tragic dimension viewed as a double reflection (the comic mask with a leer), which makes the comical-tragical mode (not tragi-comedy) the appropriate mode to describe Kierkegaard's

and Ibsen's work and to describe the especial character of modern drama. Kierkegaard, in mid-19th century Denmark, believed that because the world had lost the sense of the religious, the direction was toward the purely comic. This condition echoes Kerr who in the twentieth century inquires as to what happens to tragedy when comedy is all there is. They consider the consequences tragic because Existence is not really comic.

That Kierkegaard recognized in the comical-tragical mode the essence of an age that lacked passion, he clarifies in *Staadier*. The tragic-comic does not involve passion; neither the comic nor the tragic is essentially presented. In the comic-tragic, they are both involved and the spirit dialectically infinitized sees the two aspects in the same thing at once.

NOTES TO CHAPTER II

[1] The earliest church buildings in Norway, the stave churches, have serpent-like heads and crosses rising from various points of the edifices. One of Ibsen's water colors (from Bergen period) shows a house with crosses at the gable ends.

[2] Kierkegaard equates this condition as either the aesthetical sphere of existence or the aesthetical-ethical. See Chapter III.

[3] *Hypocrisy* enraged Kierkegaard and Ibsen. Their reaction was disdain or ironic sarcasm.

Ibsen's prominent display of his medals on his person is more easily understood as irony, than vanity, the result of the almost consistent rejection he received from his efforts to gain professional/financial support when he needed it, and his disgust at seeing lesser writers receive such support.

[4] In the pagan culture, the crippled child would have been left out to die (Viking).

[5] Arthur Miller exploits this situation in *All My Sons* and Joe does sacrifice his son. Miller is a self-acknowledged disciple of Ibsen.

[6] "Honor" is suspect in this situation.

[7] I.e. nihilism

[8] In *Kjerlighedens Gjerninger*, acts of love go beyond the family circle "loving your neighbor," a point Ibsen tries to make indirectly (also Bergman, but more directly).

[9] I.e. Hedda's suicide is shown in all its grimness—the gun to her head. I.e. Ingmar Bergman's production.

[10] There is little real difference between Valhalla and Hel in Nordic

140

paganism. In ancient poetry, there is doubt expressed as to whether the deceased went to Valhalla or Hel (Axel Olrik). Black and white horses have Biblical connotations as well as pagan. In the Ibsen play the white horses appear to be a kenning for the breaking of the waves, yet there is another interest in that the sea symbolizes the heart in Kierkegaard's work; the black horses have a pagan reference.

[11] "The Dramatic Nature of *The Poetic Edda*" (Tammany, 1970) explores the possibility of indigenous drama. The earliest and most extensive study was written by Berthe Phillpotts, supported by scholars, archeological studies, philological studies. *The Poetic Edda* is also known. as *Saemundr's Edda* and *The Elder Edda*. The manuscript dates from circa 1270, but the greater part of the contents belongs to pre-Christian Norway.

[12] "Norway's Constitutional Struggle" by Bjørnstjerne Bjørnson, in *Scribner's Monthly Magazine* XXI (1881).

[13] He made this point earlier in a letter to Bjørnson concerning *Peer Gynt* and in response to a criticism by Clemmens Petersen in *Faedrelandet* (1867). Petersen said Ibsen had disregarded the demands of reality and art and that *Peer Gynt* was full of intellectual tricks and riddles that could not be understood or unravelled. Ibsen responded with indignation and said that *Peer Gynt* was poetry and that the conception of poetry shall be made to conform to his "poem". Ibsen is not simply referring to language as poetry, but the entire work. (Rome, Dec. 9, 1867)

[14] *The Lay of Skirnir, The Flyting of Loki, The Second Lay of Hundingsbane.* Ibsen wrote a ballad of 117 verses called "Helge Hundingsbane." It was published in the *Andhrimner*, July, 1851.

[15] Because of the lateness of Christianity, the North retained its purity of form.

[16] *Skírnismál* is assigned to pre-Christian Norway. Christianity in Norway circa 1000 A.D.—Viking Age began 780 A.D. and lasted until 1100 A.D.

[17] The servant had special significance for Kierkegaard. He associated it with the man-God's presence in the world. In some situations under various guises, Ibsen did the same, as did Strindberg and Bergman.

[18] God of fruitfulness. The Sun is used conversely in *Gengangere*.

[19] The material would be recreated in Wagner's opera *Der Ring des Nibelungen* (1869-1870, 1876).

[20] The horse is viewed as a supernumerary character by Berthe Phillpotts in the sense of being a human signpost. Skirnir talking to the horse shows the changes of the scene and the movements of the main character. The pragmatic use of the horse in this situation does not convey the metamorphic possibilities of another supernumerary, the wild duck in Ibsen's *Vildanden*.

[21] Hjørdis is described by C. H. Herford ("Ibsen's Earlier Work") as a Medea. He views the *bear* as replacing the *fire* in the Eddic material as a theatrical necessity.

[22] In the ancient source, the sword lying between them indicates the

141

victory of the ethical over the allurement of the moment. With Ibsen, this is not so clear.

23 Skaldic poetry presents many such misunderstandings, and so do the sagas. Ibsen and Kierkegaard's treatment has a depth that surpasses naiveté, psychology, or happenstance circumstances. In that the misunderstanding is consonant with an evolving (or lack of) consciousness, there is a qualitative dimension.

24 I.e. similar to the *presence* of Hedda Gabler's father's (idea expressed in Tennessee Williams' *The Glass Menagerie*).

25 In *Papirer,* Kierkegaard refers to two kinds of melancholy, one occurs when a person is unhappy and shuts himself in; this could be thoughtfulness (or even petulence, as is partially so with Frey); the other kind is when a person deliberately keeps his eyes shut in order to have darkness all around him (*John Gabriel Borkman*).

26 The original Hamlet legend preserved in Saxo Grammaticus' *Gesta Danorum* (*History of Denmark*). Kierkegaard's treatment as discussed in Chapter I.

27 See "Diapsalmata" (the rotation method) in *Enten-Eller* I.

28 Archaeological evidence indicates the plates were located near the farm Hauge in Jaeren. *Norwegian Archæological* Review, Oslo, 1969.

29 He was the incarnation of evil in one sense ("A Scandinavian Aristophanes"—Andreas Heusler) while Baldur was the noblest god, beloved of the gods — incarnation of good. He was killed by Loki.

30 Loki killed Baldur, learning that the only way he could be killed was with a twig made into an arrow. Kierkegaard mentions Baldur in his journals in connection with myth, saying that legendary heroes are vulnerable only in the heel; he brings the remark into context with a similar Biblical quotation (Gen. 3:15).

31 Kierkegaard and Ibsen play on a concept to illustrate all facets of its nature. While Ibsen's Lokian figures are not the same, yet there is that essence within them that is the same, for instance, Gregers, Brack, and to some degree Hedda. Dr. Rank is a more complex characterization, a Baldur with Loki's intuition.

32 Thor was the most powerful of all the gods, democratic, ready helper. His significance in Scandinavian life is attested to by the hammer placed on gravestones; people named after him.

33 Axel Olrik. *Nordisk Aandsliv i Vikingetid og Tidlig Middelalder,* 1927. (*Scandinavian Cultural Life in Viking Times and the Early Middle Ages*)

34 The original pagan belief in immortality was that it was a rebirth in the younger generation. Kierkegaard rejects this focus and Ibsen considers it pragmatically in *Bygmester Solness.*

35 Margaret Schlauch, *Romance in Iceland.*

36 Axel Olrik points out that early Christianity had a bright spot in the idea of the salvation of the individual soul.

37 *Papirer* IX A492.

38 Ragnarok — "The Twilight of the Gods" — a new world to emerge

142

and replace the old. In the Eddic lay Voluspá — the oracle gives an account of the world as it is and her prophecy of the new.

39 Kierkegaard's essay on "the present age" attacks the public's cultural density.

40 Kierkegaard presents this point in *Krisen;* Ibsen demonstrates it in *Peer Gynt.* Consequently, Kierkegaard would not automatically yield to youth; youth has to prove itself.

41 The Eddic material does not use the chorus or monologue.

42 His illustrative play is one that had not yet been written, a modern *Antigone.* Jean Anouilh's *Antigone* (1944) portrays Antigone as a martyr bent on self-destruction.

43 I.e. a Billy Budd innocence; it would be the same if the character was insane—the consciousness is not active.

44 The Baldur/Loki concept juxtaposed.

45 Kierkegaard viewed guilt as being in error.

46 He considers tragedy and comedy from their origins down to the present. He wanted to write a book about comedy, but found it impossible because tragedy kept getting in the way.

The Nature of the
Communication —
Untying the Knot

Introduction

*"et nyt Hvorledes af det gamle Hvad"**

The function of a Kierkegaardian introduction was that it should serve to unclothe the spectators from their diverse occupations and get them ready for a real bath. In a similar way, this introduction and this chapter are intended to prepare the readers for an interpretation that illuminates Ibsen's dramatic idiom from a dialectic that considers the northern ethos as significant but also considers the method as integral to the content, so that what emerges is not only a feasible explanation, but an essential one.

Diverse *interpretations* have been written concerning Henrik Ibsen's drama (see Bibliography). Sometimes the tech-

---

* "A new how of an old what"

nique has been correlated with a particular focus; more often the technique is divorced from the interpretation, but it is rarely ignored. Consider the approach of the following studies: George Bernard Shaw's *The Quintessence of Ibsenism,* 1891, an "exposition" of Ibsen which, in actuality, lent itself to his Shavian interests, the quintessence being that there is not any Ibsen formula; *The Blight of Ibsenism* (1915) by James Leatham, a negative reaction to Ibsen. Leatham writes that Ibsen not only assails the virtues but also the natural feelings such as maternal love, the social sentiment, and the instinct for self-preservation; William Winter and James Huneker represent the critical dichotomy respectively on the American scene during the same period.[1] With *The Modern Drama* in 1960, Herman Wiegand presents a "creative" interpretation with his designation of the second half of Ibsen's work (starting with *Et Dukkehjem*); *Catiline's Dream,* 1972, is a mythical-psychological study by James Hurt that does consider the form in relation to the interpretation. His analysis begins with *Brand* and relies on a mythic-psychological pattern; *The Ibsen Cycle,* 1975, by Brian Johnston introduces an evaluation of the plays from *Samfundets Støtter* to *Når Vi Døde Vågner* which he sees as "a single, Hegelian, cyclical, and evolutionary dramatic structure"; *Ibsen's Feminine Mystique* is intended by its author, Vincent J. Balice, to indicate the function of women in Ibsen's authorship — views the women in the concept of "maternal creativity" and as a surrogate for the deity. Harold Clurman's *Ibsen* (1977) is a contemporary overview and Ronald Gray presents a dissenting perspective in his book on Ibsen (1977).[2] Gray finds a lack of coherence (among other things) between the script and the stage in Ibsen's dramaturgy.

Norwegian studies are possibly more functional: *Symbolikken i Henrik Ibsens Skuespil,* by Arne Duve which concerns itself with an individual aspect central to Ibsen, the symbols; *Ibsens Rimeteknikk,* the poetic language is analyzed by Leif Maehle; *Ibsen paa scenen,* Gunnar Heiberg's study of

148

Ibsen productions he has experience with; *Henrik Ibsen og den moderne psykologi* by Ingjald Nissen; national romanticism — *Ibsen og nationalromantiken* by Frederik Paasche.

There are individual essays such as Francis Fergusson's approach to *Gengangere*, "the tragic rhythm in a small figure"; "Ibsen and the Absurd" (1975) by John Weightman, a reviewer's accounting of discrepancies in Ibsen, attempts to suggest an Absurdist's view, but does not substantiate it. Then there is Halvdan Koht's comparative study "Shakespeare and Ibsen." Koht has written a separate study on Ibsen. Of the biographical works, the most recent is by Michael Meyer. There are also numerous histories of the theatre which comment on Ibsen's place in the evolution of modern drama. Joseph Wood Krutch presents a book on modern drama in 1953, *Modernism in Modern Drama*. In it he says that Ibsen launched modern drama in the English speaking world. Referring to Ibsen as the key to modernism, he says that to be modern is to be different from anyone who has lived before. His interest is in the mature plays which he considers as beginning with *Samfundets Støtter* (1877).

Certainly there is value in a variety of perspectives, for how else can Ibsen's "infinite variety" be illuminated and how else

149

can selectivity be exercised? There are, however, problems, in that many critics are not as intuitively blessed as was Kierkegaard, and numerous approaches have a tendency to overwhelm. Another consideration is that not all of the studies cited take into consideration the theatrical space as a part of the Ibsen dramatic idiom.

Most books on *playwriting* or those concerned with dramatic structure consider Ibsen's dramatic technique as the focal point. For instance, *The Development of Dramatic Art,* 1928, by Donald Clive Stuart, a work on the growth of Western drama, contains solid studies of changes in dramatic structure. Then there is *The Scenic Art* by Henry James and *Dramatic Method,* 1956, by Harley Granville Barker, and *Playmaking,* representing the period between 1880 and 1912, authored by the "famous or infamous" early Ibsen translator, William Archer. Because most modern plays fall back upon clumsy methods of exposition, Archer does not recommend Ibsen for the practical purposes of the stage. If the object of the play is movement, he writes, a theme should be chosen which leaves nothing to retrospection. John Howard Lawson writes in *Theory and Technique of Playwriting* (1936) that technical lessons can be learned from Ibsen but that a forward movement of the drama is a logical impossibility because his ideas do not sweep onward. Lawson considers the use of material derived from Ibsen as having become repetitious and uncreative.[3] James McFarlane considers an algebraic formula an approach to the understanding of Ibsen's structure.[4] Eric Bentley recognizes that Ibsen is operating on several levels.

Concerning themselves specifically with Ibsen's dramatic technique are P. F. D. Tennant's *Dramatic Technique,* 1948, and John Northam's *Dramatic Method* (1971),[5] books which recognize the structural coherence of an Ibsen drama, but even with these studies there is a lack in the connection to a central core. It is the American playwright, Arthur Miller, who is the natural exponent of the Ibsen technique in the

150

twentieth century. In his introduction to *Collected Plays*, Miller wrote that he learned from Ibsen how to forge a play upon factual bedrock.[6]

While there is discernment in the views these different authors have presented, it is not cohesive. Either the treatment is separated from the work itself, and/or from Ibsen's aesthetic consciousness.

In most studies of Ibsen, Eugene Scribe more than any other dramatist is cited as a determining factor in Ibsen's "apprenticeship years." George Bernard Shaw's assertion is that modern drama began when Ibsen's Nora compels her husband to sit down and discuss their marriage; indirectly, he confirms the Scribean premise: "Up to a certain point in the last act, *A Doll's House* is a play that might be turned into a very ordinary French drama by the excision of a few lines and the substitution of a sentimental ending for the last scene."[7] Shaw sees the well-built play—with the exposition in the first act, situation in the second, unravelling in the third — as having been altered by Ibsen.

151

Not only was Ibsen exposed to Scribe on the Norwegian and Danish stages, but he produced Scribean plays at the Norwegian theatres in Bergen and Kristiania. Kierkegaard's criticism of Scribe in *Enten-Eller* was well-known and Ibsen read that work.[8] Recent scholarship concedes that the 19th century Danish stage received its impetus from Scribe. However, not only were Holberg's comedies clearly visible in the 18th century and the foundation of the Danish stage, they were still being presented in the 19th century. Holberg was frequently cited by Kierkegaard in his authorship, and Ibsen's admiration of Holberg is confirmed by his membership in the Holberg circle and the nickname Geert Westphaler. Yet, Scribe is more frequently associated with Ibsen than is Holberg. Ibsen's verse play *Kjaerlighedens Komedie* contains Holbergian and Kierkegaardian cliches, epigrams,[9] and plot dynamics of a Scribean nature, and is decidedly Kierkegaardian on a conceptual level and in the theatrical presentation.

Holberg's comedies could have prepared the ground for the ready acceptance of the popular Scribean situational drama, and Ibsen's receptivity to Scribe, or Ibsen simply responded as Kierkegaard did to that in Scribe which generated another concept or approach. It is also known that Øehlenschläger[10] (who was at his best in his dramatic treatment of Old Norse material) and Shakespeare (of whom Ibsen once lectured) were appreciated by Ibsen. And, as has been previously noted in Chapter II, several of Ibsen's plays and many of his poems found their inspiration in the literature of the Middle Ages.

Kierkegaardian references in connection with Ibsen are mostly of a referential nature and infrequent. He is not mentioned by Clurman, and Gray suggests a synthesis of Kierkegaard and Hegel. Maurice Valency (*The Flower and the Castle*) does entertain the Kierkegaardian perspective, but accepts it with reservation. In connection with *Brand*, Valency concedes a debt to Kierkegaard, but he thinks that it is a mistake to consider Ibsen a Kierkegaardian. While F. L. Lucas notes a resemblance between Ibsen and Kierkegaard, he considers them to be at opposite poles. Brian Downs is cognizant of the Kierkegaardian connection but does not develop it in any great depth. Halvdan Koht presents a broad Kierkegaardian viewpoint in some of his interpretations. Valborg Erichsen has written about Kierkegaard and Ibsen (Norway, 1929) and while this treatment is more comprehensive than any of those already referred to, Erichsen does not consider Ibsen as a reflection of Kierkegaardian consciousness from an organic or internal perspective wherein Øieblikket* is a consideration. Kierkegaardian elements are mentioned in connection with overtly Kierkegaardian plays previously referred to in this vein (in Biographical Sketch): Kjaerlighedens Komedie, Brand, Peer Gynt, the poem "Paa Vidderne" and earlier poetry. Some of the similarities that are pointed out by Erichsen are the aesthetic and the religious spheres, the masses, the power of memory, and self-analysis. In Kejser og Galilaeer, Valborg sees a change, that the play is not an either-or but is a both-and. French critic P. G. Chesnais has also commented on Kierkegaard and Ibsen; Brand, Kjaerlighedens Komedie, and the poems are mentioned. Chesnais thinks that Ibsen was probably influenced indirectly and unconsciously by Kierkegaard, particularly in the language he uses.

An article which appeared in The New Age in 1908 by Dr. Angelo S. Rappoport considers Ibsen, not as a playwright, but as a moral philosopher, a preacher and a critic of life, and he compares him to Kierkegaard and Nietzsche.

According to Rappoport, Kierkegaard and Ibsen are uncompromisingly Protestant and contented themselves with pointing out the abuses of existing institutions. Nietzsche he calls a Greek to the end. He views Nietzsche as an aristocrat, while Kierkegaard and Ibsen he views as democratic. Of the three, only Nietzsche had the courage to throw the corpse in the cargo overboard.

Another article by an astute critic, Miguel de Unamuno y

---

* The Moment

153

Juga is titled "Perplexities and Paradoxes" (1945). He recognizes Kierkegaard's theology as underlying Ibsen's drama. For Unamuno, Ibsen's drama is religious rather than aesthetic or ethical and it is not understood by those who have not gone beyond the aesthetic and, at most, the ethical conception.

Kierkegaard and Ibsen were master dialecticians who played many tunes upon a single chord, "men som den gymnastiske Dialektiker frembringer og forandrer og frembringer, det Samme og dog ikke det samme."* It is expected that Chapter III will illuminate Ibsen's dramatic idiom and art through a consideration of the dialectic that has been referred to as the Kierkegaardian consciousness.

---

* "the trained dialectical gymnast produces and changes and produces again, the same and yet not the same."

The Dialectic

"Hiin Enkelte"*

Kierkegaard perceived the nature of his task as directed toward dissipating the illusion surrounding *the individual*. Everything must be done so that "den enkelte" become attentive. If he were to use a direct attack, it would strengthen a person in his illusion and at the same time embitter him. It would prevent him from making an admission privately. Therefore, he claims, the method must be indirect. While the indirect method requires time, altercation and patient "Finger-Øvelse i det Dialektiske, og en aldrig slumrende Frygt og Baeven,"** it also permits the communicator to withdraw, so that the subject can see that he has lived in an illusion. Even though the indirect way leaves it undetermined whether any result has occurred, Kierkegaard believed that it was still the only way one could achieve his or her own reality.[11] The dialectical tension and the untying of the knot could only be achieved through an understanding that was consonant with existence. With the direct way, the subject learns about the world, but nothing about himself; the moment of contemplation, the fullness in time is forfeited.

---

* "that solitary individual" (whom he considered to be his reader)
** "finger-exercise in the dialectical, and a never-slumbering fear and trembling"

"Tvetydigheden eller Dupliciteten i hele Forfatterskabet"*

In *Efterskrifter* (1846), Kierkegaard writes that where the subjective is important to knowledge, and where the appropriation by the audience, each in his own way, constitutes the crux of the matter, the process of communication is a work of art, and doubly reflected.[12] In *Synspunktet,* written in 1848 and published in 1859 — the date of Ibsen's "Paa Vidderne" (a poem which reflects their mutual desire to strip away the restraints which prevent the individual from realizing himself) — Kierkegaard writes that the dialectical is characteristic of his whole productivity, not simply of an individual study.[13]

Efterskrifter and *Synspunktet*** are significant to Kierkegaard's authorship in that they are direct statements of his intentions. The first he designates as the turning point in his work, the second he describes as an explanation; it serves as a kind of "ars poetica" to this discussion of the method.

Efterskrifter is not an aesthetic work, nor is it strictly religious, which is why it is by a pseudonym, and the reason that Kierkegaard adds his name as editor. In it, he acknowledges all the books previously written under pseudonyms. *Efterskrifter* presents the problem of how to become a Christian and it asserts that the works up to this point were written to illuminate the *problem;* they are a description of one way a person may take to become a Christian. The works after *Efterskrifter* describe the other way. The first movement is away from the poetical and it is that which constitutes the total significance of the aesthetical production; the second

---

* "The Ambiguity or Duplicity in the Whole Authorship" (heading he uses in *Synspunktet*)

** *Afsluttende uvidenskabelig Efterskrift (Concluding Unscientific Postscript,* 1846); *Synspunktet for min Forfatter-Virksomhed (The Point of View for My Work as an Author,* 1848)

156

movement is away from speculation, away from the System, "Bevaegelsen er tilbage."*[14]

The central point of Ibsen's authorship is his most philosophical work, *Kejser og Galilaeer* (1873), "Et Verdenshistorik Skuespil," which presents a world-historic view of the Christian dilemma. In *Kejser og Galilaeer*, the third way, the religious is expressed in conjunction with the aesthetic and the ethical,[15] that is, paganism, Christendom, philosophy. When he started the play in 1864, he wrote Bjørnstjerne Bjørnson that it filled him with joy. Later in 1871, he writes to Frederik Hegel that *Kejser og Galilaeer* will be his chief work and that it contains a positive philosophy of life. A year later, to Edmund Gosse, he admits that he is putting into this book a part of his spiritual life. As late as 1887, the play is in his thoughts. At an honorary banquet in Stockholm on September 24th, he denies that he is a pessimist, and he sees the tendency of the age as being directed toward the ideals of the third kingdom.[16] The plays following *Kejser og Galilaeer* become more adroitly conceptual artistic expressions of the individual in an existential dilemma with attention directed more pointedly to the *nature* of the awakening of an individual consciousness.

Ars Poetica

Synspunktet, which is essentially "an accounting" (not unlike Somerset Maugham's *The Summing Up*), affirms Kierkegaard's position. He thought that it should be read as devoutly as a religious work, "Dette lille Skrifts Indhold er hvad jeg som Forfatter i Sandhed er."** In a little over one hundred pages, Kierkegaard makes it clear that the book is not a defence or an apology; it is an *explanation* of his work as an author. An explanation was felt to be necessary to affirm

---

* "The movement is BACK." (*Synspunktet*)

** "The contents of these little writings are what I as an author truly stand for."

157

158

the fact that his duplicity was always ready to serve the religious. In *Synspunktet* and the supplement to it, *Den Enkelte.**[17] his task is stated "simply" (simplicity he viewed as an inevitable consequence of his method). The movement of his task is one that goes toward the simple, for a communication that reflects one out of one thing and into another eventually has to end in direct communication. More often than not, Ibsen's plays end with the protagonists coming *face to face* with themselves. When they do not arrive at this recognition, the ironical is expressed in that the audience comes face to face with the character's self-delusion, and indirectly with an aspect of its self.

Part one, A. of *Synspunktet* reads "Tvetydigheden eller Dupliciteten i hele Forfatterskabet, om Forfatteren er en aesthetisk eller en religieus Forfatter."** In the first sentence, Kierkegaard states that the duplicity is the essential dialectical distinction of the entire authorship. The point he wishes to make is that the fact of the aesthetic and the religious works was not a question of change on his part, but that the duplicity was there from the beginning.[18] Consequently, to understand his authorship, it should be read in the order of its production. Writing a note directed to his readers in 1898, Ibsen expressed a similar view in reference to his authorship, that it should be read in the order of its production, as it is "en sammenhaengende, kontinuerlig hélhed."*** With Kierkegaard, the aesthetic is juxtaposed with the religious simultaneously, that is, a religious piece would be contemporaneous with an aesthetic piece. He presents an inverse image, not unlike Ibsen, who in an individual play or in the sequence of his authorship will have one theme or view counteract another.

---

* *The Individual* (1855)

** "The Ambiguity or Duplicity in the Whole Authorship: As to Whether the Author is an Aesthetic or a Religious Author."

*** "a continuous, coherent whole" Note in Centennial edition of Ibsen's works, "Til laeserne" Kristiania i Marts 1898.

Kierkegaard was aware that the dialectical reduplication was difficult for some people to grasp and he recognized that other people did not desire to resolve the dialectic to be presented. Nonetheless, he still insisted upon maintaining the ambiguity that the indirect engendered. His audience was that individual who did wish to untie the knot, a consideration which accounts for the intimate tone of his writing, "Taenk en Knude, der er bunden. Saa ere der Nogle ville have den løst."* Continuing the thought that even though some people do not want anyone to touch it, and that, in spite of the fact that it is so loose it cannot hold together unless it is tightened, he suggests that someone must knot the thread. Since Kierkegaard's efforts are directed to opening "Inderlighedens Borgport"** a door long shut (similar in concept to the door Ibsen's John Gabriel Borkman [1896] did not open for eight years).[19] Kierkegaard admits that he

---

* "Imagine for a moment a knot. Some people wish to untie it."
** "the castle floor of inwardness (introspection)." See footnote 19.

knots the thread and pulls it tight, otherwise the "untying of the knot" has no significance. But Kierkegaard does not want to strangle or tranquilize his hearer; rather, he wishes to make him aware of his own existence. This end cannot be achieved with direct communication, the communication that men would prefer because it is comfortable.

Even in his direct authorship, the stratagem of the maieutic art is maintained. By his personal mode of existence, Kierkegaard tried to support the pseudonyms, the aesthetic work as a whole. He deceived inversely in the interest of the truth, deliberately creating the impression that he was an idler (an image Knut Hamsun epitomizes in his comic-tragic "wanderer" who touches so many lives, but whose own pain is unalleviated).[20] The aftereffect of his deceit, Kierkegaard was to utilize as an aspect of his dialectic. He knew that in turning to the religious works, he could count upon the negative support his conscious deception had engendered; the response would ensure that the religious communication would not be too direct. Instead of the pseudonyms giving him the aesthetic distance he needed, he had the grins and laughter by which most people are frightened away.

Section B. of the first part of *Synspunktet* reiterates the fact of the whole authorship being dialectical. Using an image of a flower, he differentiates the difference between the first simultaneous presentation of a religious and an aesthetic work, *To opbyggelige Taler** by S. Kierkegaard and *Enten-Eller* by Victor Eremita. *To opbyggelige Taler* was thought of by Kierkegaard as a little flower hidden in a great forest, not sought for its beauty or for its scent, or because it was nourishing. The image that is conjured forth is not unlike the one Ibsen evokes in *Olaf Liljekrans*. Olaf is seeking the loveliest flower of all and he wonders how he will know it, "Hvad heller er den lagt i lønlige Kraefter."**

---

* *Two Edifying Discourses*
** "What if it resides in some secret ideal?"

161

For Kierkegaard, the irony is that he held out the aesthetic work *Enten-Eller* to the world with his left hand, and in his right, the religious work *To opbyggelige Taler,* and all grasped with their right hand what he held in his left. The metaphoric possibilities that the left and the right engenders on a metaphysical level, that is "the right hand does not know what the left hand is doing" (Matthew 6:3), is cited by Kierkegaard and suggested by Ibsen in *Vildanden.* Ibsen's inversion of the context as used by Kierkegaard engenders an irony that underscores the misunderstanding that has prompted Hedvig to

take her life. Hedvig clutches the gun that kills her in her right hand and is carried off stage on the left through the kitchen door. Ibsen was emphatic about these points and he was explicit in his direction that when Hedvig is carried from the loft her right hand should be hanging down and toward the audience. He reinforces the image in the text through Relling who cannot release the gun from her hand without force. Ibsen's articulation is not only concentrated and related to the staging, but it also recalls the principle behind medieval "simultaneous staging" concepts wherein Paradise was at the extreme left and Hell was on the extreme right. Hedvig's exit through the left door is appropriate.

Kierkegaard believed the public response to his work was based upon ignorance and blindness and his conscious dialectic is based, in part, on what he knew the crowd would do. His intention was to entice it with the aesthetic work in the left hand, the left symbolizing the God-relationship, and then, eventually, to turn it in the other direction. On the artistic level, the juxtaposition of the left and the right simultaneously in *Vildanden* underscores the misunderstanding (also a result of ignorance and blindness) that prompts Hedvig to take her life. Ibsen suggests that it is not Love or the God-idea that is in operation. What motivates Greger's interference with the Ekdal family life is a desire to ease his own dissatisfaction with life. Although Kierkegaard and Ibsen are communicating in a different context and on different levels in this instance, they are articulating through the metaphysical association of the left and the right image and because the principals lacked the appropriate knowledge their choices do not have validity.

The predisposition to the theatrical and the dramatic which Kierkegaard has demonstrated in his authorship (See Chapter II) is consonant with the basic premise upon which his work is built — that transcendent existence cannot be attained through thought; he replaces philosophical contemplation with philosophical activity, demonstrating, wherever possible, his vision. However, he does not simply use the maieutic form as a desirable means of communication; for him, Christianity was maieutic communication. The duplicity inherent in the maieutic form enabled Kierkegaard for a moment, as it did Ibsen,[21] to make the invisible visible, "in concreto."[22] In Christendom, which he viewed as a caricature of Christianity, people are confused since they are supposed to be Christians. But Christianity, as conceived by Kierkegaard, was a way of life based upon decision, something that Christendom did not know; Christendom played at Christianity. In reality, these "pseudo" Christians are involved in a refined aestheticism, an intellectual paganism that has a dash of Christianity thrown in. These people must be deceived into the truth because "de vide ikke hvad de gjøre"* — and this deception can be done most effectively through "imitation" as in a theatre.[23] Consequently, Kierkegaard uses drama and theatre consciously and meticulously to support his point of view.

---

* "they know not what they do"

163

Pseudonymer og den Enkelte*

The pseudonyms were a deceit that aimed a blow at the System with the category of the individual. They enabled Kierkegaard (as his characters did for Ibsen) to embody the truth of a person in a particular mode of existence, "En Pseudonym er just ypperlig til at marquere et Point, en Stilling, en Position. Han er en digterisk Person."** Not only were the pseudonyms part of the activity to communicate alternate existential possibilities; they also permitted him to remain incognito. He wanted to stand in a poetical relationship to his work, and he, therefore, felt himself to be a pseudonym. Besides giving the views of existence dramatic power through the invention of characters who spoke for themselves, he also had these personae interact with one another; each is a particular existing individual in the concretion that existence brings to it.[24] The pseudonyms were the means to express the matter of the individual which for Kierkegaard and for Ibsen constituted the decisive thing. Concerning his

---

* Pseudonyms and the Individual.

** "A pseudonym is excellent for accentuating a point, a stance, a position. It creates a poetic person."

164

characters, Ibsen admits that he proceeds from the individual, the individual in every aspect of humanity.[25]

"I ethvert af de pseudonyme Skrifter forekommer paa een eller anden Maade dette om den Enkelte; men der er overveinde den Enkelte den, aesthetisk Bestemmet," while "I ethvert af mine opbyggelige Skrifter forekommer, og saa officielt som muligt, dette om 'den Enkelte', men der er den Enkelte hvad ethvert Menneske er eller kan vaere."* He further associates his dialectic with the treatment of the individual in the pseudonymous works and the edifying works, in that the starting-point of the pseudonyms is the difference between man and man with respect to intellect, culture and individual differences. In the edifying works, the starting-point is the edifying thoughts of the universal human. It is this double meaning that is precisely the dialectic of the single individual. The single individual can mean the one and the only and it can mean every man. Without this category, reduplication would be lacking in Kierkegaard's work. Of "hiin Enkelte"**[26] he writes, who he is he does not know, yet he is his hope, joy and pride.

Dialectically, Kierkegaard regards the individual as a category that can be used with a double lash to provoke attention. Whereas the pride of the one view is inciting (i.e. the aesthetic) to some, the humility of the second view (i.e. religious) deters others, the dichotomy creating a confusion, a confusion which is inherent to the double reflection. Those who work with this category of the individual tend to become more and more dialectical in proportion to the confusion which becomes greater and greater. The consequence is such that to discern the qualitative in a person or in a character requires

---

* "In every one of the pseudonymous works, this theme of the *individual* comes to evidence in one way or another; but there the individual is predominantly the pre-eminent individual in the aesthetic sense."—"In every one of my edifying works the theme of the individual comes to evidence, and as officially as possible; but there the individual is what every man is or can be."

** "that solitary individual"

165

a developed consciousness. For instance, the action of the pseudonyms are presented in a provocative way that has a certain persuasion (most particularly the aesthete of *Enten-Eller*), not unlike some of Ibsen's more arbitrary characters whose immediacy attracts and repels: Furia, Hjørdis, Bishop Nikolas, Bernick, Gregers, Rebekka, Hedda. There is a double meaning to the interpretation of the pseudonyms and the characters which cannot be arrived at *en masse*. The masses put a stamp on Dr. Stockman's "folkefiende"; conversely the individual recognizes the enemy of the people as the masses, and understands their power as the dissembling force for Stockman, dissembling in that he begins to play to the crowd. In the individual's interpretation of an existential dilemma, God, synonymous with Love, referred to in *Efterskrifter* as the God-idea, is the middle term which renders the meaning intelligible, "Jeg er overbevist om, at Gud er Kjaerligheden,"* — precisely the quality lacking in the aforementioned Ibsen characters and in the masses. Ibsen's dialectic has complexity in that people and situations are not always what they seem. He gives an ironical twist to Kierkegaard's conviction in *Brand;* Brand does not hear the voice that cries out through the thunder, "Han er deus caritatis."** A further irony is that *Brand* has often been considered the antithesis of *Peer Gynt,* but in these plays, the protagonists are both on the aesthetic plane of existence.

Den Enkelte og Ofringen***

Unfortunately, *the individual*, a category Kierkegaard cites as having been introduced by Socrates to dissolve paganism, was subsequently castrated by society. Nevertheless, Kierkegaard considers the only salvation for man is to become an individual, with the understanding that the established order

---

* "I am convinced that God is Love."
** "He is the God of Love."
*** The Individual and the Sacrifice

166

167

does not have any use for the individual because inwardness is not their concern. To sacrifice or to be sacrificed, which is a possible consequence of being an individual, does not interest the world. A *Papirer* entry differentiates the validity of the sacrifice.[27] The formula for the person destined for the sacrifice is *Begeistringen** but it is an enthusiasm which has an equally powerful negative reflection. It means that this individual is marked for suffering: he is like a sharpened note, and his life is sharpened for him. He is the sacrifice which is something quite different from the thousands of spontaneous enthusiasts who have been sacrificed, for instance, Dr. Stockman in Ibsen's *En Folkefiende*.[28] The issue of the polluted baths is undermined by Stockman's enthusiasm. The idea of *Begeistringen* as possessing an aesthetic quality, Kierkegaard develops in the edifying essay "En Leiligheds-Tale."** He suggests that if a man would live and die for an endeavor, sacrifice his all for it, this endeavor cannot in the deepest sense be good.[29] In Knut Hamsun's novels, the protagonists are more in tune with the individual who has a natural propensity to be a sacrifice, the man who is not impressed with the crowd's response; his enthusiasm is in touch with the infinite.[30]

Because Kierkegaard regarded his age as the age of dissolution and he wanted to make his generation aware that it needed eternity, that it had nothing but the temporal, he was willing, for a time, to be a sacrifice to their laughter, *"at jeg, som en sig Devoverende vovede en Stund at blive.**** But it is the category of the individual, the category of spiritual awakening, as opposed to politics or wordly interests that is his immediate concern. Ibsen was also a political conservative. He denied his involvement in the social rights of women, saying that his interest had been with humanity.[31] Kierkegaard associates the modern with the pagan notion that to

---

* *enthusiasm*
** "An Occasional Address"
*** *"that* jeg, as a self-immolated man ventured for a while to be"

168

be a man was to belong to a race endowed with reason. To belong to it as a specimen so that the race or species is higher than the individual — which would be to say that there are no more individuals, but only specimens — was a thesis that he could not accept any more than Ibsen could.

Den Enkelte og Maengden*

The danger of yielding little by little to society, to *Maengden* was a possibility Kierkegaard recognized. Its perniciousness he develops in the first note to *Den Enkelte,* entitled "Til Dedicationen 'hiin Enkelte'."** In the note to

---

* The Individual and the Crowd
** "Concerning the Dedication to 'the individual'"

Den Enkelte, he uses the expression "hiin Enkelte" rather than "den Enkelte"* the term he uses in the second note, indicating with the differentiation, the necessity of standing alone. The view of *Maengden* is developed in several paragraphs reflecting his concept from different angles; *Maengden* stands for number; *Maengden* weakens the individual sense of responsibility to a fraction; *Maengden* is an abstraction; *Maengden* is an untruth; *Maengden* excludes God (Love). The individual witness for the truth[32] is recognizable by the fact that he is the object of attack and persecution; the pernicious influence of the crowd Ibsen was to treat in *En Folke-fiende* (1882). Yet, not withstanding the negativity and the force that the crowd exerts (and each Ibsen protagonist comes up against an element of this force; his people are tempted, intimidated, or led astray by this mortal poser whether it be manifested in terms of recognition, wealth, conventions or some other form of public approval), Kierkegaard believed that it was possible for every man to be *the one,* the awakened individual who experiences "Angestens Skrig"** and who has recognized his solitary state.

---

* "that solitary individual" — "that individual". Note: the edifying essay "En Leiligheds-Tale" is also dedicated to "hiin Enkelte."

** "scream of dread" (actually a necessity)

170

The Design of the Work

In *En Literair Anmeldelse* ("Nutiden")* Kierkegaard expresses the idea that artistic production is full of secrets. He builds upon the premise that every man who has a *real* experience at the same time experiences its possibilities in an ideal sense, including the opposite possibility. Whereas aesthetically, these possibilities are the person's property, it is not so in respect to his private and personal reality. His talk and his *productivity* will rest upon and correspond to his *silence*, the content of which only he has possession of, and the absolute expression of that silence will include the qualitatively opposite possibility. If a man prostitutes his own reality by not including all of the ideality in his endeavors, he is no longer essentially productive. Therefore, he must be true to the work or to himself and reflect the entire expression with the same affection.[33] Within the holistic view of experience, the comic-tragic manifests itself and with Kierkegaard and Ibsen it is the form they were to use.[34]

Another instance of Kierkegaard's artistic balance (which must not be construed as simply synthesis and completion for the balance is in constant flux, yet always steady) is the representation of the aesthetical and the ethical spheres of existence in Part I and Part II of *Enten-Eller*. Also, in *Chris-*

---

* *A Literary Review* ("The Present Age")

telige Taler,[35] he reflects ideas in pairs. Using an existential situation, he presents the connection between ideas in a way that is psychological and indirect, "et nyt Hvorledes af det gamle Hvad."*[36] For instance, misfortune is good fortune. One example of this paradox concerns the seaman who is assured that the wind which is blowing is the wind that will carry him to the *goal.* Even though it is called a contrary wind by others, he knows it is a fair wind. Ibsen develops the ironical repercussions that can occur in an existential situation which recognizes the human fraility involved when the goal is misunderstood. For instance, in *Et Dukkehjem,* Nora has the possibility of transcendence on the earthly plane when the miracle she has waited eight years for, does not occur; the misfortune is good fortune. Nora was sure that Helmer would assume the blame for her "crime" if it came out, that he would say, "jeg er den skyldige."** And so that he would not be hurt by the consequence she would have taken her own life. Helmer would not accept her "crime" as his;[37] and, moreover, he did not believe anyone would relinquish honor for love (as Nora had done). Kierkegaard would describe this unfulfilled wish of Nora's as an inverse miracle, the change that occurred in Nora as a result of the shock she experienced was the miracle and her good fortune; the shock dispelled the illusion and opened the door of inwardness for her and permitted her to experience "the fullness of *Øieblikket.*" The *miracle* being that every infinite change in *quality* is genuinely a miracle.[38] Using the art form of the present day, Ingmar Bergman reflects the idea of losing all to gain all. With the film *Viskningär och rop (Cries and Whispers),* he shows the servant who has given so much of herself to her Mistress (Agnes) and to the family, as inheriting nothing of value in the material sense when Agnes dies. The ending evokes the nature of what she does inherit, the memories of past happiness, the love of her mis-

---

* "a new how of an old what"
** "I am guilty." ("I am the guilty one.")

172

tress. She never questions her role in life and she is secure in the love that she and Agnes shared. Bergman's statement is direct, but rendered poetically (in a way that Ibsen's later plays do) the truth that God is Love. Contrary winds do not affect Anna — where she will go or what she will do. The sister's shallowness and selfishness emphasize the emptiness of their lives and the lack of love in their lives.

The concept that the weaker is the stronger is also expressed in *Christelige Taler;* Ibsen has Fru Helseth (*Rosmersholm*) articulate the idea. The plunge of Rebekka and Rosmer into the swirling waters below is described by her in the last speech of the last act. She comments upon the shame of Rebekka and Rosmer embracing each other before the *fall* (her interpretation), then she refers to Beata, the dead wife, "Salig fruen tog dem."* Rebekka's daemonia was overpowered by the "Rosmer" way, the "other" way. In *Hedda Gabler* (1890), Thea's inner strength is shown as more durable and positive than Hedda's daemonic strength (as was Hjørdis' pagan strength unable to stand up to Sigurd's Christianity in *Haermaendene paa Helgeland*). August Strindberg also dramatizes

---

* "The blessed mistress (wife) took them."

the stronger in the Kierkegaardian sense. In his one-act play, *Den Starkere* (*The Stronger*, 1889), he presents two women as personifications of the idea that the weaker is the stronger. One woman by imitating the other regains her husband and it seems that she is the stronger;[39] actually, it is the silent rival who is the stronger. As the one imitated, she gains a kind of immortality.

The obvious is generally suspect with Kierkegaard as it is with Ibsen. Ibsen's drama reflects the balance that Kierkegaard has called "Loven i Forhold til digterisk Frembringelse"* and, in his dramatic art, there are an infinite number of possibilities generated other than *the one* that resides in his silence *which* is the content. It is the empty space — this

nothingness — where what is most important is conceded.[40] The possibilities that are set in motion by this law account for the many interpretations that it generates. Consider *Brand* and *Peer Gynt*, often regarded as the antithesis of each other, the one religious, the other aesthetic: *Et Dukkehjem* and *Hedda Gabler*, the woman who could let go and the one who could not, a metamorphosis occurring in the first play

---

* "the law governing artistic production"

174

but not in the second (*Gengangere* could also be discussed in this context); with *Gengangere* and *Vildanden,* revelation and repetition are side by side and sacrifice is absurd. The sacrifice is one of Kierkegaard's essential categories and it assumes the properties of living tableaux with Ibsen reflecting a bittersweet *irony* in a kind of frieze of life, the last scenes of his dramas recalling the art of Edvard Munch in particular, but also Ingmar Bergman's cinematic artistry. [41] The genius of Kierkegaard and Ibsen is that their work can be examined from so many different directions and still retain itself. In a reference to Aristophanes, Kierkegaard wrote "Som Ironien derfor beseirer Alt ved at see dets Misforhold til Ideen, saaledes ligger den under for sig, idet den bestandig gaaer ud over sig selv og dog bliver i den."* So it is with Ibsen's plays. Georg Brandes' analogy of a mirror chamber, an expression by which he designates the many facets of Kierkegaard's writing, is also appropriate to Ibsen's drama.

The tension created by the law governing artistic production enables Kierkegaard's and Ibsen's audience to experience an inwardness that they did not know before without their recognizing how or through whom the communication was expressed; each writer turns the comfortable way of thinking topsy-turvy. Nor is there simply an individual concept involved in the content; there is also a categorical consideration.

---

* "As irony conquers everything by seeing its disproportion to the Idea, so it also succumbs to itself, since it constantly goes beyond itself while remaining in itself."

176

The Categories

In dissecting the human consciousness, specific categories, other than the category of *den Enkelte* and *Ofringen*, are essential to the design. These categories are implicit, not only to Kierkegaard's authorship but also to Ibsen's drama. The categories under consideration are: *Existents-Sphaerer, Valget, Springet, Metamorfose, Gjentagelsen,* and *Øieblikket.* * The examination of these categories (along with the other two) is expected to reveal "et nyt Hvorledes af det gamle Hvad"** within a conceptual pattern that reflects upon the aesthetic consciousness of Søren Kierkegaard and Henrik Ibsen.

So significant was the category of the individual to Kierkegaard that in a *Papirer* entry, he wrote that if he was to carve an inscription on his grave, it would be none other than "den Enkelte." (See "The Individual" in Introduction.) The reader is asked repeatedly in one of the edifying discourses if he lives his life like an individual. Kierkegaard understood that *the way* of the individual was difficult and often thankless. Moreover, he realized that the existing individual was constantly in the process of becoming. He saw that striving infinitely while at the same time living existentially was comic-tragic.[42]

---

* *Spheres of existence, the Choice, the Leap, Metamorphosis, Repetition* and *the Moment.*

** "A new how of an old what"

177

His own task he viewed in terms of prompting; it was to prompt the hearer to come close to himself and to be observant of who he was and where he was. Although the spheres of existence stressed in *Synspunktet* are the aesthetic and the religious (the spheres of existence he had experienced), he designated three levels of consciousness as expressing life's various possibilities: the aesthetic, the ethical and the religious. These spheres of existence represent a category which is essential to the dialectic of Kierkegaard and of Ibsen.

THE SPHERES OF EXISTENCE AND THE INDIVIDUAL	THE DIRECTION	STASIS R- HEDDA GABLER E- KJAERLIGHEDENS KOMEDIE A- PEER GYNT	MOVEMENT ET DUKKEHJEM
RELIGIOUS Higher Conciousness	R	R THEA	R R NORA II.
	SPRINGET/VALGET STANDNINGEN		
ETHICAL Conciousness	E	E GULDSTAD	E NORA I. TORVALD
	SPRINGET */VALGET** ***STANDNINGEN		
AESTHETIC Lack of Conciousness	A	A PEER	A A
	* The Leap ** The Choice *** The Pause	At the Beginning of the play.	I. Nora at the Beginning. II. Nora at the end. Torvald Throughout the Play.

"The Spheres of Existence and the Individual"

178

Den Enkelte and Existents-Sphaerer*

In positing his doctrine of existence (the life of the individual), Kierkegaard's contention is that the individual exists in one or the other of these spheres with a possible, permissible, overlapping in terms of the ethical and the religious.[43] That does not mean that the individual will necessarily experience each sphere of existence in a life-time. Another point in considering the spheres is that there is a transition point, a *pause* between them. In some characters there is not any change, hence *no* pause; in others the transition is germinating; in still others the appearance of change seems to be occurring but is not; and in others yet, change is rejected. Locating the pause or its absence can intensify the theatrical reality in an Ibsen play, and the pause plays a significant part in the end of *Gengangere*. The spheres of existence affect the interpretation of a person's existential condition and the determination of an Ibsen character is of singular importance to the characterization and to the interpretation of the play. For instance, is Brand on the aesthetic level of existence or on the religious level; is there a significant change in the `Allmers (*Lille Eyolf*); is Hedda Gabler aware of her existential situation; does the Master Builder fall or jump, and so on? Ibsen prompts his audience continually and this gentle guidance is essential to the Ibsen director if he expects to re-create the author's vision. Art is not spelling out everything nor is it making the meaning so oblique that there is nothing but frustration.

In connecting the idea of the *aesthetic* and the *religious* spheres to *Begeistringen***[44] a quality that is inherent to both of them, Kierkegaard distinguishes the underlying principles within the first sphere of existence and then, finally, a difference between the spheres. Firstly, comes immediate enthusiasm, then follows the stage of cleverness which, because im-

---

* The Individual and the Spheres of Existence
** *enthusiasm*

179

mediate enthusiasm does not calculate, assumes a calculating cleverness, and then, there is the appearance of something higher, the religious. This higher degree of enthusiasm is able to see the shrewdest plan of action but to disdain it, and thereby, receive the intensity of an eternal enthusiasm. This really intensive enthusiasm will remain completely misunderstood because an enthusiastic action is always the opposite of shrewdness and never obvious.[45] That Kierkegaard does not regard the ethical sphere of existence as possessing enthusiasm is a consideration that serves to define an aspect of its nature. It is this lack of passion in the ethical stance that is its strength and its weakness. Whereas the ethical person lacks the creative sensibility, he or she is sometimes able to respond positively as Tesman does when he starts to re-create Løvborg's manuscript. Tesman, at this point in the play, is straining toward the religious sphere. But, because it is unlikely that he ever was in the aesthetic sphere of existence, that is, he did not have to make the ethical choice, there is a missing link in his personality.

Whereas the spheres of existence are successive steps to a richer life, they are not mere developments. Each sphere has its own specificity and is not conceived of as absorbing the other; it replaces the other. Although Kierkegaard acknowledges the ethical-religious stance as an appropriate mode of existence, he did not accept as viable the premise of existing in an aesthetical-ethical category; such an existence violated unconditionally the pattern that should be the model, the way of life demonstrated by Christ. However, he thought that the majority of people were existing in the aesthetic category, and they were at the very most on an aesthetic-ethical plane. Examples of aesthetic enthusiasm in Ibsen's characters accentuate the dimensions involved in the concept. Such characters as Skule and Nikolas (*Kongs=Emnerne*) and Hjalmar and Gregers (*Vildanden*) show the two degrees of enthusiasm involved in the aesthetic view of life. The naiveté of the first character in each pair is coupled with the shrewdness of the

180

other (shrewdness constituted a sin for Kierkegaard). Consequently, the second degree of aesthetic enthusiasm is more dangerous.[46] With other characters such as Hjørdis (*Haermaendene paa Helgeland*) and Hedda (*Hedda Gabler*), the characters are not presented against a lesser degree of enthusiasm. Therefore, the *malevolence* of their acts posited against another foil, the *religious,* represented by Sigurd's acceptance of Christianity in the one and Thea's expression of Christianity in her being, in the other, permits the negativity of Hjørdis and Hedda to dominate, but not gain ascendency. In *En Folkefiende,* Ibsen allows the aesthetic enthusiasm of Dr. Stockman to be played against the pseudo-ethical existence of his brother and against the crowd who act *en masse.* The lack of enthusiasm and ethical responsibility coupled with some degree of shrewdness characterize the aesthetical-ethical stance of the brother, Peter Stockman; with the hysteria of the crowd, he provides the milieu he and Kierkegaard were rebelling against — Christendom. Viewing the spheres of existence and enthusiasm in this context emphasizes the subtlety of the interpretative force that is contained in Ibsen's characterization, and it also indicates how deceptive surface reality in itself can be.

Delineating the Spheres of Existence

The Aesthetic: Constantine Constantius, the pseudonym of *Gjentagelsen*, refers to the aesthete as unformed. He says that the personality has not yet been discovered, that only the imagination is awake to the dream of personality and in such a dream, the individual is a shadow. At one and the same time, the aesthete is a multiplicity of possibilities and a single possibility because the ego is invisible. The aesthetic stage indicates a life of sensuality and pleasure with gradations (as

has been indicated in the consideration of enthusiasm). Ibsen characters as vastly different as Bishop Nikolas, Peer, Brand, Dr. Stockman, Judge Brack and Hedda are delineations of an aesthetic existence.

What is significant about this stage is that it is attended by such unpleasant phenomena as *angest* and *fortvivlelse.*[*][47] Kierkegaard regarded man as a synthesis of body and spirit, the temporal and the eternal, the finite and the infinite, necessity and freedom. The aesthete overemphasizes one side of the synthesis: the body, the temporal, the finite, the necessity. However, the other side is there and makes itself felt by an anxiety, and this call of the spirit is *angest* or dread. *Angest* indicates that man has the eternal within him; as such, angest is a positive force. If man persists in the sensory although experiencing dread, he will end in *Fortvivlelse* because he is denying himself. Like Narcissus, he has not chosen himself; he has fallen in love with himself. Such preoccupation with self, Ibsen shows in some of his characterizations. Consider Hedda, John Gabriel Borkman, and Bygmester Solness' absorption with themselves.[48] The first stage leads to despair because man has something else within him that cannot be satisfied solely by a sensory life. One despairs as soon as one is aware that the aesthetic consciousness encompasses possibilities, but never actuality. The awakening begins the *moment* consciousness is aware of the finite (real) as such. This does not occur with Dr. Stockman because he allows the pressure of the masses to overwhelm his initial motivation. He is swept away on a wave of enthusiasm that has become directed to righteous indignation.

When the aesthete becomes conscious of himself, then there is no recourse but the ethical choice. In choosing the ethical, one chooses one's self. It is not a question of choosing good or evil; rather, one chooses good *and* evil or excludes them. The aesthetic sphere is not evil; it is neutrality or indifference;

---

* Dread and despair.

183

it is the ethical which constitutes the choice. The choice is no more than the awakening of a man's consciousness whereby he becomes aware of his own determinants.[49]

The Ethical: Nothing finite escapes the ethical consciousness and everything finite finds in the ethical view continuity and a frame of reference which gives meaning to that sphere of existence. For the ethical man, the emptiness that characterizes the aesthetic sphere has been transcended into a life task.[50] Kierkegaard saw the ethical level of existence as necessary to the metamorphosis of the individual (although not to himself), for on this level, decisiveness is exercised in regard to the self and to others, that essential which was lacking in Peer and which was one-sided with Brand. It is through the ethical life that an individual becomes interested in the world and those around him. As a result, the personality becomes more open to the rich content of reality, and this content gives to the individual the possibility of reaching the higher form (Svanhild, for instance, in *Kjaerlighedens Komedie*). From this point, the individual can move in a more individualistic, that is, religious, direction. Ibsen dramatizes the movement with Nora. In other plays there are by-paths, omissions, distortions, and/or complications which obstruct the movement.

Closely related to the ethical is the idea of the tragic hero whose deeds are geared to the universal. Ibsen depicts a facet of the transition in *Lille Eyolf*. Allmers and his wife, Rita, are completely absorbed in themselves, he with the book he is writing on "human" responsibility, and Rita with an ever increasing sensuality, prompted, in part, by her husband's diminishing interest in her. The death of their crippled son, Eyolf, by drowning, causes them to take stock of their loveless life and finally to decide to devote themselves to educating unfortunate children. There is a certain irony involved in their resolution as it is not certain that either of them at this point in time has sufficient maturity to fulfill such a responsi-

184

bility. Kierkegaard and Ibsen emphasized the necessity of enlightened parentage in their authorship. Ibsen was to say more
directly that which the plays indirectly intimate, that the
future of the world rested with the mothers.[51]

While the *aesthete* is self-centered, the *ethical man* is conscious of being a member of the community, and this factor
constitutes the principle of his conduct. He is a fighter and an
optimist who thinks that he is fighting for a good cause.
Kierkegaard believed that the two spheres of existence were
frequently conjoined. Ibsen plays on the duality in *En Folkefiende* when he juxtaposes and combines the aesthetic and
the ethical spheres. In juxtaposing the spheres of existence,
Ibsen is reflecting Kierkegaard's view of the age "I vor Tid
blandes Alt sammen, man besvaerer det Aesthetiske ethisk,
Troen intellectuelt o.s.v."*

There are gradations within the ethical sphere of existence
just as there was with the aesthetic sphere. The highest level in
the ethical sphere is achieved by he who realizes that the
world of sensuality and desire has power and that one cannot
achieve anything by one's own strength. The audience senses
in *Gengangere* the dismay that accompanies Mrs. Alving's
awakening to the uselessness of her striving to nullify the past.
And, although her own responsibility is made clear to her,
since the past was a result of error, her guilt is dissolved.[52]
This is where Ibsen stops. He does not continue the action.
However, it is with this admission to one's self that the ethical
can be viewed as bordering on the religious sphere of existence
as with Mrs. Alving who does experience *Øieblikket*. Just as
the aesthetic can culminate in despair, the ethical can culminate in repentance. Both of these positions are divided by a
fine line. During the ethical stage, immediacy is dissipated
but returns as consciousness becomes aware of itself; then

---

* "In our age, everybody is mixed up together; the aesthete is treated
ethically, faith is dealt with intellectually, and so forth."

the finite is grounded in transcendent existence. The person who realizes this is ready for the next level of consciousness, the religious sphere, wherein one recognizes himself in a relationship of unconditional obedience to the God-Idea (Love).

The Religious: This stage is the ulterior immediacy. Kierkegaard writes in *Frygt og Baeven** that faith is not the first immediacy but a subsequent immediacy; the first immediacy is aesthetic. Aesthetic immediacy is equated with direct experience as it is simply given and had before reflection. It is a natural spontaneity; this kind of immediacy Kierkegaard associates with art which he believes cannot be savored except in fantasy. The ulterior immediacy is brought forth by reflection upon the infinite which finally leads to a new actuality. However, the new actuality cannot be achieved through reflection in itself, since reflection is in the form of possibility. The second immediacy can be achieved only through a leap of faith. Whether Bygmester Solness leaps or falls to his death becomes more than a quizzical question to bait an audience's curiosity or intellect; the act by its very ambiguity throws the audience back on itself and *forces it* to reflect. In sensing the strangeness of the action, the audience is coming closer to its own depth and to Ibsen's *raison d'être*.

The religious sphere of existence is not opposed to the ethical sphere which it transcended, but rather duty is infused with love and love becomes a duty. Such a love is portrayed by Ibsen on two levels in *Kongs=Emnerne*. He shows Haakon's marriage to Margrete becoming something more than a pragmatic and/or political move and the transition is shown as a natural development. With Skule the situation is different. From the beginning he loves his son who comes lately into his life.[53] But, blinded by his own will he does not see the necessity of disciplining him. The child's willingness to kill for his father initiates a change in Skule and love becomes a duty. However, in fulfilling the duty, the boy is sacrificed.

---

* *Fear and Trembling*

Man relates himself not only to his self in the religious sphere but also to the "Other," that is, transcendent existence, and this "Other" is man's actual origin. The passage from the ethical to the religious stage of life is more striking than the passage from the aesthetic to the ethical. Kierkegaard uses the Biblical story of Abraham and Isaac to demonstrate how the passage occurs. This story of a father's sacrifice of a son is very different from Skule's story. With Abraham and Isaac love and duty are in perfect balance.

In demanding that Abraham sacrifice his only son, Isaac, God demands something that is absolutely forbidden from the standpoint of the ethical. Man must suppress the ethical and choose as an individual, as one who is higher than the community. The man who can renounce the universal in order to become the individual has the potential to be the knight of faith. Humanly speaking, he is crazy, for if he were not, he would be a hypocrite and be unable to make himself intelligible to anyone. The leap he makes is rooted in *faith* and that is why it is called the leap into the absurd; it is not predicated on human reason; its logic is outside the reach of human consciousness. The act of faith occurs in *Øieblikket* (this category is developed later in this chapter) which is the synthesis of time and eternity. At this time, the believer is contemporaneous with Christ. It is the memory of a primordial unity that belonged to man and is now lost. Only in this instant does life begin for man.

The spheres of existence represent halting places and one passes from one to another only by a leap. Central to the concept of the leap is that man has a choice, and choice presupposes a freedom of will. Man has the freedom to live life on ethical principles or not to do so.[54] At times, Kierkegaard brackets the ethical and the religious spheres of existence together as a single way of life indicating a lower and a higher phase. He wants to show people that choice is necessary by showing what choice is and that at the moment of decision, man is alone.

187

A Note on the Boundary Zones Between the Spheres of Existence and Their Relationship to the Dialectic

There are boundary zones which correspond to the three spheres of existence; considering them is essential to the dialectic and relevant to understanding the *comic-tragic* dramatic form which Ibsen and Kierkegaard viewed as the one appropriate to their age. *Irony* is the boundary between the aesthetic and the ethical spheres and *Humor* is the boundary between the ethical and the religious spheres; thus the ironist follows immediacy, the ethicist comes next, then the humorist, and finally the religious individual.

*Mulighedens virkeliggjørelse!**[55]

Kierkegaard and Ibsen reflect in their authorship the incommensurability of the inner life with the outside reality. In point of fact, according to Kierkegaard, the tension that the incompatibility causes is an assurance that one is in tune with the infinite. Their characters live and try to survive in a world where Christendom is the milieu, a world wherein the words of the New Testament are mouthed, but not lived. Kierkegaard views the situation of the 19th century as far worse than paganism in that paganism did not know about Christianity; consequently, it was more honest; it lacked the hypocrisy that the pseudo condition propagated. The *difficulty* of achieving actuality in the sense of becoming that which is the essence of Christianity, an individual, is the base note that resounds throughout Kierkegaard's and Ibsen's creative efforts.

In addition, the tendency of the age was directed toward the materialistic values which bombarded man with extraneous concerns, baiting him with possibilities of not much consequence, and denying him the sensitivity to be selective. Out of the multitudes of possibilities, how could one know which

---

* The possibility made actual!

188

was the one for him (and what of the unborn possibilities)? Kierkegaard and Ibsen recognized how the vision could become blurred from the diversions and the pressures of "Nutiden,"* the most insidious pressure being that of the System, which rewards its members and punishes its deviates without impunity. Its rigidness obliterates the individual, the human element in existence.

Irony

Kierkegaard writes in *Efterskrifter* that irony arises from the placement of the particularities of the finite within the ethical requirement, and allowing the contradiction between the two to become visible.[56] Ibsen's plays, in presenting mundane details of the finite world alongside of the existential situation, which is rooted in the ideal, mirrors the irony that is implicit to the 19th century. In Kierkegaard's and Ibsen's efforts to show their audience how the possibility is or is not made possible in such a condition, irony is the natural constituent of the dialectic. It would be a mistake to suggest that Kierkegaard and Ibsen thought of irony as a device. Its root is in the consciousness which dominates their authorship, the existentialism of Christianity, a life based on decision, on decision that fulfills the human potential on an individual level, *not* en masse.[57] Irony is one of the fruits of their vision which they use pragmatically, thus bringing into play along with "creative intuition," the practical intellect.[58] Therefore, irony also has an artistic (opposed to poetic) function; it becomes an entity not unlike the painter's materials — the paints, the canvas. Irony extends itself to every aspect of their idiom: the titles, the punctuation, the scene, the material details of existence.

The true ironist (and an ironist can be an aesthicist or an ethicist) is not ironical because of a superiority (as Gregers' is in *Vildanden*) to the group he is associated with. What identifies the ironist who is an ethicist is the movement of the

---

* "The Present Age"

spirit by which he sets his outward life in juxtaposition with the infinite requirement of the ethical — which is something that is not immediately apparent.

The ethicist is ironical enough to realize that his interests and the world's are not in harmony, yet he is able to hold fast to the ethical in himself. Men will think that for such an individual, nothing is important. The aesthetical ironist, on the other hand, assails the world with his energy, expecting to transform the world, not realizing that the order is to transform himself. Accordingly, when such a person meets with a true ironist, the latter will know how to utilize him as comic material, as Ibsen does with Dr. Stockman, Gregers, Allmers, and others.

Kierkegaard points out the possibility of misinterpreting the ironist as to whether he is a true ironist or an enthusiast as occurring because *irony* in itself is only the possibility thereof. It is this possibility that Ibsen found indispensible to his vision. Misunderstanding[59] has an organic significance in his work that overrides the Scribean *quiproquo* sometimes associated with him.

The essence of irony is described by Kierkegaard in *Om Begrebet Ironi*:

190

Det Formummede og Hemmelighedsfulde, den har
ved sig den telegraphiske Communication, den aab-
ner, fordi en Ironiker altid maa forstaaes langtfra,
den uendelige Sympathi, den forudsaetter, Forstaael-
sens flygtige men ubeskrivelige Nu, der fortraenges
øieblikkelig af Misforstaaelsens Angest — alt dette
faengsler med uopløselige Baand.*

After the ironist raises the individual out of his immediate
existence which is his function, he lets him hover suspended
between attraction and repulsion. It is this kind of irony that
Ibsen portrays.

Humor

Kierkegaard views religiosity with humor as its incognito,
as a synthesis of absolute religious passion — because the
believer is a particular existing individual situated in the concretion that existence brings to it.

In his writing concerning the theatre (see Phister reference
in Chapter I),[60] Kierkegaard pointed out that the comic is
brought to the surface when inwardness comes into relationship with the environment. Consequently, the experience that
the religious person must express is comic, although Kierkegaard also admits that he cries while others laugh. Nevertheless, the humor evolving from the incongruity that the
finite imposes on the religious person is constructive; it insures
him against martyrdom.

Some of Ibsen's characters resemble the religious person
outwardly, but, in actuality, they are situated in the aesthetic
sphere of existence (for instance, Brand, Dr. Stockman, Pastor
Manders, Allmers, and to a certain degree Rosmer). They are

---

* "The disguise and the mysteriousness which it entails, the telegraphic
communication which it initiates, inasmuch as the ironist must always
be understood at a distance, the infinite sympathy it assumes, the elusive
and the ineffable moment of understanding immediately displaced by the
anxiety of misunderstanding — all this captivates with indissoluble bonds."

so absorbed with self that they are humorous without knowing it. Possibly, with Solveig (*Peer Gynt*), there is what Kierkegaard terms a "suffering" character. Kierkegaard calls this kind of person suffering and tragic; the contradiction is a suffering contradiction as opposed to a humorous one. In earlier Ibsen plays, this kind of pure solemnity is more apparent, for instance, Dagny (*Haermaendene paa Helgeland*), Aurelia (*Catilina*). With the later plays, there are characters who suffer but not in the same way—Aline, Bygmester Solness' *sick* wife; Irene, sculptor Rubek's disoriented "muse" *Når Vi Døde Vågner*.[61]

Those characters who appear to suggest the religious individual possess an inwardness that sometimes elicits humor. Such characters are not easily found in Ibsen. Tesman, for instance, in *Hedda Gabler*, has a seriousness (humor is unconscious), but his concern is more closely connected with the universal. It would be more accurate to view him as an ethical person, with possibly a leaning toward the ethical-religious. Dr. Rank (*Et Dukkehjem*) reflects the idea of the religious person who possesses humor. In expressing his love for Nora, Ibsen portrays him as unselfish and whimsical. He cries while others laugh — he will be "invisible" at the party the next year; he knows that he will be dead.

*Valget**[62] — "to Be or not to Be"*

The category of *valget* constitutes the core of all human existence for Kierkegaard. It is through choice (and the repetition of choice) that a person becomes a self. Both he and Ibsen start their work from various points of view, but their thought always moves in the same direction — toward choice.

Kierkegaard says that in life there are cross-ways. He sees man as standing in the beginning at the cross-ways; this, he considers, is his perfection, not his merit. But, where he stands

---

* the Choice

192

at the conclusion, that is his choice. It is to the conclusion of each of Ibsen's plays wherein the significance lies — to whether a choice was made.[63]

Kierkegaard believed that only through choice did man have the right to speak of existence, only then, through choice, could he think of himself as an individual. The credo is *not*: I think, therefore I am, *but* rather: only when I begin to exist can I begin to think. Choice initiates the individual into existence. Its criteria is that it does not have any criteria because it is *not* logic that determines a person's position and there are *no* objective standards where human existence is involved.[64]

Considering choice as the center of existence means that the communication is direct and indirect, as is the authorship of Kierkegaard and Ibsen. The purpose is not to annul one form of communication at the expense of another, but to preserve the equilibrium, the simultaneity and the plane in which they are united in existence. This is not the Hegelian synthesis.

In *Forførerens Dagbog*, Kierkegaard differentiates the nature of choice. In making a distinction concerning tragic guilt, he writes that the tragic guilt which is incurred voluntarily (as a result of choosing) is ethical while that which is forced on a person by circumstances of inheritance is aesthetic,[65] because it is there only for the purpose of the play.

He believes that choice cannot properly be made until the middle years (the point where Ibsen's characters are generally at a point of crisis) because it is only when life has furnished a text that a person can find the theme.

A further differentiation as to the nature of choice is the idea of the right person for the right task so that it is not simply blind will (as with Skule in *Kongs=Emnerne*) that is in operation. Kierkegaard uses an analogy in reference to the Annunciation to indicate that *choice* is not simply an arbitrary act. His theme is the reason that Mary was the chosen one (as was Haakon in *Kongs=Emnerne*); the Angel chose the right person because Mary chose rightly.

193

Springet* — possibility to actuality

Springet presupposes *Valget*,[66] *if* a choice has been made. The choice and the leap are acts of the whole man, that is, the total self committing itself into what its understanding is confronted with. Not only is one's understanding confronted but one's existence (which includes understanding) is also confronted. Since a person cannot know completely through understanding and existence, he must make the leap in faith, by virtue of the absurd. It is only with the leap that man has the right to speak of existence.

In considering the decisive actions of an Ibsen character, this condition is significant as to the validity of decision. The leap is itself the decision. To be near making the leap is nothing. With the leap quality emerges, as it did with Nora.

Hegel differs from Kierkegaard in connection with the leap and the qualitative. Kierkegaard saw the leap as having reality in an existential situation. Hegel's dialectic is not the existential dialectic, but rather, it is a rationalistic one. .He sees reality within a logical system of thought. His concern is with the infinite *quantitative both/and* rather than the infinite *qualitative either-or*. In that Hegel does not consider the existential dimension in his dialectic, he does not come to an understanding of the human ethical problem. In equating existence and thought, he does not move beyond the speculative point of view. Hegel does not view life from the point of existential participant, but only from the point of view of speculative thinker, and from this point of view no ethical problem really exists. Furthermore, nothing absolute exists in his monistic understanding of reality; all that exists is relative and constantly in the state of change; there is no room for faith and the absurd. It would seem that Ibsen in *Vildanden* is debunking a similar possibility. In actuality, he is pointing up *misunderstanding* as the comic-tragic dimension in the contemporary world.

---

* *the Leap*

Kierkegaard writes about the impossibility of carrying through a continuous movement either in thought or in existence in *Papirer*. Definite limits are encountered as in connection with the next sphere of existence which is accessible only through the leap.

The difficulty of the leap, he acknowledges in *Synspunktet*; in his admission, he uses the physical difficulty of the leap as an example. Everyone knows, he says, that the most difficult leap is when a man leaps into the air from a standing position and comes down again on the same spot. However, the leap becomes easier in the degree to which some distance intervenes between the initial position and the place where the leap takes off. And it is this point which he compares to a *decisive moment* in the realm of Spirit; the most difficult decisive action is not that in which the individual is far removed from the decision, but when it is as if the matter were already decided (Rebekka — *Rosmersholm*). In this instance he is referring to a non-Christian compared to a Christian who is a Christian in name only really becoming a Christian.

Whether the person be close to the leap or removed from it, an essential requirement in making the leap is that when one is about to act, one must be alone. Assistance cannot be given or taken, such as the prompting from another person, i.e. Gregers prompting Hjalmar and Hedvig in *Vildanden*.

Gjentagelsen*[67]

The category by which one enters eternity forward. Kierkegaard examines repetition in different contexts, and to further the essence of it, compares it with *recollection* which he considered a backward movement. In his essay, *Gjentagelsen*, he describes recollection as the pagan life-view and he describes *repetition* as the modern view. He affirms that all that is, has been; therefore, it can never be repeated. Yet, he can say that repetition and recollection are the same movement, only in

---

* *The Repetition*

opposite directions. Socrates is brought into the differentiation that Kierkegaard is presenting. Unlike Hegel, Kierkegaard sees Socrates as taking seriously the infinite qualitative difference between God and man. But he does *not* recognize the inability of the human understanding to know the ultimate truth about life, and the necessity of a divine revelation of that truth to be shown. With his view of *recollection,* Socrates believes that God has given each man an understanding of the ultimate truth about a prior existence (hence, Kierkegaard's designation of the pagan entering eternity backwards), and that divine assistance is not necessary to the understanding of this truth. However, to come into possession of such a truth, man must seek and exist in the good life.

BACKWARD   *The Pagan Life View – Recollection* / *The Modern Life View – Repetition* / *eternity* ....   FORWARD

In *Gjentagelsen,*[68] wherein Kierkegaard presents variations on repetition in a contemporary context, a young man's love affair is the means by which he expresses various aspects of the concept. The young man cannot marry the girl because the poetical impulse has been awakened (ironically, by her) within him. In relinquishing his love, he experiences *a* repetition.[69] There is a reintegration of self and a kind of renewal and change, but this is not actually *the* repetition (i.e. a religious repetition) because the surge of life that the young man experiences occurs when the girl marries someone else (i.e. *Kjaerlighedens Komedie*).

196

In discussing the metamorphosis of the actress in *Krisen,* Kierkegaard shows another aspect of repetition in a contemporary instance. As the metamorphosis unfolds, it is a return to the first condition for the actress and this is a repetition in a sense, although it is not a repetition in the religious sense of being received back again to be reconstructed as a new condition; that is, it is not a new birth. Mrs. Linde has a similar experience in *Et Dukkehjem.*

True repetition affirms *existence* which has been, and that *now becomes.* It looks forward to a transcendent reality eternally repeated in time. The repetition is not merely one of particular instances such as those Peer Gynt feverishly pursues in *Peer Gynt.* True repetition does not look backwards with melancholy recollection to a glory which cannot come again as Hedda Gabler does. Hedda's desire is to have those she is closest to see her in the way she wants to see herself, as she was. A similar condition is dramatized with Strindberg's *Fröken Julie* except that Julie's will becomes mesmerized by the "new spirit" as represented by Jacques. She becomes powerless to act and asks to be put out of her misery, while Hedda will be her own agent of annihilation — neither woman is able to accept the present.[70]

The repetition occurs when one's existence has been raised to a higher level. Then, when actuality and Ideality are put in contact with one another, a new qualification emerges of a kind Nora experiences in her encounter with reality. Whereas ethical repetition finds continuity and identity, it does not receive anything back; for instance, consider the resolution of Rita and Allmers to devote themselves to unfortunate children in *Lille Eyolf.*[71] They identify themselves with the universal, but the religious subjectivity is lacking. Faith by virtue of the absurd has no place in the script. Kierkegaard acknowledges that it is possible to live a useful life in the ethical category, but it is not to be confused with Christianity. Christianity is Existence *par excellence.*

197

True repetition differs from the pagan view in that paganism does not allow for any new spiritual principle to come forth; paganism brings out what is already there. Kierkegaard contends that with *the* repetition, one does not pine for what is not as in paganism (Hedda Gabler), but for what "was", "is" and an evermore "shall be" by virtue of the Incarnation. The lack of suffering or suffering in itself is not the criteria for repetition, although suffering is inherent to it (Abraham, Job, Skule, Nora).

Øieblikket* "in and out of time"

Øieblikket is for the individual *the Moment* of consciousness wherein he comes into existence. It is the category which Socrates and Hegel do not recognize in the way that Kierkegaard does — (and which is the *tour de force* of an Ibsen play) — that a *real* moment of existential encounter is a *Moment* in existence as well as in thought. What happens in this atom of time is that one becomes another person, one of a different quality, expressing the kind of qualitative difference that Nora experiences. Kierkegaard uses the expression of *Tidens Fylde*** in *Philosophiske Smuler* and *Begrebet Angest* to describe this decisive *Moment.*

> Og nu Øieblikket. Et saadan Øieblik er af en egen Natur. Det er vel kort og timeligt som Øieblikket er det, forbigaaende som Øieblikket er det, forbigangent, som Øieblikket er det, i det naeste Øieblik, og dog er det Afgjørende, og dog er det fyldt af det Evige. Et saadant Øieblik maa dog have et saerligt Navn, lad os kalde det: *Tidens Fylde.****

---

* *The Moment*

** *the fullness of time*

*** And now the Moment. Such a moment has a peculiar character. It is brief and temporal indeed, like every moment; it is transient; it is transient as all moments are; it is past, like every moment in the next moment. And yet it is decisive, and filled with Eternal. Such a moment ought to have a distinctive name; let us call it the *Fullness of Time.*

Øieblikket

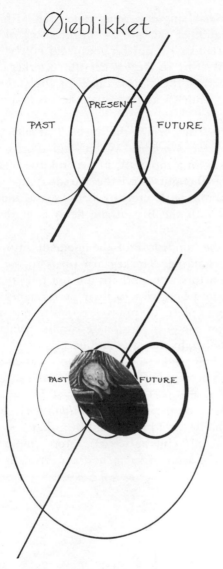

"in and out of time"

Øieblikket has singular importance for within this time span, this glance of the eye as the meaning of the word is rendered in Danish,[72] a person goes from non-being to being, consciously. Writing in *Øieblikket* 10,[73] Kierkegaard says that *Øieblikket* is when the man is there. In *Øieblikket,* man must venture forth, which was not what the world and mediocrity sought to do.

Kierkegaard cites from the *New Testament,* a poetical paraphrase of *the Moment.* When Paul describes the world as passing away in a moment, in a twinkling of an eye, he is expressing the thought (and the Paradox) that the moment is commensurable with eternity because the moment of destruction (as with the lily of the field) is at the same time *eternity.*

To bring the condition of the moment into the contemporary understanding, Kierkegaard turns to the theatre. He describes two actors who perhaps did not reflect that a deeper significance could be given to their performance. They come upon the stage, place themselves opposite one another and begin a pantomime of a passionate conflict. When the pantomime is at its height and the audience is deeply involved in the outcome, they come to a sudden stop and remain motionless as though frozen in the expression of the moment (reminiscent of daguerreotypes and possibly the studies the Ekdals arranged in their studio [*Vildanden*]; or early film stills; or, perhaps, the kind of tableaux that are an aspect of Ingmar Bergman's cinematic art). More important is that Øieblikket is the kind of moment Ibsen brought to the stage

— *tableaux vivants**[74] —; such Moments as Edvard Munch created in studies for Ibsen's plays (Osvald, Peer, Gynt og Knappestaeren,** the Ordeal of Fire in *Kongs=Emnerne,* at the end of *Gengangere* the collapse of John Gabriel Borkman) and in his other work — epitomized by *Shrik, Melankoli, Maengden, Livets dans.*

When the eternal expression is expressed eternally, accidentally, as it was with the actors in the foregoing example, Kierkegaard regards the expression as comic. But, when the expression expresses eternity *consciously,* as in painting and sculpture, it is eternal. In his last play, *Når Vi Døde Vågner,* Ibsen gives importance to a grotesque sculptured group; it is neither an accidental expression of the eternal nor is it an eternal expression of eternity; it represents another dimension, a dimension that reflects a distortion of *the Moment* viewed as frozen in time although it reflects the history of man and of 19th century Norway.

Kierkegaard differentiates the fullness of *the Moment*[75] from an ordinary moment which will be referred to as the *Instant.* When the present is not filled with significance, it is only an instant of time and is filled with emptiness. These are the kind of moments that Peer Gynt's life is filled with. Referring to Plato, Kierkegaard says that what we call *the Moment,* Plato called *the Sudden.* The difference is that the Greek concept of the temporal lacked the concept of spirit. *The sudden* brought a man out of a state of ignorance whereas *the Moment* brings a man out of a state of guilt which is what sin is in the Kierkegaardian consciousness.

Man's dwelling in faith's opposite, Sin, is what prevents man from achieving existence. In *Sygdom,* Sin is said to be not willing to be oneself or to be in despair at willing to be oneself. It is not that man is ignorant of the external truth as it is that he is not able to know it or to exist in it. Considered in this way, Sin is potential weakness or potential defiance

---

* staged paintings — levende Bilder
** the Button Molder

(*Peer Gynt; Brand*). Without the experience of *the Moment,* man continues in a position of non-being; he lacks consciousness which only appears when reality and ideality collide in *the Moment.* The concept of Sin as the opposite of faith (not virtue) is what distinguishes Kierkegaard's view of Christianity most decisively from that of paganism. Because the pagan cannot know what Sin is, *the Moment* has no eternal significance for him. Revelation is recollection for the pagan; therefore, it is within the human situation and the natural understanding is capable of knowing it. Ibsen sometimes juxtaposes *the Moment* of existence with the *Instant* and *the sudden* by placing a character in a human situation and showing how he or she interacts with other characters who are in different spheres of existence at different points in time — presenting in some plays a virtual comedy of errors.

The nature of *the Moment* is that it comes swiftly. Writing in *Christelige Taler,* Kierkegaard expresses its ephemeral quality. It sends no messenger before it to announce its arrival because it comes too suddenly for that. When it comes, there is not a moment's time before its coming nor, however significant it is in itself, noise and outcry do not accompany it, a consideration which would further an interpretation that the avalanche in *Brand* negates the possibility that he heard the final words of the play, "Han er deus caritatis."* The idea that God is Love was also expressed by Kierkegaard, "Jeg er overbevist om, at Gud er Kjaerligheden."** *The Moment* comes with a light step; consequently, one must be quite silent if one is to experience it. If one is not silent, *the Moment* is lost. Some people (and some Ibsen characters) never even sense it because the eternal and the finite are separate entities in their lives. Through a stream of characters from different walks of life, Ingmar Bergman's *Det Sjunde Inseglet**** pre-

---

* "He is the God of Love."
** "I am convinced that God is Love."
*** *The Seventh Seal*

202

sents the dichotomy (the persuasion of the finite) that limits the individual from experiencing the Moment. Through parallel action, the faith of Jof is contrasted to the lack of it in the others. In the last scene, Bergman shows the Knight as having undergone a change. The knight is playing chess with

Death. He distracts him by sweeping the chess pieces from the board, thus permitting the family to escape. With his sacrifice he has transcended existence. As was portrayed in *Det Sjunde Inseglet* and in *Kejser og Galilaeer*, God is hidden although present in the world and the Word. He is revealed only in the *Moment* of faith.

NOTES TO CHAPTER III

¹ They are discussed in Chapter V.
² *Ibsen — A Dissenting View* (a study of the last twelve plays) by Ronald Gray.
³ However, he wrote in 1960 that conceptual understanding is the key to the mastery of dramatic technique.

4 McFarlane does not neglect the humanistic.

5 Northam is in disagreement with Tennant in several instances.

6 Arthur Miller is treated in Chapter V.

7 *The Quintessence of Ibsenism.*

8 Grimstad—see Biographical Sketch and Chapter II.

9 *The Proverb in Ibsen,* Ansten Anstensen.

10 *Nordens Guder* (*The Gods of the North*) (1819), a series of poems summarizing Scandinavian mythology. P. M. Mitchell states that these were accepted as a surrogate for the old mythology. Johan Ludvig Heiberg in his Scandinavian mythology of 1827 drew on Øehlenschläger's work in addition to Old Norse material.

11 "Al dobbelt reflecteret Meddelelse gjør modsatte Forstaaelser lige mulige." "All doubly reflected communication makes contrary interpretations equally impossible." *Om min Forfatter-Virksomhed* (*My Activity as a Writer*).

12 Kierkegaard emphasizes the art of Art and Christianity as being by their very nature maieutic. Both are imitation, one of an action, the other of another reality (see Chapter I).

13 The life of the problem is in the dialectical issue.

14 The attempt of Hegel to systematize the whole of existence was attacked by Kierkegaard, who believed that a system of existence could not be constructed inasmuch as existence is incomplete and constantly developing.

15 Kierkegaard presented the three spheres of existence—the aesthetic, the ethical and the religious in *Staadier paa Livets Vei.* Prior to *Staadier,* the aesthetic and the ethical are treated in *Enten-Eller* with the religious hinted at. It is significant that the aesthetic and the religious spheres are stressed in *Synspunktet;* it is also significant that, for himself, the ethical sphere was not essential.

Christendom, on the surface, has many of the characteristics of the ethical.

16 Ibsen's speech, September 24, 1887—Banquet in Stockholm. At an earlier speech September 10, 1874, he compares Julian to himself—that he too wanted loving appreciation.

17 *Synspunktet* was written in 1848 and the supplement 1855; both published in 1859. A less comprehensive statement was written in 1851, *Om min Forfatter-Virksomhed.*

18 He acknowledges the criticism that he does not know what comes next—says that in spite of men knowing about his maieutic carefulness and his slow evolvement of content, which seems as though he does not know what comes next—he does. "I have presented one aspect sharply and clearly, then I affirm the validity of the other even more strongly." (from Papirer VIII'A4) cited in Introduction to *Kjerlighedens Gjerninger.*

19 Kierkegaard says that the genuine life of the spirit comes out with introspection. The castle door of inwardness is organic part of *Drömspelet* —Strindberg, 1901.

204

20 I.e. the comic-tragic figures in Hamsun's *Sult* (*Hunger*) *Mysterier* (*Mysteries*) *Pan.*

21 The expression is also associated with the purpose of the morality play and the purpose posited by Artaud and Peter Brooks.

22 "In concreto" term used by Kierkegaard in *Efterskrifter.*

23 See footnote number 12.

24 He asks his reader to note that his inquiry is not on paper but in the medium of existence.

25 Ibsen's concern: the "primacy of character."

26 *hiin Enkelte* is the special concern of Ibsen and Kierkegaard.

27 Kierkegaard contends that "Christians" live off others; their Christianity is to *receive* sacrifices.

28 Dr. Stockman is a too willing sacrifice. However, it was the crowd that was the *Evil.*

29 It is not right to sacrifice all for something—Brand.

30 The individual who is in touch with the infinite has a natural propensity to be sacrificed.

31 Ibsen's interest in *humanity*—emphasized over and over again.

32 The "witness for the truth" (in the world's eyes) who did not rebel against the hypocrisy around him was a fraud.

33 Violation of a work in the aesthetic sense is appreciated in connection with Ibsen and Bjørnson. Ibsen will permit the ending to be a natural consequence of his character's existential situation and will require something of the audience; Bjørnson's concern was that the ending of a play should be positive (easily seen) and manipulated his endings to this purpose, even when they were anti-climatic or false to the dramatic situation. See Chapter V.

34 Note: The term is *comic-tragic*, not tragic-comic in this study. *Also*: a religious *work* in sense of purpose is direct communication.

35 Hegel deals with opposites also but not existentially (i.e. the passing over of thoughts or concepts into their opposite and the achievement of a higher reality).

36 "det Nye er ikke et nyt Hvad, men et nyt Hvorledes af det gamle Hvad." "The new is not a new *what*, but a new *how* of an old what." *Papirer* 593.

37 Strindberg play *Fordringsägare* (*Crimes and Crimes*, 1888).

38 In *Papirer*—Kierkegaard mentions inversion in connection with miracles—making something small out of something big.

39 A pragmatic view, that the imitator is the stronger, is advanced by Birgitta Steene. Kierkegaard felt that a person was strongest when he seemed to be overcome. Ibsen presents different views of this concept.

40 About Socrates' replies, Kierkegaard claims that his words mean exactly as they sound, yet it is in the empty space that what is most important is concealed (*Ironi*).

41 Recalls medieval "simultaneous" staging and the theme of the dance of death—also Kierkegaard's essays on crucial situations in life.

42 In *Øieblikket*, Kierkegaard admits that God is paradoxical, that He

205

is the most comical being that ever lived and His Words — the most comical book to set heaven and earth in motion, to threaten with hell, eternal punishment in order to attain what is understood by being Christian — this is the most comical thing that has ever occurred.

43 Whereas he speaks of people living in the aesthetic-ethical sphere, he does not accept the combination as a viable mode of existence because an awareness of the ethical sphere is present, thus the combination is hypocritical. Existence on the aesthetical level he regards as more honest.

44 Kierkegaard did not see *enthusiasm* in the present age—here, everything was measured finitely.

45 Kierkegaard's conception of enthusiasm was that a genuine and persevering enthusiasm is possible only in relation to that which is of enduring value and that the finite and temporal were not worthy of enthusiasm.

46 See discussion of *Don Juan* and Johannes "Forførerens Dagbog," Chapter II.

47 *Angest* deals with the experience preceding the emergence of freedom. *Fortvivlelse* is "Sygdommen til Døden" (the sickness unto death) —man has chosen to exist in a sinful way, that is, not to realize himself— as such, despair is associated with defeat.

48 A note to the reader: Ibsen never presented the same pattern even in the characters that can be said to be of a kind. See Chapter I—a similar characterization is seen with the love-sick Frey in *Skírnismál.*

49 Choice and awakening are related.

50 The ethical man has a life task.

51 Ibsen's speech concerning the responsibility of mothers.

52 Guilt is the result of error for Kierkegaard. When the error is recognized, the guilt is dissolved. This does not presuppose the experiencing of *the Moment.*

53 This aspect of Skule's relationship to his son recalls the Abraham and Isaac story.

54 Choice is an ethical principle.

55 Irony is delineated in *Efterskrifter;* subject of his Master's dissertation *Om Begrebet Ironi.*

56 Incongruity of this kind is discussed by Kierkegaard in reference to Phister — see Chapter I.

57 This point brought out in Chapter V-B.B.

58 Jacques Maritain.

59 Note misunderstanding in connection with Scribe.

60 See Phister — Chapter I, critique.

61 Hedvig (*Vildanden*) is an echo of this earlier purity. With later plays there are characters who "suffer" but not in the same way.

62 Note: *Existents-Sphaerer, Valget, Springet, Gjentagelsen,* are inextricably entwined and related to *Øieblikket.*

63 Where a man stands at the end of his life is what is significant to Kierkegaard.

64 i.e. Existence, not thought, is the requisite. Kierkegaard's view of

choice is in opposition to Hegel's in that there are no rational or logical guidelines for the choice. Rather, with the acquisition of intelligence, one is confronted with numerous possibilities (to choose from). Hegel thought that the many alternatives could be reduced to a unity by a more enlighted reflection. See Stack. Kierkegaard, on the other hand, believed there would always be objective uncertainty in the area of responsible choice. For instance, the validity of Nora's choice can only be posited in actuality through a voluntary action (in this context, actuality is a specific existential existence).

65 A person in the ethical sphere of existence may repent what was chosen on other occasions. It is through repeated decisiveness that one comes to his self.

66 *The leap* presupposes *the choice.*

67 Ibsen will use the play on repetition for the movement of the play; each movement differs as the nature of the idea differs. He will also dissect the essence of repetition in another category.

68 Kierkegaard also makes use of the Job story in this essay.

69 Kierkegaard had undergone a similar experience with his engagement to Regine Olsen. See *Forførerens Dagbog.*

70 To relinquish her *will* is not possible for Hedda.

71 See ending. The point is that this may not be a reliable sphere of existence for considering their resolution.

72 In *Angest,* he says that nothing is so swift as a glance of the eye and it is a designation of time.

73 *Øieblikket* was the name he gave to a periodical he authored in 1855. Georg Brandes considered the ten issues of *Øieblikket* to be a unique achievement in his writing because it in the shortest condensible form contains his views *(Samlede Skrifter* B, II, s. 360). Of the title, Kierkegaard stated in one issue he had nothing ephemeral in mind. By *Øieblikket,* he means the present.

74 Staged paintings—groups of people—immobile—representing a scene from a painting.

75 *The Moment* is treated explicitly in *Philosophiske Smuler,* and related to Greek thought in *Angest.*

Øieblikket

paa scenen

Øieblikket

The Interpretation

IV

* "on stage"

Mulighedens Virkeliggjørelse*
"in concreto"

Artistic communication is indirect communication and it is this dimension that accounts for the so-called Ibsen-Kierkegaard "paradox." In point of fact, with Ibsen and Kierkegaard, there is not a paradox, nor is there an "either/or."[1] Quite simply, *hiin enkelte*, that solitary individual who is the epitome of the Kierkegaardian-Ibsen realization, once she/he comes *face to face* with destiny does not have a choice; there is but one way, one path and that is "to love Guden,"** not a personification of God, but the concept that God represents, *Love*. The paradox is the finite view, the perspective of the majority, to them, "the bearer of the ring is rewarded."[2] In *Kjerlighedens Gjerninger,*** Kierkegaard refers to love's hidden life and the discovery of it by its fruits. He and Ibsen were to reiterate this concept over and over inversely, believing that dissecting the context of the concept does not dethrone the concept, but enriches it. Ibsen's dramas are "works of love," although in each one love is misconceived, misconstrued, violated or negated, "the fruits unripe or rotten"; the very inversion, however, renders the truth more apparent than

---

* The Possibility Made Actual
** the God
*** *Works of Love*

direct statement could. Artistic communication emphasizes in a convoluted and seemingly absurd manner this truth. Kierkegaard dedicated an essay on tragedy to "the fellowship of buried lives."[3] He imagines himself addressing people who for one reason or another are spiritually and mentally entombed or isolated. His purpose, as with Ibsen, was to awaken these people to possibility, by disturbing their naive beliefs. In order to accomplish this, they had to be confronted with different modes of existence, be alerted to crucial situations that could, by analogy, apply to their own lives; the method is not explication, *but* demonstration and provocation.[4] Consequently, the process of communication is indirect. The ambiguity of the method evokes a response on a deep level in the personality which *generates activity,* if not change.[5] Ibsen and Kierkegaard considered most people to be living in a state of illusion or as being victims of illusion, having little idea of their place in the world.

The effort to have the audience participate actively is achieved by Ibsen through the presentation of characters in an existential encounter which generally permits one of them to come face to face with him or herself; at the same time the audience is afforded a unique theatrical experience through the dramatic irony that is consistently engendered. The audience can see and know what the characters cannot.

It is not the quantitative but the qualitative, the existential dialectic, not the rationalistic, that concerned Kierkegaard and which Ibsen articulated. Ibsen's plays dramatize the meaning of *Øieblikket* (*the Moment*) in the individual existential situation.

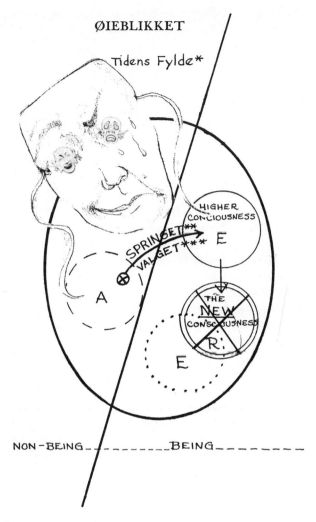

ØIEBLIKKET

Tidens Fylde*

HIGHER CONCIOUSNESS

SPRINGET** VALGET***

E

THE NEW CONSCIOUSNESS

R.

A

E

NON-BEING _ _ _ _ _ _ _ _ _ BEING _ _ _ _ _ _ _

* FULLNESS OF TIME
** THE LEAP
*** THE CHOICE

A = Aesthetic
E = Ethical
R = Religious

213

The Interpretation

The consideration is that *Øieblikket* (*the Moment*) or a refracted image thereof is the *tour de force* of an Ibsen play. It is the heart of the play. *Crisis* and/or *climax*, terms often used to describe the most intense part of a play, are not sufficient to describe the condition of *the Moment* because they lack the significance of the individual existential act. With the category of *the Moment*, the choice, the leap, and repetition are brought into perspective. Each *Moment* is an occasion of decisive significance; it occurs when man is confronted at a time and a place by that which is crucial for him. It is letting go. This little *Moment*, brief as it is, is the action that unties the knot. It is the leap, because existential choice is the leap. The leap is necessary because of the qualitative difference between time and eternity. Only by leaping across the chasm through the leap of faith (by virtue of the absurd) can *the Moment* be had. In *the Moment*, the person becomes contemporaneous with the highest sphere of existence and the past, becoming, in this atom of eternity, a person of a different quality. All this occurs in a twinkling of an eye. When *the Moment* does not occur in an Ibsen play, the enormity of the omission is experienced.

The plays selected for comment can be regarded as pseudonyms in the Kierkegaardian sense, that is, as a means of detachment, explicating the essence of the play through a play on *the Moment,* demonstrating what *the Moment* is and what it is not. Therefore, in some instances, what is the hub of the play is *THE MOMENT,* while in others, the hub is *the* Instant, *the* Sudden, or *an* Acoustic Illusion. *The Instant* is when the present is not filled with significance; *the Sudden* refers to that which brings man out of ignorance, but lacks the concept of spirit; and *the Acoustic Illusion* is that which looks like what it is not.

THE MOMENT   THE INSTANT

THE SUDDEN   THE ACOUSTIC ILLUSION

What Øieblikket Is and is Not.

A play is pure existence; it is the present tense. Kierke-

---

* *The Moment* (rather than *Øieblikket*) will be the textual choice more often in connection with *the Instant, the Sudden, the Acoustic Illusion* — the terminology in this chapter.

gaard pointed out that the occasion of the play is its total reality. Its ephemeral nature is what sustains the fascination with the theatrical experience. The form is so condensed, so immediate that it is incomplete — except when considered in actuality. Writing about a play from a dramatic/theatrical point of view is vastly different than writing about imaginative literature that was not intended for "live" performance. While the immediacy of the performance can be savored in memory, it must be re-created and communicated through the mind's eye as though for an audience. As has been shown in Chapter I, Kierkegaard found in drama and theatre the objective correlative that enabled him to bring a sense of immediacy to the exposition of his existential view.

In considering Ibsen's drama, it is his creative sensibility that is vital. He did not regard the theatre simply as a place of spectacle, but used the empty space as an adjunct to the text. Knut Nygaard points out[6] that Ibsen had insight and understanding into the working of the stage and used it as an instrument, learning to shape good theatre. But, beyond that, he saw in the theatrical reality (the stage conventions, the actual stage) the means to mold a complete work of art.

Because Ibsen's income was also derived from a reading public, intensive stage directions were necessary to the script. His minute explication of detail does not detract from the theatricality of his work; these are not closet dramas. While Ibsen was interested in fulfilling a need for those who enjoyed reading and discussing plays, the stage directions are more than a reading aid; they recreate many of the images that are significant to this interpretation, and they are an organic part of the work.

The opening discussion concentrates on *Gengangere* and *Vildanden* because these plays treat *Øieblikket* inversely. With the *inversion*, its special nature is illuminated. Even though the entire play is treated, it is the concentrated event in the last act that will receive the emphasis. Subsequent discussion will consider *Øieblikket* in other plays.

216

Gengangere*

"*Ghosts* aroused a tornado of abuse unequalled, doubtless, in the entire history of the drama since the beginning of the world . . . It is generally conceded to be the strongest, most terrible play of the nineteenth century," wrote an American critic, Archibald Hendersen, in 1910.[7] Twenty-eight years earlier, *Gengangere* had its première in the original Norwegian at Aurora Turner Hall in Chicago on May 20, 1882 with Fru Helga von Bluhme as Mrs. Alving. It was not to reach Norway for another year and then only through the efforts of Swedish actor-manager August Lindberg. Ibsen, in a reference to Georg Brandes, attributes the Scandinavian aversion to his seventeenth play as occurring because the protest of the theological critics was the most violent.

Americans were excited by the furore the play caused in England where it was produced by J. T. Grein in March, 1891, and in 1894 America presented its first English performance with Mrs. Ida Jeffreys-Goodfriend playing Helena Alving.[8] Charles Gay organized a company in 1906 and took the play on a tour of the Mid-West that covered sixteen thousand miles of territory, playing to an audience that was largely Scandinavian. Joseph Dannenburg coined a phrase to describe the tour in an article titled "Playing Ibsen in the Bad Lands."[9]

---

* *Ghosts*

The critic of *Theatre* (1917) considered *Gengangere* a marvelous display of Ibsen's technique. By 1922, the play, with Mary Shaw playing Mrs. Alving, was referred to as boring, and as having aged. Eleonora Duse appeared in the lead in 1923 and Mrs. Fiske in 1927, Eve Le Gallienne in 1948. In 1973, a performance was given at the Roundabout, a tiny playhouse on 26th Street in New York City. Beatrice Straight interpreted Mrs. Alving as a portrait of wasted feminity. A performance in 1977 in New York presents Mrs. Alving as "a figure of awesome pity." She cannot bring herself to end Osvald's life.[10]

Gengangere — Viewed as a *Moment* in Existential Encounter[11]

Ibsen's plays are concerned with the need of the individual to find out what kind of person he or she really is, not in isolation, but in the reality of existence. Within the form of the plays, Ibsen questions the nature of self. Not unlike Falk (*Kjaerlighedens Komedie*) who explores the nature of love from all sides and through the eyes of different people, each of Ibsen's plays displays a different facet of the essence that is involved in self-realization. In 1884 he wrote to Theodor Caspari, a young poet, that none of us can have a higher goal in life than to realize ourselves in spirit and in truth. The necessity to be one's self Kierkegaard insisted upon earlier, believing that to be a self was not only the greatest concession made to man, but that it was, at the same time, eternity's demand upon him.

While Ibsen recognized the weight of the past to be debilitating in the realization of one's self, he did not intend for it to be considered a necessary impediment. What he demonstrated through Osvald's disease in *Gengangere* is not so much that it was a result of his father's debauchery as it was the result of Mrs. Alving's having obeyed the immoral ethics of

218

society in continuing with a union that was unacceptable to her. In Notes to *Gengangere,* Ibsen wrote that the play was not simply the tragedy of the Alving household, but the tragedy of 19th century Europe. One of his underlying purposes was to demonstrate how a series of out-dated conventions, unwittingly perpetrated, could result not only in the destruction of an entire family, but also of an entire world.

Gengangere can be considered as a reflection of the tragic vision on a small scale, as a play of interaction, as a mind defining itself against its own surroundings, as a woman question.[12] It is a play that contains all of this, and infinitely more.

Gengangere is about a human being who experiences a *Moment* in an existential encounter . . . a moment when the past is brought into contact with the present and the future. The art of Ibsen is that he could bring into play all the currents of his day: biology, social issues, psychology — without losing the essence of his vision.

The Moment brings the present under constraint and it opens the future; it gives the future significance, no matter how brief, in point of time, that future is. *The Moment* demands of the existing individual a decision that cannot be evaded, and it happens to an individual who is in the fullness of existence, ocurring generally at a mature age as with an Ibsen character, because it is at this point in time that decision is demanded. It is only in maturity that a script has been written. With *Gengangere* Ibsen focuses on the point when the protagonist's transition can take place, when non-being can change into being or being into becoming or possibility into actuality.

The "existential encounter" occurs on two levels — one occurring in actuality, the other ocurring internally. Without both, the subject (Helene Alving in the play) would remain in reflection, that is, non-existence.

Ibsen was interested in Mrs. Alving's realization of the human condition. She is put on trial, and the play is her struggle to escape from the spiritual as well as the physical heritage of the past, the corpse in the cargo.[13]

The succinct structure of *Gengangere* recalls the form of *Skirnismál*, and of course, the classical tragedy. It is constricted in time and place and action (unlike Skírnismál and Greek tragedy where this last unity, the unity of place was not really a requisite) centering on one character and one situation. The past is amplified by every word and underscored by each character with the action forwarded by each exchange. The action of the play is Mrs. Alving's awakening. There is a gradual unfolding of the action that reaches a high point at the end of each act. The unfolding starts over again with almost ritualistic precision in the first two acts and in the succeeding one; each ending serves as an alarm and indicates change in a way not dissimilar from the function of the alarm clock in Genet's *Les Bonnes* (*The Maids*), but lacking the complete reversal which takes place there. [14] With the repetition of new insights at the end of Act I and II, the play projects the kind of repetition that Kierkegaard wrote about and referred to as the rotation method (see Chapter III) which is not the true repetition which occurs in *the Moment*.

Ibsen also reveals the past in interspersed fragments that are as dramatic as the action in the present, supplying a contrapuntal movement to the play's rhythm. The ending of Act I epitomizes this technique which is usually referred to as Ibsen's retrospective method. Mrs. Alving's world crumbles when she hears Regine, the maid, rebuke the advances of her son, Osvald. In that instant, *the sudden* has occurred. Not only is the past resurrected, but a new knowledge has been given to her, the information that Osvald has an affection for Regine. All she can say is "*Gengangere.*"[15]

Viewed in this context, Mrs. Alving has been enlightened but the sudden remains a mute atomistic abstraction. The past has been tapped and is a kind of foreshadowing, but there has not been a significant upheaval in the consciousness. She is thinking. "Gengangere" expresses the hollowness

220

of the play's mood at this point, a metaphor of the essence which is as yet undefined. Something "Other" in the play's fabric is indicated. Mrs. Alving is face to face with a similar happening, but not with herself.

If *Gengangere* were played without act divisions, the difference between *the Sudden* and *the Moment* would be more pointed. But, the audience would not experience the pause which Kierkegaard showed had such significance and was also movement.[16] In permitting the audience to be brought in at the end of each act, Ibsen was not only being consistent with the stage conventions of his day as well as providing suspense with a strong curtain line, he was also allowing the audience to respond to the reality of a life situation, relaxing them, and preparing them for the next stage of the play. The audience was to experience what Mrs. Alving was experiencing, to be brought into her world deliberately and purposefully. In creating this sense of immediacy and manipulating the audience in this way, Ibsen shares a common bond with Kierkegaard; he, too, is like the prompter, the hidden one who sits in the dark and prompts. Ingmar Bergman's art reflects the Kierkegaard/Ibsen aesthetic cinematically. He is closer to their consciousness than he is to Strindberg or Strindberg is to them although Strindbergian drama has many Kierkegaardian concepts and themes,[17] and Bergman is cognizant of them. It would be remiss to suggest otherwise.

The stage space for *Gengangere* was re-created by Edvard Munch in 1906 for Max Reinhardt. From the representations, which are in accordance with Ibsen's stage directions, the acting area is seen as a large room with multiple acting areas; the possibilities are diverse. At the back of the room is a conservatory with large panes of glass forming its outer wall. This division of the stage space was appropriate to the proscenium stage Kierkegaard and Ibsen were familiar with. Kierkegaard has expressed in his writings the suggestive power of the double reflection that the stage afforded as has been presented in the chapter on Kierkegaard and the Theatre.

221

222

With the proscenium stage, the audience is separate from the action on the stage; the performance is viewed two-dimensionally, primarily as a picture. One result of the audience/performance cleavage is that the contrast between reality and unreality is emphasized. Kierkegaard refers to the distinction that is achieved when the ordinary life is placed against a contrasting environment, as on a stage (See Chapter I). Although Ibsen created the surrounding documentation of social existence within the picture frame, the method of lighting in the 19th century was such that the emphasis was given to the foreground of the stage, the dimness of the background suggested a natural otherworldliness.[18] Ibsen was to use the glass conservatory wall in *Gengangere* to reflect the changes in light for each scene. In Act I, the gloomy fjord landscape was half obscured by steady rain. In Act II, the landscape is still obscured by mist; while in Act III, it is dark outside except for a faint glimmer of light. At the end, the glaciers are bathed in bright morning light.[19]

Munch's re-creation of the set that Ibsen delineated so carefully in his stage directions indicates the playing of the seven scenes of the act as taking place in all areas of the room. By simply following the action of the characters, it is possible to see the creation of movement as diversified and supportive of the text, and the silence in some instances, non-verbal communication *"filled with content."*[20] Visualize a miming of the following movements: The opening scene with Regine and Engstrand takes place in the rear of the room in the area of the garden door. After his discussion with her, he goes out the farthest door on the right as Manders enters through the garden door, with Engstrand making a hasty exit in his efforts to avoid Manders. During her scene with Manders, Regine leaves by the same door as Engstrand and returns. She moves an armchair to the table indicating that the action will be centered here. She goes out on the left to get Mrs. Alving. Manders walks up and down the room a couple of times, looks out the window which further directs the audience's attention to the weather, comes back to the table, looks at a book, puts it down in disgust. Mrs. Alving comes in at the left followed by Regine who goes out through the nearest door at the right. Mrs. Alving sits at the table. He takes out some papers, puts them on the table, standing above her, and cross-examines her about her reading, attempting to put her on the defensive as his position indicates. He sits down and discusses the legal aspects connected with the estate; they are on an equal basis in the scene physically, peers. At the mention of Regine going back to Engstrand, Mrs. Alving stands up. Osvald enters in a light overcoat[21] through the door on the left. He walks across the room in the direction of the conservatory and after his scene he goes out the farthest door on the right. Toward the end of the act, Osvald comes in again and Regine comes in from the dining room on the right. She goes into the dining room followed by Osvald; the door is ajar. From the dining room, Regine's voice is heard protesting Osvald's advances, Osvald is heard coughing and humming. It is at this point that Mrs. Alving utters "Gengangere." She recovers quickly. What follows is brief and almost anticlimatic — Manders recognizes the situation — Mrs. Alving does not want to speak about it. The impact of the scene is that just prior to the Osvald/Regine episode she had described to Pastor Manders a similar scene which took place between her husband and Regine's mother. The correspondence is a repetition that is almost like a verbal alliteration, especially in that Regine and Osvald are not seen. It is not merely an obvious melodramatic effect as has been suggested by one critic.[22]

Act II is full of information and Ibsen's exposition lifts one veil after another from the past, not in terms of reminiscences but in terms of its bearing on the present. Often the past is prologue as in Act I, but more often, the one is consonant with the other. For example, in discussing with Manders what to do with Regine, Mrs. Alving tells him how the situation was resolved with Regine's mother; she married Engstrand.

Little time elapses between the ending of Act I and the opening of Act II. It picks up after dinner with a possible lapse of a couple of hours. Mrs. Alving and Manders are discussing the problem of Regine and Osvald. In addition to exposing the past, the Kierkegaardian values concerning hypocrisy and duty are expressed, and in the process, the double standard is articulated by Manders. He considers Engstrand as having married a fallen woman, even though the "tre hundre specier" Johanne had was his motivation. Mrs. Alving points out that she married a fallen man and that there was an infinitely larger amount of wealth involved. She asks him where the difference lies.[23]

In this scene, Mrs. Alving's bitterness is conveyed to a very obtuse Manders. She rejects obligations of any kind and says she must struggle for her freedom. She admits her cowardliness and her being possessed by ghosts, the past that will not give her rest. She blames Manders for making her submit to duty and obligation when she was young and wanted to leave the marriage. This is a "wordy" scene with little action, a confessional.

A break in the rhythm comes when Osvald tells his mother about his illness. He blames himself, unwittingly expressing the truth when he wishes it was something that he had inherited. The dramatic irony is intense because the audience knows about his father's disease and they can respond with Mrs. Alving. It seems similar. The atmosphere gets gloomier; lamps are lit. Osvald speaks of the joy of life and Mrs. Alving says she sees for the first time what has happened. Another insight. Osvald senses that something is hidden from him and wants to know what it is. Mrs. Alving does not get time to tell him; the orphanage is on fire. There is no insurance. Manders calls it a judgement on this house of sin and Mrs. Alving agrees.

The ghosts walk again in Act II, the corresponding illness

225

of father and son.[24] A deeper core of understanding has been touched in Mrs. Alving and she is confident that she knows the truth. Once again it is knowledge, *the Sudden*. Something dormant in her was brought to the surface, something she had known but now knows in another way, something that makes Mrs. Alving agree that the fire is a retribution.

The last act is the same scene. All the doors are open, the lamp is still burning. It is dark outside except for a light seen through the windows. Mrs. Alving is standing in the conservatory with a shawl around her; Regine is standing a little behind her. In Act III, it becomes apparent what Mrs. Alving thinks — that she is partially responsible for her husband, for his loss of joy in life, for Osvald, for herself. A gradual transition has taken place; the past has invaded the present, but it is not until the last scene in the play that Mrs. Alving has a moment of real consciousness. Up until this point she has been rationalizing and deceiving herself. The sacrifice and the individual were significant categories to Kierkegaard and are expressed in each of Ibsen's dramas. To contemplate the significance of it in *Gengangere*, the last scene must be sharpened, and the action that leads up to it heightened.

After the fire, Mrs. Alving wants to relinquish her rights and place her affairs in Manders' hands. Engstrand is a minor Loki figure in the play and any humor in the play issues from him or from Manders (unconsciously) and most particularly in scenes which they share. Engstrand suggests to the gullible Manders that the property be used for a sailor's home and Manders agrees to consider that. Engstrand is elated with the absurd turn that has occurred in his fortune. Even though he has set Manders up for this concession by suggesting Manders was the cause of the fire, Manders thanks him for his support and calls him one in a thousand. Ibsen is throwing Kierkegaard's ideals back in his face, it would seem. But, then, Kierkegaard also used the ridiculous to make a point, not necessarily to affirm a belief.[25] If this was a Bjørnstjerne

226

Bjørnson play, the play could be resolved with **Engstrand** being put in his place, Mrs. Alving sadder but wiser, Manders less obtuse but good.[26] But, this is Ibsen, who is dramatically opposite. Therefore, in an act that seems to be tying up the loose ends, the knot is untied.

Mrs. Alving tells the truth and disillusions Osvald and Regine; they are embittered. Regine rejects Osvald to pursue her own life. One irony after another presents itself. If she needs help, she can go to the Alving Home for sailors. Osvald has also rejected the past; he feels no compassion for his father and cannot understand how Mrs. Alving has clung to those antiquated superstitions, those ghosts of beliefs. Mrs. Alving realizes that *gengangere* are not the ghosts of the past as much as they are ghosts of dead beliefs. Osvald's concern is in himself and his only regret is losing Regine who might have taken away his fear. She could have done it with one kind word. Mrs. Alving wants to know what he means; she does not understand.

The dawn is breaking and Mrs. Alving is optimistic. Osvald speaks of the sun rising and Mrs. Alving knowing what it is important to know; she does not understand. He tells her the disease is hereditary and the full implication of it overwhelms her. It will recur again and again. He wants his mother to give him morphine when it is needed. Regine would have, but, of course, Mrs. Alving will not. Osvald sits down in the armchair and asks for the sun. She throws herself on her knees beside him and shakes him, buries her head in her arms in the Munch painting that shows the horror of her predicament, a living tableau, a pieta image such as the kind Ingmar Bergman brings to life on the screen.[27] This is the moment of pain when the healing properly begins. She has ventured to hold fast to Osvald and finds that she cannot.

George Moore considered the last scene finer than any that had ever been written by man or God. "Its blank simplicity strikes upon the brain until the brain reels."[28] Osvald asks for the sun again and Mrs. Alving jumps up despairingly,

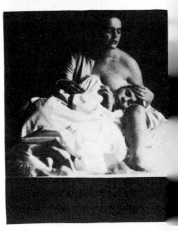

beats her head with her hands, and screams. She tries to reject the thought of the pills, fumbles for them in his coat, draws back, says "Nej; nej; nej!-Jo!-Nej; nej;"* stares at him. Osvald again asks for the sun. What does she do? One German performance with Frau Trautmann changes the ending.[29] There is no pause at all on Mrs. Alving's part. Ibsen is ambiguous, or does the open ending have other implications? He, like Kierkegaard, does not want the audience to forfeit their moment of contemplation so he does not state the answer directly.

Mrs. Alving's consciousness has been touched. The past and the present have been brought together in a new condition which goes beyond understanding. She does something. In this *Moment* of *angest,* her eyes are opened to the consequences of her lack of any real decision in the past. What was missing from her life was that she did not understand what it was that would take away the fear, what it was that Osvald was seeking. Regine could not supply it to Osvald because she would not. It was something that each individual has to give to her or himself first, and that was what Regine was doing, and what Osvald would have done if he could, and it was what Mrs. Alving should have done. She should have loved herself first and lived in the "now,"[30] not selfishly but honestly, and then she could have given of herself. The coldness of Regine and Osvald does not suggest that they will develop further, enough to treat their neighbors as themselves. However, they are, in terms of experience, at the starting point and how far they will grow is unpredictable. Osvald, of course, is shut off because of his illness.

Nevertheless, this is the only significant decision Mrs. Alving has made and she makes it in *the Moment.* She undergoes a significant change and makes a real decision *and* the audience is not permitted to see its final consequences. Whereas *the Moment* in existential encounter seems to refer to the situa-

---

* "No, no, no! — yes-no, no!"

229

tion in which it occurs, the encounter itself is internal action. The swiftness of the encounter, the moment of reflection, the leap, the choice, the new birth coalesce in this brief *Moment*. When Helene Alving runs to Osvald's coat, the decision has been made. The *no's* outweigh the *yes's* is all that Ibsen says. The sun shines brightly, too brightly. In an interview with John Simon, when asked what happened after the ending of *Det Sjunde Inseglet*,* did it imply an afterlife? Bergman responded that that was not so very interesting, and that is what Ibsen is saying. It is what has finally happened that is important. Consequently, any other ending would be anticlimatic. What is significant is that *the Moment* has occurred for Mrs. Alving. She is no longer incarcerated in the house, she has rid herself of it; she is no longer one of the fellowship of buried lives.

One could project, on the basis of the metaphysical associated with *the Moment*, that she will not give Osvald the morphine, that he will recover by virtue of the absurd.[31] After all, so much of the talk in the play has been based upon misunderstanding. If, on the contrary, recovery is impossible, Mrs. Alving will do what love requires. In spite of a flutter of uncertainty when she has her hand in Osvald's coat pocket, her horror, the horror of the situation, a change other than understanding or knowledge has occurred.

That Ibsen was also a painter is reflected in his drama — the composition, texture, the scenes, the models — the staging suggesting *tableaux vivants*** (which were so popular in Norway); especially representative is the work of Tidemand and Gude, Norwegian artists.[32] Edward Munch's art displays the same dramatic character, although expressionistically and as with Ibsen his aesthetic vision is in service to the idea. But also of significance are the poems Ibsen created, a verbal poetry in space. Through a physical symbol and succinct word choice (particularly in the nominal words), he was able in condensed

---

* *The Seventh Seal*
** (*levende Bilder*)

form to express the idea. In the 1850's, Ibsen created a poem cycle of twenty-three sonnets, appropriately entitled "I Bil-ledgalleriet."* Later some of the poems were reworked and published in *Digte*, 1871.[33] Much of his poetry reflects the Viking culture and the Kierkegaardian concepts, both of which were to become so essential in the plays — the power of memory, doubt and faith, the thought that the flower ought to die the moment the bud breaks forth (see Kierkegaard on the lilies of the field).[34] Ibsen showed in his poetry events dramatized by a conflict with the moment of action clinched by an epigram[35] at the end — "Fugle og fuglefaenger"** tells of being enclosed in a cage from which there is no escape; "Eder-fuglen"*** presents a bird's exploitation and death. The ending is changed in the 1871 edition so that the bird escapes. In "Mindets Magt"**** the bear is tortured into dancing to his master's merry tune. The poems have been honed and reveal a sculptured purity, a classic simplicity that is found in the final scenes of each act of *Gengangere* and most emphatically in the last act. Recreating the condition of the last scene of the other plays, even when there is less sophistication in the rendering, supports the consideration of *the Moment*.

* "in the Picture Gallery"
** "The Bird and the Bird Catcher"
*** "The Eider Bird"
**** "The Power of Memory"

231

Vildanden*
"with bleeding heart"

Ibsen wrote to Frederik Hegel, in 1884, that the critics would find plenty to quarrel about and plenty to misinterpret in *Vildanden*.[36] He was not mistaken. Premières in Norway, Denmark, Sweden, Germany, France, England and the first Broadway performance in America were less than positive. *Vildanden* was performed in Bergen, directed by Gunnar Heiberg, on the 9th of January, 1885, and in Kristiania on January 11th, directed by Hans Schrøder; the play was considered an artistic success but not a public one, the sentiment being that there was no message, and that the play was depressing. In the Schrøder production, the settings by Bjørn Bjørnson were applauded and appreciated for their dramatic function in the play.[37] *Vildanden* was hissed in Copenhagen in February; particularly appreciated by August Lindberg in Sweden, and generally successful in Scandivania, although the critics did not make much of it one way or another.[38] Interestingly, Ibsen did not interpret the hissing as criticism of the play, but attributed it to strained relations between literary parties; in Berlin, the play was produced by Otto Brahm (Freie Bühne) on March 4, 1888, and was considered to be an artistic achievement, but its depth was not generally rec-

---

* *The Wild Duck*

ognized. In Paris, April 27, 1891 (Théâtre Libre) *Vildanden* was presented by Antoine, who regarded it as another aspect of Ibsen's genius; the symbolism perplexed the audience and the notices were not favorable. It was produced in England by J. T. Grein, May 4, 1894, at the Independent Theatre; the response was weak. The first Broadway production was directed by Arthur Hopkins in 1918. Nazimova's Hedvig was cited as a positive blemish and Robert E. Jones' sets were said to lack atmosphere. *The New York Times* critic described the play as "shallow idealism" and gave this valuation as the reason for it not appearing on Broadway earlier.[39] Rainer Maria Rilke was moved by the play and George Bernard Shaw loved it (1897); for Ibsen, *Vildanden* was one of his favorite creations. More recently, directed by Robert Brustein, the Yale Repertory Theatre (April 1978) presented *Vildanden* in a production which stressed the photography image to the extent that a giant replica of the camera lens served as a device to begin and end scenes.[40]

Vildanden — the Acoustic Illusion

Vildanden functions like an inverse image to *Gengangere,* in that the uncovering of the truth is not a moment of Revelation as it was for Mrs. Alving; neither is it an instant of recollection as it was in the early moments of *Gengangere,* wherein Mrs. Alving's recollections are conjured forth by a corresponding situation and she receives a new insight. Whereas *the Moment* can come into being in time through Revelation as the truth does for Mrs. Alving in the last scene of *Gengangere,* the possibility of a similar occurrence is questionable for anyone in *Vildanden* (with the exception of Hedvig, who dies), although for each individual the possibility exists since the play, as with life, is open-ended.

The Moment is an advent into existence. Nothing of this nature is intimated in the characters who inhabit the milieu of *Vildanden*. It is only Hedvig who has an occasional glimpse

233

that there is something "Other" to be understood. In Act II, she reacts to Greger's remark that he would like to be a clever dog, "Jeg skal sige dig en ting, mor, — jeg tror at han mente noget andet med det."* Is is through Hedvig that attention is directed to a quickening of something "Other" in *Vildanden*.

The Kierkegaard-Ibsen premise is that in error, man exists in a state of non-being; he exists in a state of possibility, not actuality. The teacher is God and the learner is man. No third person can bring about the reality of existence for another individual. Kierkegaard suggests that such interference is hypocrisy, "for such investigations are hardly fruits of love."[41] But within the unfolding of the play, there is a Loki (the troublemaker of the gods) lurking in the background — Gregers, prodding, contradicting, not the God of the *New Testament*. Erwin R. Steinberg also notes the resemblance of Gregers to Loki and suggests that he is related to the devil.[42] Certainly, Gregers resembles the Devil as portrayed by Ingmar Bergman in *Det Sjunde Inseglet* except that he is not consciously malignant. Gregers is a strange character and the way in which he enters the household recalls a description Kierkegaard wrote in *Christelige Taler*. The situation suggests the mentality operating in Ibsen's play. A stranger comes into a room where a group of people are talking. He asks them what they are talking about; this one question shows them that they have been talking about nothing. Suppose this person is an egoist, gifted and intellectual. He seizes on the ethical ideal and poetically, under the guise of goodness and truth, he distinguishes himself with it. Gregers, the pseudo-Loki in *Vildanden*, thinks he is motivated by the ethical ideal. His entrance into the Ekdal household does not occur until Act. II.

*Mulighedens Virkeliggjørelse** is presented ironically in *Vildanden*, and in its articulation the stage (as in *Gengangere*)

---

* "I'll tell you something, Mother, it seemed to me that he meant something else by that."
* The possibility made actual.

234

is an organic part of the play. The importance of the proscenium stage is more emphatic in *Vildanden,* the duality of existence more strongly contrasted.

Berit Erbe,[43] in her study of Bjørn Bjørnson, refers to the dramatic function of his sets; for instance, his characterizing the studio against the mysticism of the loft. The double reflection appears in Act I also, but with a different connotation and the lighting reversed. It was Bjørn Bjørnson's feelings that the dark loft should be dynamic, the background, a fellow player. It is apparent from the fastidiousness of Ibsen's stage directions and from his notes, letters and other writings, that such pictorial representation and lighting were elements of his dramaturgy.[44] Not only was Ibsen's visual sense highly developed as his paintings indicate, but his "living tableaux" were three-dimensional echoes of famous paintings, such as Tidemand and Gude presented on stage and fused with poetry and music. Ibsen referred to the living tableaux in a comparison he makes between art and reality.[45]

Act I opens in a comfortably and handsomely furnished study in Werle's house. In the center of the floor is a desk, green-shaded lamps are lit and a soft light is cast over the room. Bookcases and upholstered furniture are along the sides and in the vicinity thereof. At the back, the folding doors have been thrown open and the portières drawn back. A large, richly decorated room, brightly lit room can be seen through the doors. A small private door is on the right-hand side of the study and leads to the office. On the left is a fireplace with a cheerful fire and beyond that, folding doors (closed) leading to the dining-room. The directions Ibsen writes are always from the audience point of view.

A servant and a waiter are speaking about their employer and with the exposition the background of the play is presented. Mr. Werle is painted as having been a gay dog, successful and aggressive in business. His relationship to Mrs. Sörby who is somewhat of a housekeeper-hostess-companion is considered. A dinner party is in progress in honor of Werle's

235

son, Gregers, who has spent years out of town, working at the family works in Höidal.

The chat is broken by the arrival of Ekdal, dressed eccentrically and shabbily, a comic-grotesque caricature, infinitely pathetic and somewhat comic, more emphatic because of the disparity of the setting he is in. Ekdal wants to get into the office. He is told to leave and the help informs the audience (in dialogue) that Ekdal was a fine fellow in his day, a lieutenant. He was in partnership with Werle and Werle played him a dirty trick and Ekdal went to jail.

Then the dining room doors are thrown open by a couple of servants, and Mrs. Sörby makes her entrance, talking to two of the guests, followed by Werle, Gregers, and Hjalmar Ekdal, old Ekdal's son. The relationships become clear in the scene.

Ibsen has in this quite realistic setting guests he refers to in the text as the flabby guest, the thin-haired guest, the short-sighted guest and other supernumeraries, i.e. guests. There is little individuality in these men; a great deal of gossip ensues. Mrs. Sörby is seen as being on familiar terms with the guests and they consider her as one whose favor is a value.

The guests are not to be considered as simple types or ordinary supernumeraries as this would destroy the entire act.[46] One of Kierkegaard's aggravations was the "twaddle" that most people spoke in a social situation; the kind of amenities the Werle guests were engaged in. They personify the Philistine as he appeared in the latter part of the 19th century, and they are an adjunct to the setting as well as functioning more significantly. Ibsen felt they were integral to the fabric of the play. Ibsen's interest in balancing the tensions that are contained in his dialectic is apparent in his writing about *Vildanden*. He refers to the need for an ensemble performance and the need of actors of stature in every role, actors who could subordinate their ego to the demands of the play.[47] He also stresses the necessity for the lighting to correspond to each mood of the five acts.

At this point in the action of the play, Werle observes that they are thirteen at table, and that usually they are but twelve. Hjalmar feels he is the intrusive member of the party; Gregers reassures him. The image of the thirteenth member will sharpen at the end of the play when he refers to himself as God's unwanted child. Steinberg points out that Loki was supposed to be the thirteenth at the feast of the gods and that he is responsible for Baldur's death, suggesting the Christ and Judas image.

Mrs. Sörby, Old Werle and the guests go into the inner room, the brightly lit room. There is a discussion between Hjalmar and Gregers concerning the inner and the outer man that furthers the duality of existence. It takes place midway between the inner and the outer part of the stage.

Mrs. Sörby and Werle come out of the brightly lit room because the lights are too strong for his eyes. The guests follow them. Photography, wine, existence are prattled about and there is mixture of image and subject and enough double-talk to suggest a Kierkegaardian play on words but presented so as to emphasize the ignorance of the company; it is in keeping with the social milieu. Hjalmar is seen as standing apart but not in a very admirable light. His father passes through the room and Hjalmar turns his back to him much to the consternation of Gregers. It is remembered by the group that Hjalmar was a lover of poetry and often recited; now he cannot — he has forgotten all the poems. He leaves. Mrs. Sörby and the guests go into the music room; Gregers and Werle remain to talk — the music is in the background.

The first act is exposition; the past is brought out by the various characters and most specifically by Gregers; the exposition is not as dramatically presented as it was in *Gengangere*. His revelations: his father's unjust treatment of old Ekdal, his neglect of his wife and child, and those that are revealed to him — old Werle's responsibility in Hjalmar's becoming a photographer,[48] his part in Hjalmar's marriage to Werle's former housekeeper — are presented directly in dialogue. These disclosures will be played against each other in the succeeding acts and the dramatic irony will permit the audience to share the experience. But, more important, it is significant that the information does not come to the characters by insight — by either the sudden or *the Moment*. There are instances that indicate attitudes and add new information. Consider Hjalmar's disavowal of his father, and the gradations within the revelation of Werle's approaching blindness. The dramatic expression is non-verbal or a subtle juxtaposing of action and language that appears to be innocuous.

The tone of the first act is melancholy, the brooding of Gregers dampens his father's spirits and in the end, Gregers leaves his home. Unfeelingly, he dismisses his father's admission of loneliness, saying to him that Mrs. Sörby is playing blind man's buff with the guests. The sarcasm and the repetition of blindness strikes a note that recalls Werle's previous remarks about his loss of vision and serves as a link to Hedvig's similar problem in the next act. There is an additional irony in that blind man's buff is the game that is unwittingly played by the characters including Gregers. Ending the act with a down beat in the dimly lit room, Ibsen has the game go on in the brightly lit one.

The same double vision is created in Act II as in Act I. Against the back wall to the left are the double doors arranged so as to slide to one side. Behind them is the loft. The studio is a fairly large attic room. On the right is a sloping roof with large glass windows through which the light can focus on the scene below. There is a considerable number of doors; one on the right hand corner leads into the room, and farther on the same wall is another door leading to a sitting room. In the left wall there are two doors with a stove between them. The studio is simply furnished, but comfortably so. Between the doors on the right stands a sofa and a table and chairs. On the table is a shaded lamp which is lit. Photographic equipment is scattered around the room. Near the double doors is a bookcase containing books, boxes, bottles of chemicals, brushes, paper. On the table are photographs, paint, brushes, paper. Gina Ekdal is sitting in a chair sewing, her daughter, Hedvig, is on the sofa reading with her thumbs in her ears and her hands shading her eyes.

Against this pleasant but simple background, Gina and Hedvig identify themselves and add more to the background of the play. The Werle's are respected and recognized as being gentry. Old Ekdal enters and is seen in a new light against a more congenial background. He is still a sad character but he is beloved, and understood. It is Ekdal who first draws attention to the loft and what it contains.

Other information is supplied, the family finances, the desire to rent a room. There is a sense of expectancy in the studio as Gina and Hedvig wait for Hjalmar to return. That the room on the left is the kitchen is indicated in the stage directions and the dialogue when Ekdal gets some hot water.

Hjalmar returns from the party earlier than was anticipated and the earlier part of the scene is viewed as having taken place while Hjalmar was on the way home. There is a cinematic quality in the rapidity of action. By pointing out that there were twelve or fourteen at table, Hjalmar avoids

239

saying there were thirteen guests. Gina inquires if Gregers is as ugly as ever. Hjalmar is concerned about his father, wanting to go to him. He is told that Ekdal has taken the hot water to his room and there is a tacit understanding of what that means; he is drinking. However, Ekdal comes out of his room and asks Hjalmar if he had seen him — Hjalmar says no. Hjalmar tells the family about the party and the fact that he did not recite for them. His resentment and hurt is apparent, and some measure of pride is displayed. In contrast to this gentle image is another Hjalmar, one who is boastful and conceited and admired by his wife and daughter. It is revealed that he borrowed the tuxedo from Molvik. That he has forgotten to bring her a treat from the party hurts Hedvig. She is unimpressed by the menu; her hurt is shown more strongly, Hjalmar becomes defensive. The closeness of the family group is reinforced by his interest in the loft — some kind of pet is in there. Hjalmar's sullenness is broken by the thought of a beer. He really regrets having hurt Hedvig. His hurt is seen as he wipes his eyes and plays a Bohemian dance very slowly and sentimentally. He is a man extremely self-conscious but not conscious of self. A knock is heard at the door and into this simple family walks Gregers.

Gregers immediately aims a blow; Gina is the target. To Gina, he mentions his mother. Her lack of response suggests some kind of mystery. There are apologies to Gregers about the living quarters. In quick succession, Gregers discovers that they need a boarder, that Hedvig's sight is going, that the condition is hereditary, that she is fourteen, that she is tall for her age, that she favors Gina, that the marriage occurred fifteen years ago and that Hjalmar did not realize that it was so long ago. His inquiries are quiet, subtle, and natural. He insinuates himself into the family's affairs. It is further learned that old Ekdal was a fine sportsman at one time. Gregers wants to take him back to Höidal with him, saying he must not have anything to do in Hjalmar's home. It is then that Gregers is shown the loft and the wild duck. It has grown fat and thrives

240

in captivity like the Ekdal family. There are pigeons and rabbits as well.

When Gregers asks to rent the room, Gina is upset and tries to dissuade him, mentioning the noisy men below, Molvik and Dr. Relling. Gregers is not dissuaded. After he leaves, they discuss him and it is Hedvig who discerns something else in Gregers. She does not take literally his remark about his wanting to be a dog. Gina is disturbed at having Gregers in the house; Hedvig and Hjalmar are delighted. The act closes with Hjalmar declaring he has a mission in life to which Hedvig is supportive and Gina ignores. There is no insight. They help the sleeping Ekdal up from the chair and will put him to bed.

The act ends on a quiet note, no fire or great disclosures as in *Gengangere,* but with a sense of unrest which will increase in Act III. In this act, the comic-tragic is pointed, much more so than in *Gengangere* where there was a brief side scene or two.

In the comic-tragic dimension, Kierkegaard and Ibsen recognized the essence of modern drama, a form their world-view took. In the comic, tragic is experienced more acutely because of an incompatibility. The individual who is incommensurable with his environment is comic. Ekdal was referred to in Act I as being at odds with the Werle household, and Hjalmar was uncomfortable. They were slightly ridiculous, Old Ekdal the more ludicrous because of his appearance. In Act II, they are in an environment that accepts them and their eccentricities are acceptable. But from the audience point of view, a view that is not subjective, their life is not normal and is at one and the same time comic and tragic, more so in their own environment. The fantasy world of the loft side by side with normal life is comic and yet infinitely sad. Hjalmar and Ekdal are anachronisms, unable to fit themselves into the world around them.[49] It is this vision that prompted Kierkegaard to write, "Folk leer, jeg graeder."*

---

* "They laugh, I weep."

Gregers is also incompatible with the life around him, but the laughter that his antics arouse is tinged with horror because of the upheaval he is capable of causing. This is developed as the play evolves. *Vildanden* carries the comic-tragic to its limit.

There are five acts in this play and they are of equal length. All but the first act takes place in the Ekdal home. Nothing has been missed between acts; no off-stage action has occurred. Act III begins the following morning, the sun shining through the window on the sloping roof. Hjalmar is retouching a photograph. Gina comes in dressed to go out, a basket in her hand. Gregers has settled in. There is going to be a lunch with Gregers, Relling, Molvik and the family. In this scene, Hjalmar is further characterized as being lazy. He puts aside his work and goes into the loft with Ekdal. When they enter, the sun is shining through the top lights of the loft and pigeons are flying about. It is clear that Hjalmar enjoys this simulated world as much as Ekdal does.

Gregers arrives and cross-examines Hedvig. There is a certain affinity between them; they both are sensitive to what is poetic, and express their feelings about the change in light and the effects of it on the surroundings. Hedvig no longer attends school and she tells Gregers how much she liked to look at *Harrison's History of London* (a book Ibsen read as a child — see Biographic Sketch) and mentions the tremendous picture of Death with an hourglass and a girl which disturbs her. She tells Gregers about the wild duck and that it is hers. It came from the bottom of the sea; he says the ocean depths, and she tells him that the whole loft makes her think of the ocean's depth.[50] When he suggests that the loft is perhaps not only a loft, she is astounded.

Gina comes home and Gregers' inquisition continues and he finds out that she also works on the photographs. They hear shots and Gregers is astonished to discover that Hjalmar and Ekdal are really shooting in the loft. Hjalmar comes out with the pistol, warning Hedvig not to touch it because the

242

barrel is loaded. It is revealed that the wild duck has a weak wing and trails his foot.

In the next revelation, Hjalmar has an invention; its nature he will not reveal. He also has a goal in life which is to restore self-respect to the name of Ekdal. Gregers becomes maddening in his constant prying and more so because Hjalmar is completely unaware of it. Gregers informs Hjalmar that he too has an object in life and that he will find a way to help Hjalmar. Hjalmar does not want to hear any depressing talk from Gregers. With Molvik and Relling's entrance, Gregers brings up the fact that they were thirteen at table the day before and, perhaps, there will be a need for a doctor.

The relationship between Molvik and Relling is quite compatible. Relling can understand Molvik's need to go on a spree occasionally, and he brings up Gregers' demand of the ideal when he was younger. In response, Gregers claims not to have reduced his demand when he is dealing with a man who is a man. Dr. Relling presents the picture of the life in the Ekdal home unromantically and realistically. When Gregers mentions the poisonous atmosphere around him, Relling puts him in his place.

Finally, Old Werle enters the scene. He wants to speak to Gregers who tells him that he is going to open Hjalmar's eyes. That is his object in life; the one he told his father about in Act I. Werle attributes Gregers' sick conscience to his mother. The act ends with Gregers taking Hjalmar for a long walk. Relling is upset. Gina is repulsed by Gregers and Hedvig's line ends the act, "Dette her synes jeg er underligt."*

What will occur in Act IV is catastrophic for all the members of the Ekdal family. Gregers breaks the bubble of their illusion and *forces* them to acknowledge the truth. The cruelty of the act suggests that Ibsen is asserting the necessity of *livsløgnen*** for some people. The parallel to Eugene O'Neill's

---

* "It all seems very odd to me."
** the life-line

The Iceman Cometh is striking. When the people in that play are brought face to face with their reality, they are devastated, but return to their dreams once the arch-agitator, Hickey, is removed from their existence. Hickey is the anti-illusionist, the Gregers of the piece. O'Neill goes in a different direction with the characterization; Hickey discovers that he has been living in an illusion.

The opening scene of Act IV is normal. A photograph has just been taken; the sun is on the point of setting and a little later it grows dark. Gina is at the open door with a small box and a wet glass plate in her hands talking to someone outside. Hjalmar returns from his walk and makes two assertions — that he will do everything for himself from now on and that he will never set foot in the loft again. He would like to wring the neck of the wild duck. In the wild duck, Ibsen has presented a multiple image, one which is (like Frey's horse in *Skírnismál*) a supernumerary. Hjalmar, old Ekdal, and Hedvig identify with the wild duck and as a symbol it functions in an ironic way, similar to the way the clouds function in Aristophanes play *The Clouds* (a play that Kierkegaard was interested in and wrote about in *Begrebet Ironi,* referred to in Chapter I). The clouds illuminate the empty activity of the Thoughtery, described by Kierkegaard as a directionless movement of thought which configures in every way as clouds do, resembling creatures, but in fact, they are vapor. Ibsen is kinder; the wild duck is thought of affectionately by the family but he represents a free spirit in captivity. There is only one person who can legitimately identify, in truth, with him, and that is Hedvig; the wild duck is hers. The poignancy of the image comes into play in the last act. Hedvig too is wounded in flight and when she exits from the play she will turn toward the South with bleeding breast as Ibsen's eider duck does in his poem.[51]

Hjalmar's rejection of the wild duck at this point in the action of the play is connected with Werle who winged the bird. For the first time in the play, Hjalmar is alert. He questions the finances, the household books, the money Ekdal earns through Werle. He confronts Gina about her past relationship with Werle. He uses an expression like "væv af fortielse"* telling her she has entangled him. Unlike Mrs. Alving, Gina never has been obsessed with the past. Although she had a relationship with Werle which she regrets, she does not think about it. She lives in the present. In this she is similar to Regine. It is clear that in the interval between the third and the fourth act, during Gregers' and Hjalmar's walk, Gregers has told Hjalmar almost all there was to know about the past.

A joyful Gregers comes in; he feels good about what he has done. In a scene that is a parody of the Moment, in that there are only words and no real experience, Hjalmar tells him that he has passed through the bitterest moment of his life. The scene shows the stupidity of Greger's action and the lack of consciousness in Hjalmar. He has no inner depth and little understanding of anything other than what is on the surface. In the parody, Gregers speaks of a momentous enlightenment, a new beginning, a new existence and that Hjalmar must be consecrated in a new enlightenment, all the characteristics of *the Moment*. One Ibsen critic wondered what would happen if everyone followed the blind idealism of Brand.[52] Ibsen has shown again in a different setting what the price is. Relling comes in and wants Gregers out. He recognizes his influence and his concern is Hedvig. Through Relling, Ibsen connects Hedvig's emotional sensitivity to her age, creating with her puberty, a correspondence between the real world and the "Other"; any kind of mental health problem is annulled.

In *Vildanden*, Ibsen has presented each of the central characters with his own script; each identity is carefully constructed (in *Gengangere*, Mrs. Alving is given center stage and while it is clearly seen how other characters are thinking

---

* web of lies — a line significant to Bergman's *Visknigär och Rop*

245

and what their various motivations are, they are not fully developed, they function as satellites that revolve around her). Mrs. Sörby is a case in point; she has had a bad marriage, is now going to marry Werle, had some kind of earlier relationship with Relling which she rejected. She is as practical as Gina in her own way and functions in Act IV as a kind of messenger.

Mrs. Sörby arrives with a gift for Hedvig whose birthday it is. Upon her arrival at the Ekdals, she imparts more information. Ibsen has been constant in showing that these people are not discerning — or even very curious — with the exception of Hedvig. Mrs. Sörby reveals Werle's blindness. When Hedvig comes in later with a letter and a deed of gift from old Werle, Hjalmar has his first insight (which he had been primed for by Gregers). He recalls other things — Werle's help when he married, and finally he asks Gina if Hedvig is his. She does not know. He is shattered and leaves the apartment, after denying and rejecting Hedvig. Gregers asks Gina to believe that he meant his actions for the best. Hedvig is desolate.

Just before the act ends, Gregers puts it into Hedvig's head that if she would sacrifice the duck, her father would know she loved him. Hedvig says that she will ask her grandfather to shoot the duck in the morning. It is learned that Hjalmar has gone off with Molvik and Relling — no doubt, drinking; Gregers had hoped that he would be a soul fighting in solitude. There is little doubt to Gina that Hjalmar will return, and the act ends with Hedvig's tears and Gina's comforting her.

The cold grey morning light is shining in through the wet snow on the studio skylight in Act V. In between the acts, the night has passed and we learn from Gina that Hjalmar spent it with Molvik and Relling and he is still downstairs. Gregers shows up and finally Relling. While Gregers speaks about the conflict in Hjalmar's soul, Relling points out that he is snoring on his sofa. He has not seen any significant

246

spiritual upheaval in Hjalmar and in response to Gregers' remark about Hjalmar's personality, he says that if there ever had been such a tendency, it was rooted out of him and destroyed when he was a boy. Hjalmar was brought up by two hysterical maiden aunts. Relling diagnoses Hjalmar as having been looked upon all his life as a shining light. Hjalmar is painted as having been a likeable, popular student who recited other people's verses and thoughts. Relling tells Gregers that he suffers from a delirium of hero-worship; people cannot live up to Gregers' ideals. The whole world is sick, asserts Relling, and the only solution for Hjalmar is to sustain the make-believe life within himself. Relling has created such a make-believe world for Molvik. *Ideals are lies,* he tells Gregers.

After Relling's departure, Gregers prompts Hedvig about the sacrifice, which she has been reconsidering. Displaying a talent not unlike Gregers, she gets information from her grandfather as to how to go about killing the duck. When Hjalmar returns, he again rejects Hedvig; she leaves silently. Hjalmar rejects her two more times and refers to her as an outsider. He is packing to leave. She takes the gun and goes into the loft.

In the next scene Gina and Hjalmar are heard wrangling in the sitting room. Hjalmar's childishness is obvious; the gun is discovered to be missing and is believed to be in old Ekdal's possession. Hedvig receives the brunt of his complaints — she has taken the joy out of his life and he doubts her love. Gregers tells Hjalmar that he will have proof of Hedvig's love. They hear movements in the loft — the duck. Hjalmar is recovering. He starts to rationalize about the gift from Werle and is on the way to resolving the matter in his mind, but he wants proof of Hedvig's love and wonders how she would respond if he asked her to give up any life that Werle might offer her. At this moment, the pistol shot is heard.

Gregers is happy and tells Hjalmar that was the proof he

247

desired, that Hedvig has sacrificed the wild duck. Hjalmar is moved. They think old Ekdal has shot the duck for her. When they find out that he has not, Hjalmar goes to the loft door and screams "Hedvig." She is lying on the floor. Hjalmar calls for help — it is thought that there has been an accident. Hjalmar wants at least one moment to tell her that he loved her. Relling tells him that Hedvig died on the spot. All the lamentations around him evoke little faith in Relling. He believes that Hedvig will be but a beautiful theme in eight or nine months; that will be the extent of her significance to these people. Ibsen is expressing a bitter — less than sweet — irony that plays on the Kierkegaardian idea of love living in memory. Neither the instant, the sudden or the Moment has occurred. There is only *an acoustic illusion* that something significant has happened to any of these people.

It is Relling who blames the ideals of fools for creating such situations. And the act ends with Gregers saying it is his destiny to be thirteenth at table; Relling agrees. Gregers is not really a Loki or a Devil in that his maliciousness is not conscious. He has the same qualities but he is much more a misguided fool.

One significant consideration in this play concerns the sphere of existence each character is in. The aesthete, the self-indulgent, non-participating individual is the essence of the Hjalmar and Gregers characterization, one without a will like Peer Gynt, the other with too much of one like Brand. Gina is centered between the aesthetical-ethical sphere and Relling reflects the ethical sphere. Hedvig is not yet defined and never will be. She is naive and innocent. In a state of innocence, Kierkegaard writes, the spirit is characterized as a dreaming spirit.

Only through experience can a human being be said to be on a specific level of existence. Considering Gregers and Hjalmar from the aesthetic point of view counteracts the image of the Kierkegaard idealist. They are seen to be stunted,

249

withdrawn characters who fantasize and never see possibilities around them. While Gregers is shrewder, it is a shrewdness that is dangerous but not less so than the emotionalism of Hjalmar. Kierkegaard saw the age as characterless with the aesthete foremost in the social milieu so that what existed was a refined aesthetic, an intellectual paganism with a dash of Christianity.

Is Hedvig's death a sacrifice or is it a suicide, or both,[53] or an accident? If it is a sacrifice, it is a sacriligeous act, although there is a distorted analogy to the idea of being forsaken by God. If suicide, a wasted effort — stemming from what Kierkegaard called a pagan lack of self, and if an accident,

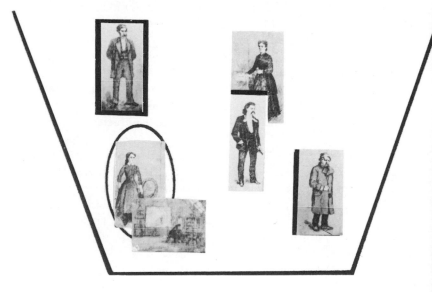

the action is horrendous. Whichever interpretation, the truth is that some gross misunderstanding that has no foundation or value is involved. This is not an Abraham and Isaac situation, an act of faith by virtue of the absurd, yet the play is comic-tragic in the early acts. There is no possible thought that this is the case. A meddler of dubious enlightenment and purpose has seduced a young girl's poetic fancy with an act of no consequence. The light from the skylight focuses on the scene. She is to be taken out through the kitchen door, to the left — the direction the medieval stage designated for Paradise,[54] her right hand holding the pistol hanging down, the father holding her under the arms, the mother the feet. There is not any "fullness of the moment" for Hedvig, or any of the characters in the play, and the acoustic illusion is weak.

The negative print is presented, the photographic image which for Kierkegaard and Ibsen lacked reality and truth. The possibility frozen in time, the photograph, which like the clock that does not tick, is static, and the tragic dominates, the tragic that is found in misunderstanding, and the pain is acute.

Considering *the Moment* as the Archimedean point upon which to determine the heart of the play has significance for the theatrical presentation, not only for the interpretation of events leading up to the play's center, but for how that center is to be played. Even though the ending of an Ibsen play is usually open-ended,[55] there is a final action in the play and the actress or the actor must know how the last action is viewed by the character to give it credibility.

The interpretation that Mrs. Alving has made a decision in her moment of consciousness, that a qualitative difference has occurred, demands a certain resoluteness of attitude on the part of the actress, but she must also show that as a human being she shrinks from what may be required. The action of the German actress who did not pause when she was fumbling for the pills in Osvald's coat pocket was the result of a directorial determination and in omitting the pause, a dimension of the human is missing. Ibsen did not ever want that element to be lost. In *Vildanden,* the obliqueness of the misunderstanding prompts Hedvig to sacrifice herself and is contrasted against the denseness of those she leaves behind, people who lack selfhood. If the ending is presented as a possible accident and that possibly a change has occurred with Hjalmar, Gina or Gregers, the statement of the play is undercut and assumes a Bjørnsonian optimism. The parody of *the Moment* and of love in *Vildanden* is biting as well as comic, and reflects the absurdity that has no basis, other than ignorance.

"Et sideblik" through "den bule hand"* — the eye of the motif

To gain a better perspective, the boy in Ibsen's "Paa Vidderne" holds to his eye the hollowed hand and looks down from the mountain top to the humanity below. It was *perspective* that Kierkegaard considered to be the differentiating feature of the artist. It has been mentioned in the Chronology, the section on the Creative Consciousness and elsewhere that Ibsen was an artist.

As conjured forth in his poetry verbally, Ibsen's art shows the strength of image and meaning/form. This sensitivity accounts for the suggestiveness of visual detail (organically related to the whole) which is to be found in the stage directions[56] and in the visual suggestion of the language. Ibsen is an artist who creates with his eye as well as with his mind and his ear. Seeing with the mind's eye was natural for him.

The background of his artistic production (painting and other media) is presented in a study by Otto Lous Mohr. In 1850-51, he did primitive woodcuts and later landscapes of Hardanger,[57] costumes sketches, [58] settings. The early work has been called naive, but it shows that Ibsen conceptualized in images.

In a letter to J. B. Halvorsen, he tells how he systematically went about trying to get instruction in the art of painting, and Bergliot Ibsen, in her book about the Ibsens, writes that Ibsen intended to be a painter. The majority of his best landscapes were fjords, a lake encircled by mountains, frequently

---

* "A sideglance through the hollowed hand"

252

snow-clad mountains which appear in *John Gabriel Borkman*[59] and others. Waterfalls which played such an important part in *Rosmersholm* interested him. Ibsen referred to Skien as the town of waterfalls. Some of his best work was done in 1862 and his friend, Lorentz Dietrichson, says in 1863 that Ibsen was at his easel.

Ibsen said in his speech concerning the task of the poet that to write poetry was "to see." The importance of his paintings to himself is demonstrated by the fact that five paintings bear his signature. When he was in Rome, he wrote to Georg Brandes (1869) that he recognizes the laws of beauty but that he does not care for the conventions, and of Michelangelo, although he has sinned against the laws of beauty, all that he has created is beautiful because it is full of character. An observation (not on Michelangelo but other art he encountered) comments upon the lack of artistic concentration in a motif, something that was not lacking in his own work. What is affirmed in Ibsen's visual art is the primacy that the image held for him and that it was inherent to his natural expression no matter what form it took.

There is one painting from the Grimstad period that has a *unique* place in his work and which is significant to the perspective of this study. It is titled "Propheten Elias under en gyvelbusk i ørkenen."* One of the unusual features of the painting is that it is the only religious subject that Ibsen painted, and according to the Biblical rendering in the first book of Kings it is an account of Elijah's awakening, how an angel came and touched him, not once but twice, and how later he was told to go forth and stand upon the mount before the Lord. When the Lord passed, a strong wind rent the mountains breaking it into pieces, and there was an earthquake and a fire but the Lord was not there.[60] After the fire,[61] he heard a still small voice.

Ibsen, like Kierkegaard, wanted to awaken the alienated

---

* "The Prophet Elias under the juniper tree in the desert."

person, to be in an unpretentious way *the still small voice.* Ibsen's dramatic work is not subordinated to a mission but is enhanced by the concentration of motif.

The Other Plays

the still small voice "paa scenen"

In the earlier plays *the Moment* is seen to be germinating and obvious. Its presence is appropriate to the context of the play. The first two plays that Ibsen wrote indicate this: *Catilina* and *Kjaempehøien*.

Catilina (1850)

Catilina, Ibsen's first play, written in Grimstad,[62] shows a phase of *the Moment*. The play is about a rebel who is disillusioned with the corrupt rulers of Rome and who dreams of greatness. He wants freedom and he wants to restore Roman honor. He speaks of restoring Rome very much in the same way that Kierkegaard writes about restoring Christianity.

From the very beginning of the play, Catilina is aware that he is not being true to himself. He is torn between this knowledge and the dream of glory and manhood unrealized. This is not an obtuse character. Catilina recognizes the times in which he lives for what they are, that might, not right, has the upper hand, and that the good man is overshadowed by naked power. He is married to a devoted woman, Aurelia, and he is attracted to a strong-willed Vestal Virgin, Furia. He recognizes that his life, like hers, is without a goal. While Aurelia personifies love, Furia is the personification of hate and Catilina is caught in the middle. Catilina is the first of the misguided Ibsen reformers.

This is a pagan play and there is a strong belief in fate. Furia voices Catilina's choice and tells him to choose saying that one path leads to quiet solitude, a life that is part death and part lethargy, the other path to a monarch's throne. In the last act, Catilina is described as standing alone among the crowds who cannot understand him. The idea of the stronger is brought forth in a dream in which the two women in his life are contrasted: the bold one seems to be triumphant, but part of the dream is missing. The Kierkegaardian overtones other than the choice, the path, the man alone, the stronger — continue. There are references to midnight's silent hour and to fear and trembling (all the action takes place at night). The Phantom comes from the grave (or the deep recesses of Catilina's being)[63] and points out how he is revered.

When his friend, Curius, betrays him, Catilina is disillusioned.[64] Catilina rejects Aurelia and Furia thinks she has won. Undaunted, Aurelia asserts that love will win. He is crowned with a wreath by Furia (as Hedda Gabler wanted to do for Løvborg); he gives Furia his dagger and she stabs him in the breast. An understanding of an earlier prophecy comes to him — that he will die by his own hand (Catilina is responsible for the death of Furia's sister and this is Furia's revenge).[65] There are two paths, he says, and by rejecting Aurelia, he has to go to the left (the direction Hedvig was carried off stage),[66] but Aurelia whom he stabbed earlier comes in and says no, that he will go to the right, toward Elysium and that breast to breast they will sink into their own grave. As in the Helgi lay, the lovers sleep together in a grave; Catilina and Aurelia like the lovers in *Når Vi Døde Vågner* — but unlike the lovers in *John Gabriel Borkman* and the Helgi lay — will remain together. Aurelia says that their love dispels the gloom of dusk, "Lyset seirer."* And it is in this moment that Catilina remembers the rest of his dream, that the darkness of the halls was dispersed with light from the new-born day; the repetition that is invoked in the image is that of renewal. Catilina and Aurelia die entering eternity backwards, the pagan way, through recollection.

---

* "Light has conquered."

There are other moments of enlightenment in the play, for instance, when Aurelia finds out that Catilina had seduced her sister. Another example is a reference to a moment and occurs in Act II. All that Catilina wants is to shine forth for one single moment, "nei-for et øieblik at lyse klart."* He does not want to vanish from the earth without leaving a trace. At the end of the last act when Furia stabs him in the breast, he understands the prophecy . . . that he will die by his own hand. These are examples of the sudden when some insight is gleaned — excluding the moment he wants to shine forth which has the immediacy of the instant.

In the second version of *Catilina* (1875), there is more emphasis on the immediacy of the moment in regard to life and Furia is given a new line. When she thinks that he is between life and death, hoping that he is dead, "Det vorder nat et øjeblik påny før dagen kommer."** In this version of *Catilina,* there is more suggestion of the pagan-Christian dichotomy than in the first version, and Catilina's repentance is emphatic; the stage directions are more detailed.

*Kjaempehøien**** (1850)*

The pagan/Christian dichotomy[67] is succinctly dramatized in the one-act drama. *Kjaempehøien* (original title *Normanerne)*[68] was written under the pseudonym Brynjolf Bjarme. It is placed in the period just after Christianity has been introduced into the North and takes place off the coast of Normandy. The North and the South representing paganism and Christianity are contrasted. With the opening scene, in the setting itself, before any action occurs, the dichotomy is shown. The burial mound which represents a

---

* "no . . . just to shine forth for one single second"
** "For one brief moment night will fall again before day comes."
*** *The Burial Mound*

Viking grave has a cross on it that recalls the stave churches noted in Chapter II, the chapter on the Ancient and the Modern.

Bernhard, an older man, is writing and speaking at the same time; his audience is a young girl, Blanka. He speaks about what will happen after Ragnarok, the twilight of the gods (when a new world would emerge), has purified this life (the story is set down in another lay of *The Poetic Edda*, "Voluspá").[69] According to the story, Odin, Baldur (the god of light who was slain by Loki; with his death evil came into the world) and the goddess Frejia will rule again. This is a tale he says and he enjoys the lore but does not believe in it. Blanka is fascinated.

Bernhard found Blanka after a Viking invasion when she was a little girl. They have lived alone for many years. She refers to the dead man's grave and says that she will put a wreath on it later.

They leave the stage and Gandalf, a young Viking chief, enters with his followers. His purpose is to avenge his father's death and bring his ashes to his homeland. He takes an oath to kill whoever is responsible for the death.

Blanka returns with flowers which she plans to use for the grave. Gandalf is enchanted with her and falls in love immediately. The instant in its immediacy has occurred. She speaks of gentleness and might. It is beyond his understanding that she can decorate an enemy's grave.

Valhalla is discussed and Gandalf tells her it is the home of the brave dead warriors; friends and enemies meet there. Blanka, views Valhalla as a place of strife. If strife gives life meaning, she tells Gandalf, then she does not understand its meaning. He does not understand her, but his soul is lit by insights. Ibsen is very obvious in this play, telling more than is shown.

Blanka speaks of Baldur's death and Loki's tricks and Baldur finding himself in Hel. But, she adds, Baldur was united with the gods and evil was like a leaf that was swept off. In the

259

exchange between Blanka and Gandalf, there is an affirmation of goodness overcoming evil. Gandalf cannot deny the story and Blanka is touching a truth that he has knowledge of (if not understanding of) although the aggressiveness of his world has dominated his life.

Blanka compares the Viking world and the Christian world in which love and faith contain the prize. She confuses Gandalf; he is unsettled; his spirit is divided.

In the next scene, Gandalf's men come in with Bernhard. He explains his position — that he is a Christian, as is Blanka, and that he is her foster-father. Bernhard learns that Gandalf is the son of the Viking who killed Blanka's father. Gandalf hesitates in carrying out the revenge he has pledged himself to. The seeds of doubt[70] have been sown by Blanka. When Bernhard confirms that he is the man who struck down Gandalf's father, Gandalf calls him Loki, suggesting with the connotation that the good has been annihilated by evil. There appears to be no reason for him not to carry out the punishment, but Blanka protests and Gandalf asks that Bernhard be spared. Bernhard restrains Blanka from further pleas, saying that all will be clear soon.

His men remind Gandalf of his oath — if he does not carry it out he has pledged himself as sacrifice. Calling Blanka the woman who has awakened his soul, he states that there is no choice, he must die. Kierkegaard made this point about *hiin enkelte*: the solitary individual, once he comes face to face with his destiny, does not have a choice; there is but one way and that is to love God, the concept that God represents, *love*. This is what Gandalf is doing. Blanka believes that they will meet in Heaven, but Gandalf does not agree.[71] His death will be a Viking death at sea. Blanka wants to go to the North and spread the word of Christ there.

At this point, Bernhard asks for her forgiveness and announces that he is Gandalf's father. It is the moment of crisis in the play. But Bernhard is more than a *deus ex machina,* arriving to save the day. There is a sense of immediacy in the act as it was when Gandalf fell in love with Blanka.

Bernhard tells his story; how he was unconscious after the battle and that the five-year old Blanka had nursed him and that he learned about Christ from her. In the burial mound is his armor and sword. There is a reconciliation and Bernhard (Audun) decides he will not leave; Hemming, the skald, will stay with him. This moment is engraved on Hemming's soul. Blanka will go with Gandalf and spread Christianity. Christianity reflects the new day and serves as a link to the prophecy of the seeress in "Voluspá." Axel Olrik (see Chapter II) has pointed out that later paganism could have predisposed the Vikings to Christianity.

Another point in this play is that Gandalf refers to his office as a calling, an expression which Ibsen uses frequently in regard to the mission of the individual in life. Kierkegaard also stresses the idea of the right man for the job and it being related to an inner right.[72] In later plays the idea develops into the problem of self-realization.

The opening of the second version of the play is not as obvious as the first.[73] The burial mound has a monument on it reflecting the Viking custom and it is decked with garlands. Blanka's foster-father's name is changed to Roderik and the action takes place off the coast of Sicily instead of Normandy. The difference between the South and the North is voiced more emphatically by Blanka and there are more references to Christ. When Gandalf speaks of a blight in the present age (this occurs in the second version of *Catilina* also), Kierkegaard is brought to mind.[74] There is more of a link within Blanka to the vitality of the North; she dreams of Norway and calls herself a warrior's bride. In addition to the fact that more information is given in this version, Blanka places oak leaves on Gandalf's helmet and refers to him as a sunbeam, "Et flygtigt Øieblik, saa blegned Straalen — Blomsten maate"!*

---

* "And one brief moment, and then the sunlight paled—the flower died!"

261

further recalling Kierkegaard, his essay on the lilies of the field. Dream and reality coalesce in this action; Blanka once dreamt that she did the same thing and she is not quite sure that what is happening is real.

Even though in both versions the main thrust, the contrast between heathendom and Christianity, is the moral factor, the main difference is that there is superior character delineation in the second version and more concentration of image as the title indicates. There is also more stress on the inner necessity that brings about the change in Gandalf.

What has been articulated in this early play is the immediacy of *the instant,* as presented in the aesthetic sphere of existence, the Viking code of honor, and a flash of *the sudden* in the insight that Gandalf receives when he is reminded of Baldur and introduced to the Christian way, a *glimmer* of the fullness of *the Moment* demonstrated by his decision, and a foreshadowing of the future.

Et Sideblik til Øieblikket — the frieze of life and death: Dødsdansen* — Simultaneous Staging and the dance of death

Subsequent plays have similar resolutions, sometimes based on the optimism of *the Moment,* rather than its fullness. Other times the sudden, the instant, or the acoustic illusion is given play. The quality of the ending is predicated upon the degree of consciousness the character or the characters possess at a specific point in time, the ending corresponding to *that* condition of being or non-being.

Brand and Peer Gynt (1866, 1867)

As has been pointed out in the chapter titled "Untying the Knot," Ibsen's dialectic has complexity in that people and situations are not always what they seem. Often *Brand* has been considered as having a transcendent ending, and the an-

---

* A side look to *the Moment* in Ibsen drama.

tithesis of *Peer Gynt* which is regarded as an aesthetic work. Actually, Brand's one-sided decisiveness is just as aesthetic as Peer's lack of decisiveness; both characters are existing in the same sphere. Where Peer stands at the end of *Peer Gynt* is similar to where Brand is at the end of *Brand*. It is unlikely that Brand has experienced the fullness of the moment. Whereas Peer peels the onion to get to the core and finds nothing, Brand's ideals are stripped away and shown to have lacked the one essential — *love*. He is full of regrets but Ibsen shows, with the avalanche drowning out the last words of the play, "Han er deus caritatis," that he has not experienced this change in his consciousness.

Et Dukkehjem (1879)

Nora's transcendence was expressed as occurring because the miracle she had waited eight years for did not occur. The miracle that did occur was its inversion. The fullness of *the Moment* was shown in the qualitative difference that occurs the moment she hears Torvald's rejection of her; *then* something happens. Ibsen builds up the anxiety prior to the change. The disclosure of Nora's forgery precipitates the action which destroys the past and Nora is left on the stage alone. Helmer goes to his study where Nora knows he will read Krogstad's letter informing him of her "crime." She is frantic, speaks of suicide, is torn between her love for him and the children. When he opens the study door and says "Nora!" she screams. He holds her and she struggles. Immediately, he insults and demeans her. She says that she is beginning to understand. He continues to berate her and she says she will be leaving this world soon, which he does not believe. When the second letter from Krogstad arrives and he learns that Krogstad will not prosecute, Helmer changes, but by this time something has happened within Nora and she can act decisively and non-destructively.[75] Later, when she slams the door, the action underscores the decision.

Rosmersholm (1886)

Rosmersholm has been discussed earlier in connection with
the idea of the weaker and the stronger. Ibsen has Fru Helseth

describe the last moments of Rebekka and Pastor Rosmer. The idea of soul affinity which Ibsen has dramatized in other plays — *Catilina, Kjaempehøien, Haermaendene paa Helgeland, Hedda Gabler,* and others — is strong in this play. Fru Helseth describes the last moments of Rebekka's and Rosmer's life,

their plunge off the bridge into the swirling waters below, and lends to it a fatalistic note in saying that the dead wife has taken them. Actually Rebekka has succumbed to Christianity, the Rosmer way, which she says ennobles and kills. The change has been radical and the moment of its finality is emphasized in Rebekka's decision to die with Rosmer. In the earlier play of a double suicide (*Haermaendene paa Helgeland*), the conclusion shows that the pagan strength of Hjørdis cannot withstand the power of Christianity. In *Rosmersholm,* the same thing has happened with the difference that the pagan has been converted. The fullness of *the Moment* has not been shown, but the aftereffect of it has. There is a qualitative difference in Rebekka that permits the ending.

Bygmester Solness (1892)

The question of whether Solness jumped or fell off the tower in *Bygmester Solness* can be answered when it is determined if he experienced the Instant, the Sudden, the Moment,

266

or an Acoustic Illusion. Was it simply regret at the way he had lived or was it the desire for transcendence or a pagan glory that made him jump — or was it disgust with the world? Solness finds people have no need of houses, that they are not worth anything to them. The physical aspect of the leap is in itself not conclusive even if it is decisive, and an act of suicide, if it is that, would seem to negate transcendence. Solness believes he has killed Aline, his wife, that he is responsible for his children's deaths, and that he is living with the dead. There is a foreshadowing of what may occur when he learns that Ragnar's father has died without having read the long overdue letter commending Ragnar's work. He becomes, with Hilde's arrival, more fully aware of his past actions and his denial of self. She is like the phantom who came to Catilina, the vision that came to Brand, or the Gregers who came to the Ekdals. To murder God or the good was, from Kierkegaard's point of view, the most horrible form of suicide (and suicide in itself was a rebellion against God). Entirely to forget God is man's deepest fall, and that is what Solness has done. With Hilde, Solness talks about retribution. He takes the wreath to the tower and is described as climbing to the top. Hilda says that he is struggling with someone and that there is a singing in the air, and then he is falling. The suicide is after the fact;' Solness has committed suicide long before but the physical act is indicative of his awakening.[76]

Hedda Gabler (1890)

Hedda Gabler will take her own life. There is no doubt that her action is suicide. Her rebellion is unemotional. She is her own angel of annihilation. When she listens to Tesman and Thea recreating Løvborg's book, she realizes the futility of her existence (her insight reflects the Sudden) and rejects life; she has no functional reality to stand in. In Sygdom, Kierkegaard writes that the pagan praised suicide because

267

she/he was not conscious of self as spirit and felt that what one did with one's life was one's own affair.

One point that signifies that Solness' fall was a conscious leap predicated on revelation other than knowledge, and not a fall resulting from dizziness, is that his guilt is ethical guilt (the weight of what he has done to others deliberately) as well as a personal one (what he has done to himself). Although Hedda's guilt was also an ethical violation, she was dominated by the guilt of inheritance which is an aesthetic guilt and is reflected in her adulation of the past which should have no power, according to Kierkegaard, to stunt the individual. For Hedda, the past was everything and her responsibility was only to herself.

The dichotomy of the pagan and the Christian has made its appearance again in these later plays. There is the grandeur of the act of will and the awareness in *Bygmester Solness* of guilt, ethical and personal; in *Hedda Gabler* there is cognizance that the wrongs Hedda has committed are being rectified but there is the aesthetic guilt of inheritance — and Hedda's rebellion against her situation and a determination to be her own master. A glimmer of *the Moment* has affected Solness and *the Sudden* has prompted Hedda. Kierkegaard's view would be that when a human existence is brought to the pass that it lacks possibility, it is in despair.

Fruen fra Havet (1888)

A softer note is heard in *Fruen fra Havet*. Ellida Wangel (as with other Ibsen women — Margit, Hedda Gabler, Svanhild) has entered into a marriage of convenience with a solid and kind man. It is immediately shown by her actions and the staging that she is moody and that she is separated from the group (her two step-daughters and her husband). Her entrance prepares the audience for the fascination that she has for the sea. She enters the scene dripping wet like a mermaid, having been swimming in the fjord. It turns out

269

that she has an obsession with something from her past, a strange man she had encountered ten years previously and with whom she has entered into a pact, a symbolic marriage. She had put him out of her mind, but the death of her child brought it back. She exists in a half-life, neither wife, mother or lover, sustained by drugs and swimming.

Her step-daughters act antagonistically toward her and she feels herself to be an intruder. The man returns. He is a Finn and is referred to as a Finn or a Stranger, although he has a real name. When Ibsen wanted to evoke the exotic, he referred to the far North or to Finland (Dr. Stockman practiced in a funny little quarter of the North; Rebekka came from the North.) The Finn's coldness suggests the Stranger who prevailed upon the boy on the heights to separate himself from those below. He is a reflection of the Socratic, the Kierkegaardian and Loki, rather than of the Christ figure.

It is suggested in the play that the occult is involved — a baby (with the eyes of the Finn whom Ellida has not seen in ten years) dies. There is a kind of Swedenborgian correspondence that was to obsess Strindberg who became deathly afraid of thinking certain things for fear they would come true. But the Finn is *also* a personification of a possibility unrealized, a Kierkegaardian idea. What happens to those unrealized possibilities?

The fascination with the sea is explicit; the Finn is described as being like an undertow, the pull pervading the mood of the play as it did in Eugene O'Neill's *Anna Christie* and *Long Day's Journey Into Night,* or *The Moon for the Misbegotten.* Ellida associates man's sorrow with the fact that man adapted himself to the land and not the sea (Kierkegaard has associated the sea with the heart as Ibsen does here and in *Vildanden*).

The crux of the play is Ellida's decision. Her mesmerism with the past is broken by a decisive act. Ellida is afraid of the Finn and voices her terror to Wangel whom she says she

270

loves, although she has rejected him for the past three years of their marriage. Finally, she meets the Stranger again and his eyes (like those of the Stranger on the heights) frighten her. He has come for her. She calls upon Wangel to help her. The double reflection between a strange, unknown existence and reality are side by side — the possibility and the actuality.

The Stranger will not use force. She must decide which man she wants. Wangel points out that Ellida did not recognize the Stranger until she saw his eyes and he says a new image is replacing the old one. She believes that neither she nor Wangel married of their own free will, but married out of necessity.

When the Stranger tells her that she must choose of her own free will, everything is clear to her. The first marriage had possibility but never became complete. She requests her freedom, claiming that if she does not have it, she does not have a choice.

Wangel is reluctant to give her up and in the next scene she discovers that the girls do like her, that the youngest has been waiting for an expression of love from her. This disclosure makes Ellida feel she has a purpose in life; knowledge has been given to her.

The time of the final meeting with the Stranger occurs. Wangel calls Ellida's obsession the hunger for the infinite and he dissolves their contract because he loves her. The release transforms everything. She strikes her hands together like a cymbal. Her decision has been made; she cannot go with the Stranger. *The Moment* has occurred. The past is brought together with the present and the future is posited in the decision. The idea of the stronger is brought into play and the need to love proves to be stronger than will. The play ends with Ellida and Wangel hand in hand, and the steamer gliding out of the fjord. Music is heard close in near the shore.[77] This is a rather overt, abrupt, and weak articulation

271

of *the Moment;* it lacks intensity because there has not been any serious consequences to others from Ellida's action — something is lost.

Lille Eyolf (1894)

In considering *Lille Eyolf,* it has previously been remarked that there has been no significant change in the Allmers. There is an irony involved in their resolution as it is not certain that either of them, at the point in the play where they decide to educate unfortunate children, have sufficient maturity to fulfill such a responsibility; the ending reflects an acoustic illusion and the last words an irony that suggests they have no real sense of what they are talking about. Allmers says they will have glimpses of Lille Eyolf and Asta, and then they look upward toward the mountain peak, the stars, and the great silence.[78]

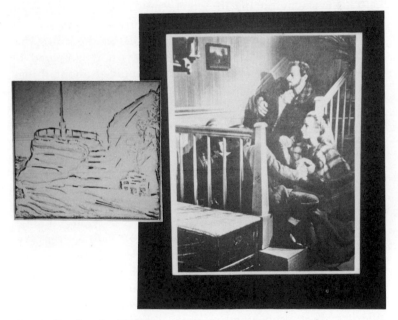

En Folkefiende (1882)

In *En Folkefiende,* a fighter and an optimist who thinks he is fighting for a good cause ends up alone with his family,

273

ostracized by the crowd and unaware of what has really occurred. In this play, the acoustic illusion suggests a transcendence, but is not. Dr. Stockman is seduced by his own enthusiasm. He considers himself one of the strongest men in the world.

De Unges forbund (1869)

The idea of hypocrisy and what it does to people enters into *De Unges forbund*. It shows that reformers are just as hypocritical as capitalists. Ibsen lampoons the idea of a certificate proving that a man is an artist, a civil engineer, or a priest (Kierkegaardian sentiment).

This is a play on the idea of being singly blessed (chosen by God) as Haakon was in *Kongs=Emnerne* (a satirical inversion). In this comedy, Stensgaard will be the voice that rises above the crowds and because he is not hampered by moral considerations he can be liberal-minded about things.

There are echoes of other Ibsen plays, that is, the masses, ghosts as new ideas, one man ruining another, and there is a Holbergian element in connection with the theme of youth. Ibsen stated that the situation in the play could be Denmark as easily as it could be Norway. Almost tongue in cheek (at least on Ibsen's part) he has Stensgaard say that he will reach his objective with the help of himself. While there is a Lokian quality in Aslaksen, the editor who cannot make a living out of a good paper, there is a stronger Lokian strain in Stensgaard. Ibsen was going to call the play *Vorherre & Comp.** (although it had nothing to do with religion). He wrote Frederik Hegel in 1868 that the play was a comedy that dealt with the frictions and the currents of contemporary life. There is a play on the idea of sacrifice. Selma is upset because she has never been asked to give a sacrifice and she would like to be sacrificed for Stensgaard's career. The doll image

---

* Almighty & Co.

is conveyed in her characterization, but there is also a maturity when she leaves her husband. Shrewdness of the kind seen in *Kongs=Emnerne* (Bishop Nikolas) is present in another context, that is, functioning inversely and successfully. Kierkegaard's thought concerning education is uttered by Dr. Fjelbo and reiterates Kierkegaard's existentialism. He draws attention to the gifted people running around in one direction and their actions in another. The reason this occurs he decides is because the emphasis is on learning, not on being.

The play opened on the 17th of May for the Norwegian Independence Day celebration. Stensgaard, a young lawyer, is the main character. He is an enthusiastic liberal ready for action and it is he who starts the League of Youth. The audience is plunged right into the action without any preparation. The conservatives in Norway thought Stensgaard was a liberal and the liberals thought he was a caricature of them.

275

Bjørnson thought he was the model, but Ibsen said that Stensgaard could be any politician.

Stensgaard uses everybody and even becomes engaged three times to get money (imagining his loved one to be financially ruined). His ambitions cannot be curtailed by time. It is predicted that he will eventually end up in parliament. The ending is a sour note to the audience — no instant, no sudden, no moment, and no acoustic illusion perpetuates any kind of change in Stensgaard. His success generates new energy in him.

Samfundets Støtter (1877)

Ibsen considered *Samfundets Støtter* to be a counterpart of *de Unges Forbund* and that it would stir up some of the most significant problems of the time. It is a study of public life based on a lie. The pillar of society is Karsten Bernik, the inheritor of a famous ship-building concern. He has permitted one man to assume guilt for a theft that he did not commit and to be discredited for a love affair in which Bernik was the culprit. It is his defence that in being a pillar of society, he cannot weaken the social structure by an admission of his guilt; this brings disrespect down on the class he represents.

Bernik's greed leads him to jeopardize the life of his son. The son is saved and it appears that Bernik has reformed, that his consciousness has undergone a change. Unfortunately, the strength of this conclusion is weak. There is a similarity in plot, although a different context, to Miller's *All My Sons;* Miller's play ends on a somber note in that Joe's son's life is forfeited.

Kongs=Emnerne (1863)

Doubt[79] about his right to the crown plagues Skule in *Kongs=Emnerne*. His striving to gain it through will leads to one violent act after another. It is only when he sees what has happened to his son that he has the possibility of transcendence. Skule has warped his son's sense of values to the

276

point that Peter is willing to kill for his father; the boy will kill Haakon's child in his mother's arms (the mother is Skule's daughter). Skule tells Peter that he (Skule) is not the chosen one, and that the idea to unite Norway — which he claimed to be the author of — was not his idea, that it was Haakon's. He has no life-work to live for. Peter understands and they go hand in hand into the path of their foes, knowing that they will be killed. Skule asks that Peter not be wounded in the face.[80] They are killed and Haakon arrives; he will have to step over Skule's body to go forward. Haakon calls Skule a riddle, God's unwanted child on earth.[81] The last action of the play is that of Haakon stepping over Skule's body.

The fascination with some phase of *the Moment* and the contemplation of the play's final image strengthens the Ibsen play from a theatrical point of view and when *the Moment* or some semblance of it in each of the plays is viewed simultaneously, the impact is stimulating; the diversity of Ibsen criticism bears witness to the provocation his idiom has generated.

Norma (1851)

Ibsen had one play end with a *deus ex machina* ending and although this play was not intended for performance, it presents another side of Ibsen. *Norma,* while a political parody, is also a parody of his own work and caricatures aspects of his dramatic idiom. Written in 1851, *Norma eller En Politiker's Kjaerlighed,* is a three act (very short acts) political satire, inspired by the Bellini opera *Norma,* and printed in the newspaper *Andhrimner.* It was a parody on the members of parliament and not intended for performance. In the Preface to it, Ibsen writes that he saw the Storting as a dramatically talented corporation, and he offered *Norma* to them to be acted out. He assigned the parts to various members. It begins in "mcd tilbørlight Halvmørke."*

---

* "in proper half-darkness"

277

There are two women, Norma and her girlfriend, Adalgisa. Norma was to be played by the opposition and Adalgisa by the Party of the opposition. Other characters are Severus, Norma's husband, and their two anemic sons; Norma's father; a chorus of male Druids (the sensible ones); a chorus of female Druids (the silent ones in the Storting).

It revolves around Severus' affair with Adalgisa. Norma stresses duty and is going to kill Severus when she discovers the infidelity. But he is saved at the last moment by a *deus ex machina* ending. Adalgisa enters in the form of an angel transforms Severus into a demigod or a cabinet minister. And everybody, including Norma, bows down to him. Nothing so obvious, of course, occurs in Ibsen's serious work, although *De Unges Forbund* in 1869 makes a similar statement.

Fru Inger til Østeraad (1855)

There are in *Fru Inger til Østeraad* as in all Ibsen's plays many Kierkegaardian echoes in the ideas that are expressed: the idea of sacrificing one for many; the best part of love is

memory; the will; betrayal of one's calling; going one's own way; turning the pictures to the wall. By going her own way, Fru Inger has suffered too long (not unlike Mrs. Alving but for less personal reasons). Her instant of recognition occurs when she sees her ring on a soldier's hand, she then knows that the boy she ordered to be murdered was her own son (prior to this point she had been in anguish over her actions). She sinks over the coffin and asks for a grave beside him.

Olaf Liljekrans (1857) and Gildet paa Solhoug (1855)

Another mother in another play (one staged and costumed by Ibsen), Olaf Liljekrans, does not succeed in destroying her son's life. Olaf is caught up in a double existence — romance and reality — and the situation is resolved through love. Faith in love does not sustain Margit in Gildet paa Solhoug.[82] She marries an older man who loves her rather than wait for the one she loves (Gudmund). When he returns, her love is rekindled. He is in love with someone — Margit or her younger sister Signe — each woman thinks that she is the chosen one. Margit even decides to poison her husband but he is killed and she is free, but Gudmund chooses Signe and Margit goes to a nunnery when she realizes what she has lost. The play reflects another concept of Kierkegaard's, that she who chooses rightly, is chosen — Signe.

279

Sancthansnatten (1852)

Sancthansnatten (1852) for shadows later developments. Julian Poulson mouths cliches from Kierkegaard and the call of the ideal is ridiculed. The action occurs on a summer night when the supernatural world will reveal its secrets, similar to *A Midsummer Night's Dream.* It is suggested that only those

who are genuinely poetic can see this world. Ibsen refused to have it printed in his lifetime; he referred to it as a fairy tale comedy (*eventyrkomedie*). Four young people are together on Midsummer Night: Johannes and Juliane, who are engaged but do not love one another, and Julian, a student friends of Johannes, and Anne, Juliane's step-sister, whose innocence is a contrast to Juliane's sophistication; Anne is regarded as "fey." A nisse or goblin lives in the loft. Anne accepts his presence; only she can see him. This goblin is a kind of Puck, puts a potion in the punch. They go to the hilltop and catch a glimpse of the other world, the supernatural. Under the influence of the night they declare themselves. The next day they realize that they are betrothed to the wrong people. Revelations are made and misunderstandings are cleared up. *Sancthansnatten* foreshadows aspects of *Kjaerlighedens Komedie*. Poulson's last words are particularly significant to *Kjaerlighedens Komedie*. He claims that when in love one takes a theoretical view of love, but when married or betrothed, there are practical considerations. The play is a reflection of immediacy and ends with the couples embracing each other.

As has been set forth in the Chronology, Ibsen read Herman Hettner's book *Das Moderne Drama* on his first study tour to Copenhagen. It was a significant study in that it turned against the modern drama of the day, that is Scribe and Øehlenschläger. Hettner rejected coincidence and mistaken identity in *serious* drama. What mattered was conflict and development of character. He set forth the idea that the historical play could be written psychologically and thus be relevant to modern times, something Ibsen did. A special point was made regarding the romantic fairy tale (*Märchenlustspiel*); its importance being that it dealt with two worlds, and the juxtaposition of the two worlds. Ibsen wrote *Sancthansnatten* on the study tour.

The loss of the idyllic asserted itself with Nora in *Et Dukkehjem* and earlier with Svanhild in *Kjaerlighedens Komedie*.

281

Kjaerlighedens Komedie (1862)

Kjaerlighedens Komedie is a sardonic play although it is called a comedy and it shows how the stage can project the image. It is written in verse and the following lines express the mood:

O Du Fortnuft-Karrikatur, som draeber
Med Galskabs Hallingdands paa Vennelaeber!*

As with *Sancthansnatten,* the setting and the people are contemporary Norwegians. The play also contains a statement about the artist and about marriage. Ibsen sets the aesthetic and the ethical spheres of existence side by side. In a letter to Peter Hansen, October 28, 1870, he wrote that the poem "Paa Vidderne" receives its expression in *Kjaerlighedens Komedie.*

Svanhild was an earlier draft written in prose. It emphasizes the importance of the name which is the name of the heroine in the play. Svanhild in the *Volsunga Saga* is trampled to death by wild horses; this Svanhild is not.

Kjaerlighedens Komedie is a play about ideas and caricatures the nature of love in various stages, mocking it and marriage. The plot revolves around Falk, the poet, Svanhild and Guldstad. Falk and Svanhild fall in love, but in the end Svanhild decides to marry the businessman, Guldstad, rather than the poet. (In a subplot, another couple fall in love and

---

* "The grinning caricature of prudence
a deadly danse macabre on friendly lips."

282

become engaged. Ibsen shows the fate of their love when it attempts to survive within the conventions of the people around them.) Falk is restored to his original position in the play; his values are the sublime. He has sacrificed the actuality of love to his poetry.

Life is bigger than Svanhild. Her decision is based on the pragmatic, *the sudden* rather than the Moment; she relinquishes the aesthetic, Falk, and the aesthetic in herself (poetry). While Falk experiences instants of rhapsody, there has not been any internal change. The irony is that Svanhild accepts in the end what she rejected in the beginning, the ethical. Their love will live in memory[83] rather than be lost in actuality. There is dancing at the end of the play, but the feeling of renewal, as in an Elizabethan jig, is not present, because of

O Du Fornuft-Karrikatur, som draeber
Med Galskabs Hallingdands paa Vennelaeber![84]

Falk expresses the Kierkegaardian belief that by releasing the claim to love, he keeps love young; in memory it increases with the years in beauty. Ibsen was to rephrase this sentiment in his poem to Fru Heiberg (see Chapter I).

Når Vi Døde Vågner (1899) — A Dramatic Epilogue; John Gabriel Borkman (1896); Kejser og Galilaeer (1873)

Når Vi Døde Vågner (1899) is Ibsen's last play. It could be called the fellowship of buried lives because of Irene and Rubek, the main characters who are buried in an avalanche in the end. Since they have not really lived, the irony is implicit. There is also a strong sense of finality in the tone. The pronoun "Vi" suggests that Ibsen had some such thought; so many of his people have sacrificed the life force, love of the good, of *the God*. The avalanche that occurs suggests that the words that Brand did not hear, "God is love," have been smothered.

When the play was performed in America for the first time

283

(March 8, 1905), it was considered to have been given an uninspired performance by Florence Kahn. Earlier and later performances by other people have not been praised any higher. It is suggested that the nature of this dramatic epilogue is the reason. *Når Vi Døde Vågner* is a mystic and poetic play and the poetic language expresses the soul affinity that existed between Irene and Rubek.[85] The reality of Maia's and Ulfheim's realistic idiom sets the poetic language in relief — this has been done before with Nora and Rank, Hedda and Løvberg, Hedvig and Gregers, Hilde and Solness — and others. The play ends with the lovers going to their grave in the mountains *together,* suggesting the Helgi lay, but lacking the separation that occurs in that lay.

The Moment does not occur in the usual sense. Irene has told Rubek that they and their love are dead. Its possibility never became an actuality because Rubek would not accept her. In the Kierkegaardian sense, Rubek has cherished Irene in memory. He believes that they can still live life to the fullest, at least one more time, and he suggests that they ascend the mountains together. The last scene lacks the poetic image that concludes *John Gabriel Borkman* — the idea of the poet

284

who wants to return to the mountains. Offstage, Maia's voice is heard singing that she is free. As in *Brand,* there is an avalanche, and Irene and Rubek are buried in the snow. The sister of mercy makes the sign of the cross and says "pax vobiscum."* For Irene and Rubek, the future and the past have been sacrificed and the present nullified. Even though the sense of personal renewal is absent, the sense of the future is posited by Maia's song but it is not a very positive future. She, like Regine, is self-centered and there is little indication that humanism will survive.

The dramas of Henrik Ibsen have not been treated chronologically but according to the ideas that have been generated. While this method does not show the development of his dramaturgical skill, it does create a vital picture of the life force. Furthermore, without the developmental structure, the concentration is heightened.

---

* "Peace be with you."

Set all these moments, these *tableaux vivants* (*levende Bilder*) together in one frieze of life as Edvard Munch did with his art, and the bitter-sweet irony of *the Moment* is seen as a medieval dance of life and death, *Dødsdansen** suggesting the pictorial representations that line the walls of the old churches in Scandinavia, the same dance that is dramatized in the morality play. Munch felt that when his paintings were side by side, not necessarily in chronological order, they struck a chord different than when shown by themselves; — they became a symphony. He says that is how he began to paint friezes. A musical note is sounded in each of Ibsen's dramas when they are set side by side as on a medieval stage, and the note is given resonance by *the instant, the sudden, the Moment* or/and *the acoustic illusion.* Dissonance is the comic-tragic tune the players must keep in step with. Ibsen's dramatic art is a study in counterpoint in which the tune changes when the plays are rearranged, but the movement does not. There is an echo of the same chord, "What does it mean to be an individual?" And, in the background the Death figure mouths the words, "Memento mori" — intoning the message over and over, "Remember, you must die."

* the dance of the dead

NOTES TO CHAPTER IV

1 Kierkegaard states that once one has been made aware of the religious sphere of existence, the question of choice is not in question. That is why he uses the dash between *Enten-Eller* and not the diagonal as used in the English translation. The *dash* indicates a pause.

2 In *Frygt og Baeven*, Kierkegaard expresses the idea that reward is not given in this world to those who live for the idea, but to him who has the ring.

3 *Symparenkromenoi* is the Greek name for the fellowship of buried lives — used in essay in *Enten-Eller*. He imagines himself addressing a society composed of people who are living lives which are spiritually or mentally entombed and isolated.

4 Pre-Artaud.

5 The activity that is generated suggests the kind of aesthetic awareness that can occur in Indian theatre, which is called the "rasa" experience. See A.C. Scott.

6 Article on Ibsen's earlier plays by Knut Nygaard.

7 It is difficult to understand such a reaction today.

8 The first English performance with Mrs. Ida Jeffreys-Goodfriend.

9 *Theatre* 6, 1906, pp. 219-21

10 Margaret Tyzack as Mrs. Alving *Time* Je. 20, 1977.

11 In its usual context encounter refers to a confrontation and/or to be faced with the unexpected. Today, it is more popularly associated with psychology, used in connection with people who wish to increase their sensitivity or relate more personally to others. A similar idea was projected in the theatrical and art scene of the 1950's with a form called "Happenings". John Cage, leading proponent of this art, considered the form a means to intensify and alter perceptual awareness, and, therefore, the consciousness. There is a similarity to what Antonin Artaud (earlier) and Peter Brook were attempting to do. With Ibsen (and Kierkegaard) the encounter was on a deeper metaphysical and conceptual level that was connected with their ethos and the spiritual.

12 Frances Ferguson, David Thomas, Inga Stina Ewbank, *Gengangere* embraces the Brandes dictum (see earlier reference to Brandes) intimately — "det uendeligt Smaa som udgjør Livet"* and "det uendeligt Store, det er Livets Aarsag, Grund og Type."**

13 A line from an Ibsen poem.

14 *Les Bonnes* — Genet's characters change identity on cue.

15 An epigrammatic expression punctuates her revelation—the corrrespondence suggests the idea of Erich Auerbach's *figura*, i.e. two events in history.

16 The significance of the pause led Kierkegaard to state that standing still was movement also.

---

* "the infinitely small which makes up life"
** "the infinitely great, which is the cause, the foundation and the model of life itself"

17 Strindberg admits that Kierkegaard impressed him, but it was Swedenborg who possessed him.

18 "Natural other-worldliness." See *Theatre* chapter.

19 Kierkegaard considered the bright light as negative as Ingmar Bergman does. In *Papirer* Kierkegaard writes that too much light and the situation becomes too serious, especially if the light does not fluctuate. (Same as in Sartre; *Huis Clos*.)

20 The importance of silence — is reiterated by Kierkegaard and Ibsen — to be silent, to wait until one hears the still, small voice.

21 The overcoat has more significance than the suggestion John Northam has made that it shows Osvald is not equipped for Norwegian gloom. It plays a significant role in the last scene of the play.

22 *The New York Times*.

23 Bjørnson wrote a play on the double standard *En Hanske* — discussion in Chapter V.

24 In Act I, Osvald's smoking of the pipe — something his father has done — has already established their parallelism.

25 Numerous examples in Chapter I.

26 His endings are sometimes trite. Discussion of his work is in Chapter V.

27 For instance *Viskningär och Rop* (*Cries and Whispers*) 1972.

28 George Moore was one of the original founders of the Irish Literary Theatre.

29 The *pause* has significance for the staging.

30 Kierkegaard believed in living life. He felt the *now* more significant than the past.

31 I.e. akin to the Abraham and Isaac situation.

32 Tidemand often collaborated on a painting with Gude—Tidemand doing the figures and Gude the background.

33 See Chronology.

34 See: "Lilien paa Marken og Fuglen under Himlen," Bind 14 *Samlede Vaerker*

35 Epigrams at end of the poems.

36 Letter to Frederik Hegel, 1884.

37 Berit Erbe—her study 1973: *Bjørn Bjørnsons vej mod realismens Teater*.

38 Ibsen had confidence in himself, did not take hissing at his play (*Vildanden*) adversely — attributed it to strained relations between literary parties.

39 *The New York Times* review considered *Vildanden* to be shallow idealism, March 12, 1918.

40 Robert Brustein, author of *The Culture Watch*, is now at Harvard University.

41 *Kjerlighedens Gjerninger*.

42 Article on Loki by Erwin R. Steinberg. "Gregers as Loki," *Papers on Language and Literature*, 1970.

43 Berit Erbe, *op cit*.

⁴⁴ He (Ibsen) took a personal interest in this play—most particularly.
⁴⁵ Ibsen thought the staged paintings an inferior imitation of the painting.
⁴⁶ He (Ibsen) wanted good actors/actresses in the most minor roles.
⁴⁷ Letter to August Lindberg who was to direct *Vildanden*.

⁴⁸ In a letter to Bjørnson, December, 1867, Ibsen writes that photography is inferior to the creation of poetry as it is only the simple reproduction of reality.

⁴⁹ They represent extremes. In referring to the comic treatment, Else Høst suggests a moral lesson can be drawn from the events.

⁵⁰ Kierkegaard compares the ocean depths to the heart — the depth determines the purity of the ocean.
⁵¹ Poem "Ederfuglen." (The Eider Duck)
⁵² Georg Brandes.

⁵³ Kierkegaard felt suicide could be dispelled if one would talk to someone but also thought the clearer the conscience, the graver the danger.

⁵⁴ Medieval simultaneous staging — the action moved from mansion to mansion; Paradise on the extreme left and Hell on the extreme right. In between were the earthly scenes based on the stories of the Old Testament.

⁵⁵ Kierkegaard is not confined to the System; therefore, it should not be expected that the last thing he says will complete the system.

⁵⁶ Stage directions cannot be ignored as Arthur Miller does in his adaptation of *En Folkefiende*. See Chapter V.

⁵⁷ There is only one painting in which the landscape is free composition.
⁵⁸ *Olaf Liljekrans* and Scribe play.

⁵⁹ Munch has said that it is impossible to paint winter after Ibsen has done so in *John Gabriel Borkman*.
⁶⁰ See last section of paper on "The Future."
⁶¹ Note fire in Ibsen play — *Gengangere Bygmester Solness*.

⁶² Ibsen was studying for his university examination, reading Sallust's Catiline and Cicero's speeches attacking Catiline. Suggests *Julius Caesar*.
⁶³ Expressionistic possibility.

⁶⁴ There are reminisces of Shakespeare in this play. A few years later Ibsen was to give a paper on Shakespeare.

⁶⁵ Ibsen had an affair during this period and was the father of an illegitimate son.

⁶⁶ Kierkegaard and Ibsen enjoyed juxtaposing the Biblical symbolism associated with the left and the right, i.e. side of God.

⁶⁷ The first treatment of the polarity that appears over and over. Paganism is poetically defined by the *eagle*, Christianity by the *falcon*.

⁶⁸ *Normanerne* — Halvdan Koht says this material on the conflict between paganism and the Christianity is from Øehlenschläger.

⁶⁹ Voluspá — a visit is made by Odin to the oracle and the account she gives of the origin of the world — its present state and her prophecy of the new.
⁷⁰ Doubt reaches its zenith in *Kongs=Emnerne*.

290

[71] The idea of lovers separated by religion comes up again in *Haermaendene paa Helgeland*.

[72] Ibsen treats this phase of the call in *Kongs=Emnerne*, Kierkegaard in reference to Mary being the chosen one. See Chapter II.

[73] Name changed from *Normanerne* to *Kjaempehøien*.

[74] He expresses himself in connection with this in "Nutiden".

[75] Simply to act is not enough; the act must be decisive in a positive way.

[76] It is not anticlimactic; however, it needs to be shown to the audience, as it punctuates the sentence. Many of Ibsen's endings make epigrammatical statements as did his poetry. An ironic overtone is posited in that the pull of gravity is a natural force. An interpretation of suicide or accident is supported by the nature of gravity.

[77] The idea of an earlier love affair, a comfortable marriage and regret expressed in *Gildet*.

[78] Ibsen has his "tongue in cheek" here.

[79] Doubt was felt by Kierkegaard to be man's undoing. Ibsen is playing on this idea (in a different vein) and relating it to the right man for the job.

[80] Abraham's love for Isaac is present but there is no reversal.

[81] Idea of Loki character expressed. He is another Loki in a different mask; a more intense Lokian figure in the same play is Bishop Nikolas.

[82] *Gildet* was Ibsen's first success in the theatre.

[83] A Kierkegaardian sentiment he expressed in his own life and writing — the same sentiment Ibsen expressed in the poem commemorating Fru Heiberg — see Chapter I.

[84] "The grinning caricature of prudence a deadly danse macabre on friendly lips" — is a theme that is present in Ibsen, Bergman and Strindberg.

[85] Although Ibsen became more abstract in his later plays, he did not place emphasis solely upon the inner drama of the emotions as Maurice Maeterlinck did. It is with the juxtapositing of the finite and the infinite that Ibsen brings *life* into relief and suggests the forces behind it. Unlike Maeterlinck who wrote during the later Ibsen period (Maeterlinck's name appears in a Bjørnson play), and he admired Ibsen's interior dialogue. Ibsen did not try to create a drama out of atmosphere and symbolism alone and he professed to dislike Maeterlinck's symbolism. For Ibsen, people were marionettes in that they were manipulated by error.

From Another Perspective:
the American Consciousness

V

A NOTE:

The contrast that is permitted when Ibsen's drama is considered from the Bjørnsonian and American perspective further illuminates the nature of the Øieblikket and sets it out in broad relief. When the point of view is examined in the context of modern drama, that which is called "modernism" suggests that what is now thought of as the "absurd" is an optical illusion, that misunderstanding has made of it something more nihilistic than Kierkegaard's meaning of the concept. Sans faith, the *absurd* lacks the double reflection and forces the comic. Its despair goes beyond the sickness unto death, it goes to death itself. Black comedy is what happens when the tragic element wanes.

Kierkegaard expressed in *Øieblikket* 7 what Ibsen articulated theatrically, the desire is to "kunde Komme bag Ved alt dette Formummede."*

---

* "get in behind the scenes of all this mummery."

Bjørnstjerne Bjørnson (1905).

Henrik Ibsen (1905).

Bjørnstjerne Bjørnson

"We now have a dramatic poet in Henrik Ibsen," wrote Bjørnstjerne Bjørnson in 1881 in an article to the American people. "I do not hesitate to say that in my opinion Henrik Ibsen possesses the greatest dramatic power of the age. I am so much the more certain of my judgment from the fact that I do not always like his drama. It is surprising to me that he is not translated in America. He is one whom contemporaries should know."[1] This praise came from a man whose drama was more popular in Norway, and even in America, a man who was a friend, a critic, a defender of Henrik Ibsen, and a sometimes adversary, especially when he felt he was a model for one of Ibsen's characters,[2] or when he thought Ibsen was too pessimistic for the popular understanding.

They met in the 1850's when they were both preparing for the university examinations at Heltberg's student factory in Kristiania. Although Bjørnson wrote in other genres than drama, his career parallels Ibsen's. He too, was a theatre critic in his early years. More fortunate than Ibsen, he received stipends to advance his professional work. Both he and Ibsen were to supply a distinctive Norwegian repertoire for the theatre in Norway and both desired to free the theatre from Danish influence.[3]

The critical commentary that has been written about his

297

dramatic art has been, for the most part, posited in reference to Ibsen. It defers to Ibsen and has a tendency to lionize Bjørnson, extolling him as a fine human being. Ibsen spoke of Bjørnson's life as the finest creation and Georg Brandes called him the spirit of Norway. It is lesser known that August Strindberg professed to prefer his art to that of Ibsen's. Strindberg admired *Mellem Slagene* (*Between the Battles,* 1855) which was Bjørnson's first play and used it as the model for *Den fredlöse* (*The Outlaw,* 1871). It ends in reconciliation. Clemens Petersen, Danish critic, admired Bjørnson's characterization, saying that he could paint the most mundane character in such a way that he or she took on life.

Bjørnson's dramatic work differs from that of his contemporary, Ibsen, in several ways, but most significantly in the endings. Bjørnson's drama offers *a contrast* to the focus in this study and illuminates a significant aspect of the American consciousness.

Unlike Ibsen, Bjørnson fights in the name of the majority, and places the family above the individual. While his early work recognizes the place of joy in life (which Brandes attributes to Grundtvigianism which permits the highest, freest human development)[4] the later plays show the anti-social aspect of individualism. Bjørnson does not view life as a few moments from the heights. Brandes describes Bjørnson's vision as representing an ascent in fair weather with a clear and beautiful view.

The protagonists in Bjørnson's earlier plays are presented from Bjørnson's point of view rather than from a philosophical position. He presents the hero as a born chief and benefactor (not unlike Haakon in Ibsen's *Kongs=Emnerne*) and within the image, Bjørnson reflects himself. He does not pierce the depths of existence in his portrayal. In presenting nature, it is not used symbolically as it is with Ibsen, but as a characteristic feature of Norway.

He paints scenery verbally. This aspect of his dramaturgical principles was given an impetus during the periods he was stage manager at the same theatres as Ibsen, the first national theatres in Norway.[5] His pictorial vision was extended through his work in the theatre. When he directed Shakespeare, he allowed Shakespeare to speak for himself and he underplayed the visual. In 1865, when he took up the directorship of the Christiania Theatre, he put on five new Shakespearean productions in addition to an older one. Francis Bull considers Bjørnson to have done Shakespeare less than justice, in connection with *Henry IV* which he compressed, but his productions of the other plays showed a profound insight into the poetry.[6]

Unlike Ibsen, Bjørnson was considered a proficient stage manager, and the experience gave his plays an added dimension other than the verbal scenery. He was very responsive to the spoken language — the actor's delivery and her/his interpretation — and to the staging of mass effects. Unfortunately, Bjørnson's work suffers in translation much more than Ibsen's, primarily because of the dialogue which depends upon versification. His sensitivity to language (the sound patterns and rhythms), rather than the image or/and the idea, is an integral part of his art. Bjørnsonian language "abounds in strong sensuous color" and is "responsive to every shifting mood."[7]

Universality is not apparent in Bjørnson's plays because he was more concerned with the problems of his country, and these are presented directly. The attitude of the 1870's in intellectual circles was that art was for life's sake. For Bjørnson that meant art had the responsibility of reform. When he received the Nobel Prize in 1903, he said that the author must not be unconcerned as to whether his motif is a source of blessing or of harm.[8] Consequently, in keeping with his conviction, the themes of his plays do not transcend that belief — if a conflict might result that would cast doubt on the moral stance he wished to perpetuate. Even before the 1870's Bjørnson was headed in that direction. According to Harold Larsen in his study of Norwegian nationalism, while Ibsen

299

with *Haermaendene paa Helgeland* wished to create a national drama, his paramount objective was to portray life as it was in Norway in the past. Bjørnson would erect a historical gallery from the romantic past in order to repeat an idea for a more lucid explanation of the present day, as opposed to Ibsen whose purpose was to illuminate the significance of life to the individual.

Bjørnson was more direct in his presentation than Ibsen was; the audience did not need to puzzle or wonder what he meant. But, it would be an oversimplification to suggest that Ibsen was not at one and the same time articulating a contemporary condition. The condition was not one that was immediate as it involved the national consciousness. In any case, Bjørnson's efforts toward reconciliation of the issue sometimes thrust the ending of the play into a synthesis that could be anticlimatic. Yet, in the work up to this point, there would be a dramatic spontaneity.

Bjørnson reacted against the "too muchness" of ideals. The dramatic perspective he articulates in some of the plays is revealing in that his plays were popular; it helps to understand the kind of audience he and Ibsen were writing for. In some of their plays there is a similarity of subject matter, and often Bjørnson articulated the subject first. Bjørnson's popularity, in part, can be attributed to the fact that he was reassuring and supportive. Bjørnson said in his Nobel Prize speech that Ibsen warned his readers too much and that he frightened them.

Bjørnson did not undercut the audience's fundamental beliefs, For instance, consider his treatment of marriage in *De nygifte* (*The Newly-Married*, 1865). In this play, Bjørnson turns to realism and anticipates Ibsen by several years, introducing the problem of the doll wife, which Ibsen treats in 1879. It concerns the problems of a young man who finds life is being encumbered by a wife who is unable to escape the childlike restrictions of her family. The play ends happily, but emphasizes the dilemma of the young man. Martin Lamm states that *De nygifte* is the first instance of a marriage play in Scandinavian drama. It had the greatest theatrical success of any Scandinavian play of that period, and it was performed in Kristiania, Stockholm, and Copenhagen in 1865. Later, it moved to Austria, Hungary, Russia and Germany.

En Fallit (*A Bankruptcy*, 1875) is considered the first successful prose play in Scandinavia and introduced the subject of money and business. It brought to the stage the problems of modern capitalistic society and it utilized the financial crisis of 1857-58 (Bergen).[9] The chief artistic merit of the play is the descriptive passages. Another first is that it is the first play in which the awareness of a strong "home" atmosphere is apparent. Lamm suggests that Ibsen had it in mind when he wrote *Samfundets Støtter* (1877). The older generation of scholars considers Bjørnson's the better play, which Lamm admits is true from the technical point of view. It is open-ended in that it permits the audience to reach its own conclusion. However, the object was to show how misfortune reunited the family.

Bjørnson was happily married to an actress, Caroline Reimers. Possibly she influenced him in that he has written some feminist plays.[10] *En Hanske* (*A Gauntlet*, 1883) appeared after *Et Dukkehjem and Gengangere* and shows a response to these plays. The double standard is articulated. A slap in the face punctuates the point. Svava slaps Alf in the face and walks out of the room when the situation is presented to her as normal. A similarity to Ibsen is suggested in that it is always the past which lies behind the play that is significant. Bjørnson lacks Ibsen's skill in involving the past into the theme. The heroine who not unlike Nora, is placed in a position where she must sever her relationship or compromise. The choice is less compelling than Ibsen's Nora's, and Svava is the same lively (but less innocent) young woman in the end, her choice verging toward the pragmatic rather than the idealistic. The plot is built upon a broken engagement. Alf and Svava are in love and they are well suited to one another

301

even though he is wealthier. But she discovers that he had seduced a married woman, now dead. Alf admits to the affair but does not consider it of importance. *The New York Times* review of the 1913 London performance states that in Norway the play had the power to set women against marriage.

When Svava asks Alf if he would marry her if she had had an affair, he says no, because he thought of her as a pure woman and that was one reason he loved her. Svava tells him she regarded him in the same way. She breaks the engagement when she discovers her father has also been unfaithful to her mother. Learning of his father's indiscretions strengthens her convictions. The play is presented from everyone's point of view including the wives who have lived with the situation. In the London review, this was considered to be a drawback theatrically. As for Svava, if she cannot have a husband who can be trusted, she will remain single. Alf is genuinely in love and at the end of the play he makes one last plea. Svava does not actually reject him. The ending is rather subtle. He asks for her hand, and instead of giving one hand, she gives him both suggesting that she will eventually compromise.

With *Over Evne I (Beyond Human Power*, 1883), there is more suggestion of Ibsen. Bjørnson concentrates on a chief character and begins after the catastrophe. In turning to mysticism and man's relationship with God, Bjørnson expresses his fear that in the insistence on the ideal, a person can become unrealistic. Pastor Sang thinks he can work miracles. The play opens with the wife lying sick; she suffers from physical and spiritual exhaustion. She is not a believer as he is but she loves him. It is her lack of faith, he believes, that has prevented her cure. He brings his twin children home from school and they are all to gather about her bed and pray. The children declare that they also lack faith; they believe there is only one Christian in the world and that is their father. They are not capable of living the way he does.

When the pastor calls his sick wife from her bed, his power lifts her up and she walks. But then she falls dead; it is

302

beyond her power. Her death breaks the forces that have kept the pastor going, and he dies too, rather *a deus ex machina* ending. There is an indication that the wife is the stronger and a recollection of Brand's one-sidedness in the husband who is a much gentler man. The ending has a moralistic tone like a proverb: Be moderate in your demands on life or your strivings will end in disaster. The awe that the North produces is presented in the catastrophe that covers the church with snow, occurring when Pastor Sang is praying for his wife. When the play appeared in New York in 1902 with Mrs. Patrick Campbell, the landslide was thought to be extreme. The play was referred to as an Ibsenist play and said to have held the audience spellbound. Bjørnson was criticized for his lack of the religious in his treatment of miracles.

In his last play, a comedy titled *Når den nye vin blomstrer* (*When the New Vine Blooms*), Bjørnson reflects his reactions to the Ibsenist new woman. It shows the effects of the new standards on the household of Mr. Arvik. His protagonist is a middle-aged man who turns to a young woman for the love his wife denied him. As with *Over Evne I* (and also in *En Hanske*), the point of view is presented from all sides (something Ibsen did with more sophistication in *Kjaerlighedens Komedie* (when) he illuminates love from the point of view of all the characters). One of Mr. Arvik's daughters gives her hand to an elderly pastor; another is toying with a passionate suitor; a third has been returned to him bag and baggage because she was an unsatisfactory wife; and his wife, who has dabbled in everything, particularly business and the children, has withdrawn her interest from her husband. Mr. Arvik leaves for other vistas, but returns in the end to a chastened household.

Bjørnson's dramatic art — if not inundated by his conviction — is, at the least, less aesthetically satisfying. He recognized his calling — that he was more humanist than artist. Øyvind Anker's estimation of Bjørnson's mission was that he knew early in his career that there was something more to an author than honor and wealth, and that was truth and justice in all dealings between people and nations. Kemp Malone considered Bjørnson as great a literary man if not as great a dramatist because Bjørnson was also a novelist and a lyric poet. It is evident that Bjørnson wanted to set up ideals for his age and to use these ideals pragmatically. His aims were lofty but not beyond the human power of the ordinary person. It was his contention that society would always harm some and they would protest as Svava did in *En Hanske;* but he believed the protest should not ignore what is important, for instance, that Svava was loved by a sincere man. Bjørnson, conceded that in Norway the protest was stronger than elsewhere (and similar to the American experience)[11] because it was bred on the national element — individualism — rather than social development. Above all, he was a realist, becoming more so in time; he accepted Darwinism and he rejected Christianity — yet he did not break with the ethical, nor was he a pagan. It would be more accurate to say he broke with the Christendom of his age as Kierkegaard had. Anker so rightly phrases it when he says Bjørnson was a believer in evolution, not revolution. While Ibsen is asking if man can live without the eternal, Bjørnson is saying that he can. But in this declaration, Bjørnson removes from his drama the Archimedean point on which Ibsen's art hangs, the consideration of *the Moment.* More often Bjørnson's endings are resolutions. The two kinds of reality are articulated by Ibsen and Bjørnson — the infinite and the finite, respectively. With Ibsen there is the terror of the unknown and sometimes the utter destruction of the known, but there is a glimmer of light at the end of the tunnel. With Bjørnson, the pragmatic is presented as being all that is within human power and human power all that there is, suggesting that that is enough.

In some of his plays, he treats the same material as Ibsen does, frequently earlier in terms of subject matter. Later, the work has Ibsenian characteristics. In his earlier plays (the

304

Romantic National period), he brought the contemporary problems into focus. His method is a comparatively direct approach enhanced by a poetic language that reflects the grandeur and beauty of Norway and extending into the theatrical effects — the handling of crowds and scenery — but lacking the sophisticated symbolism of Ibsen. In English, Bjørnson's language sounds more like purple prose than poetry, losing in translation more than Ibsen's. There is in the Norwegian a flow and rhythm that reflects Bjørnson's acceptance of the change that has occurred in the language with the Danish influence, and he describes the Danes as the most civilized people in the world. He also recognized the value in remodelling the language because in its existing state it did not have enough room. With the reform the sentences become shorter, a characteristic of Ibsen's art and the art of an earlier ethos.

With his defense of Ibsen, Bjørnson shows that he understands Ibsen's dramaturgy and he refers to the significance of *form* in modern Norwegian literature, something he pointed out in connection with *The Poetic Edda*.[12] With Ibsen, there is something new, Bjørnson says, that should be looked at. He admits to the artificial darkness in Ibsen which is similar to spiritualistic media and he admonishes those who would put down an artistically intended obscurity as a lack of clearness in the poet; rather, the fault is not with the poet but with the audience. Ibsen's cruelty Bjørnson attributes to his compassionate feeling for the misery of criminals and a condemnation of society when it seems an accessory.[13]

Bjørnson reflects, in discussing one characteristic of Viking literature, something that has become tantamount to the understanding of Ibsen dramaturgy (as expressed in this study). It is something that receives luke-warm treatment in Bjørnson's own drama. That is, in a decisive moment, when one character speaks to another the threads of life are laid bare by what they say. And because the issues involved in Viking literature

305

concern life and death, an intensity is projected that will not permit the finest shade of the expression to be missed.

Bjørnson predicts that Ibsen's art will survive and he singles out the art of the "repliquie"[14] which was prepared earlier in the far-off temperature and the events of the play, and fitted into the surroundings and the temperature of the present. That, furthermore, as a result of the whole work, Ibsen's art rises in radiancy and bursts forth in the color and the splendor of the idea. He asks who else has succeeded so completely in concentrating all the effects of the drama in speech.[15] There are no dead points in Ibsen nor are there superfluous words; everything is centered in the "repliquie." "In service to the idea" negates an ending that would soothe. The ending of the Ibsen play, generally,[16] unlike the Bjørnson play, follows through and is related to the articulation of *the Moment* directly, or indirectly. The open end is the existential and subjective character of the theatre and the Kierkegaard/Ibsen consciousness, yet in the silence lies the content.

Bjørnson points out that Europe and America first looked to Norwegian literature because of its cleanliness and poesy and then for its ideas and form. He grants that others might achieve the technical dexterity of Ibsen but the distinguishing feature with Ibsen is that his dialectic is in the service of the ideal. An American critic writing for *The New York Times* during this period reiterates Bjørnson's contention that when Ibsen is not understood, or is thought obscure, the lack is in the audience, and this is, in one sense, correct.

The American Stage, Ibsenism
and Modern Drama

*the tragic comic-tragic comedy of errors
and the "fullness of time"*

The nature of the American theatre was a contributing factor to the reception of Ibsen's work. In the 19th century, the American Stage was keeping pace with the growth of the country. More people were making money in the Industrial Revolution, the West had opened up to theatre, and playhouses were being built whether or not entertainment was available. With the thousands of immigrants who poured into the East coast cities came a greater interest in entertainment. From a handful of theatres in 1800, the number increased to 5,000 playhouses in 3,500 cities by 1885. Some of the playhouses that were built seated as many as 3,000 people. Generally, producing management and theatre ownership were in the hands of entrepreneurs with business interests in theatre.[17] The idea was to get as many spectators as possible.

As theatre for the masses became more popular, there was a change in theatrical programming. Older audiences diminished and the interests of the new populace were given first consideration. The changes involved a shift from a classic repertoire to spectacle and melodrama.[18] There was not only pressure from the audience to reflect its taste but the audience was encouraged to voice its disapproval by hissing. In this period, these professional drama critics were verbalizing their reaction.

The stage itself exerted some influence in the presentation. During the first half of the 19th century, painted wings and drops, and dimly lit stages encouraged an expressive acting style. With the building of larger theatres, spectacle was needed. In the 1880's the age of inventions, theatre was equipped with mechanical devices which lent itself to what was termed the "new realism" — a realism that was superficial and familiar. Steele MacKaye is credited with bringing the latest mechanical devices into the theatre. His Madison Square Theatre in New York included a double stage which permitted a change of scene in seconds. He thought of drama in terms of spectacle, pantomime, and verse.

The popular audience was described by Henry James in 1875 as one that goes to the theatre to laugh and cry, not to think. They wanted diversion. There was also native drama such as minstrel shows, vaudeville, and circus acts. In the 70's and 80's, Harrigan and Hoyt presented broad farces about Irish and German immigrants.

As it is now, theatre in the 19th century was a commercial enterprise; it had to support itself or go under. Competition was intense and the theatre placed reliance on the actor (especially mid-19th century) and upon breathtaking spectacle to attract theatregoers.

In addition, America partook indirectly in the European revolt against rules because the romanticism of the American life was sans rules. American theatre did not have the same traditions as Europe in respect to drama and theatre, despite European ties. The romantic artist responded to the romantic spirit in the life around him. Form was thus dictated by the immediate subject matter and the momentary inclination of the artist.[19] Subtlety of expression was sacrificed to direct presentation of striking and suggestive actions and settings.

Theatrical and melodramatic entertainment persisted until the end of the century, yet in 1880 a new vitality was discernible. Stimulated in part by the experimental European theatre, American drama gradually acquired social responsibility and seriousness along with a surer grasp of psychological and spiritual realities.[20]

The American Bicentennial exhibit of America on Stage[21] at the John F. Kennedy Center for the Performing Arts showed the nature of the American theatre. It was not conceived of as a historical presentation but rather as an exhibition that conveyed *the essence* of the American experience in two hundred years of performing art. In presenting a visible expression of theatrical modes and personalities which were "on the boards" from the colonial period, a panoramic vision of social change was asserted but also expressed was the romantic nature of the American people.

The theme that controlled the exhibit was American impulsiveness, courage and naiveté. It was a metaphor of the American theatre, individualizing its essence which is a *deceiving* "centerless diversity," and suggesting its promise. The program text expressed the uniqueness of the American ethos:

> A pioneer spirit bound together the many national strains in the American spectrum, democratizing and diversifying the arts, liberating old theatre forms, modifying and amalgamating traditions, daring the new.

Ibsen was definitely not an immediate success on the American stage. Fife and Anstensen[22] attributed conservatism and suspicion of the new as a factor in Ibsen's unpopularity; rather, the response or lack of response was grounded in the nature of the American condition, of which moral censorship was also an ingredient.

Dion Boucicault described the American stage at the time Ibsen came to it as "an unweeded garden that grows to seed."[23] American types were being presented by such playwrights as Steele MacKaye, Bronson Howard, William Gillette and Charles Hoyt. Mary Caroline Crawford observes in *The Romance of the American Theatre,* "In an analysis of the plays presented in New York between 1884 and 1888, when Wallack's, Daly's, the Madison Square and the Lyceum were all equipped with permanent companies playing serious drama, it was observed that every one of the enduring successes were plays of American character."[24] The audience was not cultivated and it was dedicated to easy entertainment; it disliked pessimism. Ibsen was not well thought of, "the whole theatre of Sardou is as much below Hamlet in stagecraft as all of Ibsen is below it in intellectual content."[25] Show business techniques accompanied the promotion of the play. Even in 1887, when an adaptation of *Ghosts** was produced in the larger American cities, it was entitled "Phantoms, or the Sins of His Father," and it was advertised as "forbidden in Germany" to make it more tantalizing.

While spectacle drama continued to develop, changes were going on in American drama during the last third of the 19th century. There was a tendenccy toward realism. Whereas melodrama continued, it became social melodrama, occasionally shocking the audience with a realistic portrayal of life. Farces showed interest in the social community and social comedy was stimulated. Poetic drama nearly disappeared. Long runs could be as long as one hundred and fifty nights,

---

* Ibsen's titles as they appeared on American stage will be used in this section.

311

the length of time of Bronson Howard's *The Young Mrs. Winthrop.*

Bronson Howard's importance to the development of playwriting goes beyond his own success. Although a syndicate[26] dramatist, he was to give the American dramatist greater importance. He founded the American Dramatists Club in 1891 and, later in *The Autobiography of a Play,* 1914, he cites the "Laws of Dramatic Construction." He associates a well-made play with a play that is satisfactory. The subject matter should be universal; the heroine should not die; the play should end happily[27] (certainly at odds with much of Ibsen and even with some of Bjørnson, although more in tune with Bjørnson).[28] Howard's laws were contingent upon audience expectation rather than artistic considerations. In this he was similar to Bjørnson but for different reasons. With Bjørnson, the audience was an ethical consideration related to the way life was.

The playwright closest to Ibsen was James A. Herne.[29] He was a realist who attempted to create a drama of ideas in a realistic vein that went beyond the authenticity of a performance. In 1897, he wrote "Art for Truth's Sake" and stated that art should emphasize humanity. His was not art for life's sake as with the Norwegian intellegentsia, but art for truth's sake. His most realistic drama, *Margaret Flemming* (1890) is about a strong woman who goes blind, and would like to forgive her husband's weakness. The ending is less final than it is in *A Doll's House.* It shared the same fate as Ibsen's *Ghosts* and was rejected.

Ibsen came to America's attention by way of England, and most particularly through the enthusiastic voice of George Bernard Shaw. Although Ibsen had met opposition in Norway and in Europe, the opposition was more intense in England. The English became acquainted with the later plays first and were shocked by the subject matter as well as by the form.[30] His supporters included such figures as William Archer, Edmund Fosse, J. T. Grein, George Moore, Henry James, and Sir Beerbohm Tree.[31] Ibsen attracted performers and particularly actresses who found a strength in the women's roles that gave them the opportunity to display their art. Through performances, theatrical criticism came to America, and, eventually the actresses themselves recreating the roles: Mrs. Patrick Campbell, Ellen Terry, Janet Achurch, the American-born Elizabeth Robins. Actresses from other European countries also made their appearance: Eleonora Duse, Frau Agnes Sorma, Mme Rejane, Mme Alla Nazimova, Mme Modjeska, and, finally, the American actresses: Miss Ida Jeffreys Goodfriend, Mrs. Minnie Madden Fiske, Miss Mary Shaw, Blanche Bates, Nance O'Neill, Florence Kahn.

While interest in Ibsen was present before the event of the theatrical scene — readings, the universities, the Scandinavians in America (such astute critics as Clemens Petersen, a well-known critic in Denmark before coming to America and a friend of Bjørnson and Ibsen) — these interests reached only a small section of the American public. The more popular criticism that attended the plays was a rehashing of the English critics with the sensational elements receiving the emphasis. Ibsen was not immediately seen as a voice raised against the hyprocrisy of modern society. There were many misconceptions about Ibsen and his work.

Mme Helene Modjeska's performance of *A Doll's House* in 1883 at Macauley's Theatre in Louisville, Kentucky, was the first professional performance of *A Doll's House*.[32] The way in which it was produced gives some indication of the dilemma the outcome of Ibsen's play caused. The title was changed to *Thora*, and the play was given a happy ending.

It had been Modjeska's feeling that, with the taste of the times veering in the direction of realism on the stage, Ibsen's play would be appropriate. She was wrong. She was forced to withdraw the play from the repertory; "Macauley's had to have audiences." When it was given again in 1889 with Beatrice Cameron as Nora (in Philadelphia), because of the title *A Doll's House,* it was thought to be a play for children, and the audience, in fact, was populated, for the most part,

by nursemaids and children.[33] In 1889, Minnie Maddern Fiske recreated Nora and her Nora is considered the best-known Nora in the 19th century. Montgomery Phister described her as "the most intellectual actress of the American actresses." As a creative artist, she was always concerned with the last moments of Ibsen's plays, and in *A Doll's House,* the play ended with the slamming of the street door "and the audience settled down to wait for a fourth act and the return of the penitent wife." Archie Binns[34] in his writing about the American stage, claims that through her (more than anyone else), Ibsen had become an accepted fact in America.

It was in 1894 with the first authentic performance of *Ghosts*[35] with Miss Ida Jeffreys Goodfriend at the Berkeley Lyceum in New York that the Ibsen movement got under way. William Dean Howells hailed it as "a great theatrical event," but the critics called it "unwholesome." A year later, Howells was to say that the least dramatic of Ibsen's pieces was more dramatic on the stage than any work by any other author. He considered that the average playgoer did not share Ibsen's views and that unless the audience was given action, incidents, and "the usual hysterics and heroics" it would not feel it had received its money's worth.

One of Ibsen's strengths, he writes,[36] is that he forces one to put himself in a similar situation, and that it is then difficult to pull oneself out of it. This imposition, Howells feels, does not endear Ibsen to the audience.

Howells does not foresee any great acceptance of Ibsen on the stage by the public, but for Ibsenism there is a great acceptance. Ibsen's simplicity impresses him; it is a simplicity that actors like. They find in Ibsen an understanding of the stage and a support that is in the work itself. For this reason, Howells contends, it is very difficult to fail Ibsen in performance. On the other hand, the influence of Ibsen on dramatists Howells does see, and cites Pinero, Shaw and Jones. He could wish that they centered their interest in conduct rather than in action (as Bjørnson also did)[37] because an Ibsen problem is as wide as the whole of life and seeks a solution in the conscience of the spectator in the future rather than in the present. He acknowledges that puritanical narrowness cramped the race; consequently, it cannot go beyond personality which Ibsen transcends.

At the end of the 19th century the serious drama critic came into existence. Writing for the *New York Sun* was James Huneker. In one article, "Ibsen the Individualist," he refers to him as a thinker, an artist, a critic, and a true Viking. The thinker sometimes overrides the poet, but the theatre man is always there, even to the point of sometimes wrecking the psychological. Huneker admits that the artistic precipitation is sometimes cloudy.

He points out that with Ibsen, man is stupid because he is bad. Mentioning Kierkegaard, Huneker says that he agrees with Kierkegaard that the average sensual man will ever "parry the ethical chain." The power that Ibsen has is that of "the artist doubled by the profound moralist, the philosopher doubled by the dramatist"; the crystallization of these antagonistic qualities constituting the triumph of his genius.

Another important drama critic was William Winter who wrote for the *New York Tribune*. He was not impressed by Ibsen's drama, and in fact, he did not consider Ibsen a dramatist in the true sense of the word. Of Ibsenism, it "is rank, deadly pessimism, it is a disease, injurious alike to the Stage and to the Public, in as far as it affects them at all, and, therefore, an evil to be depreciated."[38] Winter dislikes the didactic tendency of the social plays because human nature is presented as universally vile and human society as corrupt. To present such subject matter is to exploit the theatre and to offend persons who respect the theatre.

For Winter, Ibsen's work lacks sensitivity which is a requisite of art and Ibsen's ability Winter does not consider extraordinary. He considers art as beauty inseparable from morality and this point disqualifies Ibsen for Winter. In one criticism, the "Ibsenite" James Huneker is reprimanded for lauding Ibsen. An indictment against Ibsen ends the article; his gospel assessed as the gospel of a disordered mentality and his mind "diseased."

Huneker and Winter represent the sharp division of thinking concerning Ibsen in America. He was either extolled or rejected. Daniel Frohman,[39] theatrical producer sometimes referred to as the "Little Napoleon," saw the problem simply: "Debatable plays, problems, fantasies of the character dear to

316

the heart of Ibsen, Bernard Shaw, and the rest of them, are never financially successful in America. These are relegated to special audiences, and these special audiences are 'pious playgoers.' Such an audience is a temptation to the Ibsen scoffers, and would have been irresistible to Ibsen except that Ibsen was humorless."[40]

What has been revealed in connection with the American stage and drama foredoomed a favorable reception to Ibsen; the nature of the American audiences was not predisposed to the paradoxes and intricacies of his dialectic or his theme; they liked action and were optimistic. Most important is that the predisposition of the American dramatist to the happy ending — the recommendation of Bronson Howard and one of the demands of the Syndicate — also contributed to Ibsen's rejection.

Even in the Scandinavian community which had access to Ibsen earlier in the original Norwegian and with whom the ethos would suggest a bond, there was a distortion of the final scene. Of *A Doll's House*, Arthur C. Paulson writes that "the new techniques of the third act puzzled the Norwegian-Americans, that it did not grow out of what had gone before; it was no ending at all." Lack of religion was one reason for the problem, wrote P. P. Iverslie, drama critic for *Norden* (August 25, 1880). He considered Ibsen's play an attack on the foundation of society. A little play titled *Hvorledes Nora kom hjem igjen* (*How Nora Came Home Again*) brings Nora and Hjalmar together over the sick bed of their child.

Another Scandinavian critic, Ole S. Hervin, upheld Ibsen. He disapproved of Nora's action but believed the point that Iverslie missed was that Ibsen did not write the play to uphold any moral or ethical code. Hervin was one of the few perceptive people who recognized this facet of Ibsen's aesthetic.

For whichever reason (commercial or moral), these early interpretations missed the significance of *The Moment* in Ibsen's work.

Baron de Stampenbourg, in 1901, mentions the voluntary clubs established and the interest in maintaining the esthetic standard of Ibsenic ideas. Mrs. Fiske, one of the few who did understand Ibsen, produced *Rosmersholm* in 1907. As an example of some of the blatant errors critics made about Ibsen, one called Ibsen's work a novel adapted by Charles Archer. Rosmers was played by the matinee idol Bruce McRae, Rebekka by Mrs. Fiske and George Arliss portrayed Ulrik Brendel.[41] Binns credits Mrs. Fiske with an interpretation that brought out the comic elements.

318

Ibsen's death, May 23, 1906, served as an impetus in terms of further interest in his work and in the number of performances. It was in this year that *Peer Gynt* was produced at the Grand Opera House in Chicago with Richard Mansfield.[42] Mme. Alla Nazimova returned to New York in 1908 as Nora in *A Doll's House* and Hilde in *The Master Builder,* while the year before, Ethel Barrymore had played Nora at the Lyceum. Some performances prior to World War I were given intermittently until the twenties. In 1923, Joseph Schildkraut appeared in an expressionistic production of *Peer Gynt.* Eva Le Gallienne took her production of *The Master Builder* and *John Gabriel Borkman* on the road; Mrs. Fiske, in 1926, presented *Ghosts*; *An Enemy of the People* played to one hundred and twenty-eight performances.

In the twenties, there had been a change — theatrical diversity, experimentation, a new acceptance of moral values that would not have been accepted earlier, and a drama not easily identified. There was also an interest in discussing plays of not only Ibsen, but of Shaw, Synge, Barrie, and Rostand. As a genre, drama had come into its own. The playwrights were more serious; there was a new interest in playwriting through such a figure as George Pierce Baker of Harvard. A change in stagecraft and the little theatre was also seen, and Eugene O'Neill, a student of Baker's, made his debut at the Provincetown Players "little" theatre and wrote *Anna Christie.*[43] He wanted to write tragedy within the American experience. O'Neill admits to Strindberg's influence and showed an interest in Ibsen and European Expressionism.

Sidney Howard wrote *They Knew What They Wanted* (which later becomes the musical comedy *Most Happy Fella*), and O'Neill cast a reflection on it in *Desire Under the Elms.* There was Paul Green's indigenous, symphonic drama and Heywood's *Porgy and Bess;* Elmer Davis related to the naturalistic impulse in *Street Scene* (naturalism was not popular in America)[44] and in his expressionistic work, *The Adding Machine,* Mr. Zero goes berserk. The happy ending is not

319

requisite and when Rice arrives at the final scene, he adds an ending that suggests Rosie's future. With Harrigan and Hart the slums are central, and Philip Barry is a kind of Neil Simon with such plays as *Holiday*.

In the thirties, there is the reality of the depression, Hitler, the golden age of the radio and the awakening. Steinbeck's *Of Mice and Men* reflects the melancholia of dreams unrealized and there is no happy ending, but in the midst of the seriousness of life there is the optimism of William Saroyan's *The Time of Your Life*. American drama's strength is its ability to articulate reality and experience. Plays are not openly didactic in the thirties and they do not look for solutions.

Toward the end of the thirties, Thornton Wilder wrote *Our Town*. His work expresses the humanism of Kierkegaard's Christianity. He found *love*, as did Kierkegaard, Ibsen and Bergman, to be the answer to life. For Wilder there was no impediment to presenting the theatrical reality of his vision. He regarded the stage as a pretense upon which other pretenses were to be placed. It is a bare stage, imaginary scenery, and colloquial speech that is his preference. The conventions of the past are significant to his art; he admits that he is not an innovator. In *Our Town*, there are morality play "types" in the characterizations, Brechtian echoes in the use of film and the direct address; the places shift from the present to the past and the "Other" dimension.

Wilder had come in contact with Kierkegaard in 1945 through his friend Walter Lourie, who had translated Kierkegaard.[45] Wilder felt that the "shudder and awe induced by the presence of the numinous" was one of the most powerful effects that had been lost in the theatre. He too believed that a sacrifice must be inspired by love, to be in the religious sense of Kierkegaard — a trial.

In *The Skin of Our Teeth*, Wilder wanted to illuminate, to stir Plato's idea of "recollection" perhaps of a racial past, so he presents "moments" (of a more theatrical and less personal

320

kind) that do this; for instance, the reference to Abel, the mother putting a message — that only women know — into a bottle. His play, while not expressing the fullness of *the Moment* as a singular experience, is the hum of the universe in motion. His theme is that man will never be destroyed, that he will always try again.

In the forties, the American drama reflects the anger and the pain of the period. Of significance is Lillian Hellman, whose play *The Little Foxes* has a character who suggests Hedda Gabler. She does not destroy herself, however, but others. There are sporadic performances in the forties, notably with Eva Le Gallienne in *John Gabriel Borkman* (1946), *Gengangere* (1947), *Hedda Gabler* (1948).

But more central to this study is the drama of Arthur Miller. Speaking at Harvard in 1953, he stated that Norway's greatest dramatist Henrik Ibsen's significance for him was "in his remorselessness, his hard logic, the clear edge of his work." A few years later he wrote in his introduction to *Collected Plays* that he learned how to make the moral world real and evident by observing Ibsen's ability to forge a play upon a factual bedrock, "a theatre of ideas like Ibsen's must discuss the complexities of life and man's fate."

Theatrical criticism is unanimous in pointing out the similarity of Miller's work to Ibsen's. Consider the following critics; Frederik Lumley, *New Trends in 20th Century Drama,* writes that Arthur Miller is the prose writer in the tradition of Henrik Ibsen; George Steiner, *The Death of Tragedy,* says that "playwrights such as Arthur Miller have observed the technical means of the Ibsen play and adapted some of the conventional and defining gestures"; Allen Lewis, *The Contemporary Theatre,* remarks on the hope of order reflected in Miller's northern austerity, and his closeness to the social concerns of Ibsen.

The source of Miller's interest in Ibsen is probably Professor Kenneth Thorpe Rowe, his drama instructor at the University of Michigan.[46] In Professor Rowe's class, Miller came into contact with Ibsenian ideas and the anatomy of play-writing. Three aspects of Ibsen's drama particularly impressed Miller: the social implications, the techniques, the economy of language. He was to express the belief that "social drama dealt with the evils which can be changed." He was to articulate a dramaturgical principle pertinent to Ibsen's dramatic idiom, that "the antecedental material is no longer introductory, but the center of the immediate conflict." Professor Rowe recalls how Miller came to him with a method of revision: the last rewriting was for the purpose of eliminating every superfluous word, and especially to eliminate expository analysis for the direct revelation of character.

The debt to Ibsen from the point of view of technique is most apparent in *Death of a Salesman*, 1949. The play was hailed as a thought-provoking social document, a drama full of psychological and sociological insight. Miller was awarded the Pulitzer Prize and the Drama Critics Award in recognition of this play which examines the downfall of Willy Loman, salesman, a man defeated by the American dream.

Through the realistic treatment of the social situation, Miller recalls Ibsen. But, what is more clearly presented in Miller's interpretation of Ibsen's "retrospective technique"[47] is an explosive situation which occurs in the present and is explained and brought to a head by something which happened in the past. In *Death*, it is Willy Loman's adultery which alienates his son, and when Willy is confronted with this reality, he is brought face to face with his own inadequacies, but he never really accepts them. *Death* parallels Ibsen's *Gengangere* in the manner in which the past is interwoven with the present. Miller's insertion of the past into the present is more expressionistic than it is with Ibsen. However, when compared to *Gengangere, Death* points up expressionism as being very much a part of Ibsen's dramatic idiom, and the condition of *the Moment* as being incompatible to Miller's dialectic.

Certain objects in *Death* activate events; for instance, the silk stockings his wife is mending stirs Willy's memory and he recalls the stockings he gave to the prostitute. In a similar way, the pipe Osvald smokes in *Gengangere* stirs the memory of Mrs. Alving and Manders; they are reminded of Captain Alving. Miller does not consider the correspondence between object and the past as flashback technique, but views it as the past distorted by the character's mind. That the memories occur simultaneously with events is more like a double exposure to Miller than a flashback. His method suggests the double reflection that is so significant in Ibsen's drama, although with Miller it occurs on a more realistic level which erases the mythic aspect.

The gradual emergence of the hotel bedroom and the prostitute has been unconsciously repressed by Willy as opposed to Mrs. Alving's conscious repression of Captain Alving's infidelity. Miller recreates the memory physically on stage, unlike Ibsen; Miller does unveil the past in interspersed fragments and the past as a dead weight on the present is amplified by word, action, and character. The past, however, does not have the same significance it did for Ibsen. Miller's concern is principally with the social environment while Ibsen is also concerned with the emergence of self. Both plays are tightly constructed and the compressed space strangles Willy. Dennis Welland, in his book on Arthur Miller, compares Miller's method with what in psychiatry is called "the return of the repressed." In *Gengangere,* Mrs. Alving's repression of the past is intentional and is illuminated by Osvald and Regine's relationship and Osvald's illness. She is not permitted to forget and that comes to have a positive value. Willy's blindness denies him transcendence as it did other Ibsen characters; he emerges as victim, done in by the capitalistic system.

Miller's social ferment led him to adapt *En folkefiende* in 1950, transferring it to a social pamphlet attacking repression and the lack of individual freedom. Although Miller calls his work a translation, the word adaptation is on the title page.

He admits to three changes: the translation of the language to a "new" spoken English, cutting some scenes which he considered uninteresting and superfluous, and changing the third act structurally (he considered Ibsen to have been guilty of over-writing). The result is a play neither Ibsen nor Miller — the language is *pidgin* English and the connotations are lost.[48] In the interest of relevancy, he ignores the stage directions and deletes lines and injects his own business into scenes, obliterating much of the poetry and some of the comic-tragic edges that are significant to Ibsen's final scene. Miller's Dr. Stockman is a crusader for democracy; his enthusiasm has been given its head with Miller.

T. E. Kalen in his review of the play in 1971 calls Miller's attempt to tone down or elevate some of the speeches an attempt to spotlight Stockman (played by Frederic March) as a pioneer spirit of the ethical life and he reminds the audience that Miller was interested in attacking McCarthyism when he wrote the play. As a result, in 1971, the play has become a tirade against the venality of small town existence rather than an examination of whether the democratic principle of majority rule may be legitimately abrogated by a single individual. Kalen also thinks that the interest in the seventies to be in the ecological aspects of the play.

Ibsen is not noticeably on the boards in the fifties although there are performances here and there; for example, Luise Ranier played in *Fruen fra Havet* in 1950 and in *Vildanden* (1952), *En Folkefiende* remained popular and *Gengangere* is performed in 1951 with Mildred Dunnock as Gina (later, she played Willy's wife in *Death of a Salesman*). A revival of interest in the sixties is created by Claire Bloom in *Et Dukkehjem* and *Hedda Gabler;* she gets a round of applause from the women. Liv Ullmann experiences the same thing with *Et Dukkehjem* in 1975 (her American debut in Ibsen), and Jane Alexander rewrites the text and plays Hilde in *Bygmester Solness* in 1976, and Robert Brustein directs *Valdanden* for the Yale Repertory Theatre in 1978.*

---

* Maggie Smith — *Hedda Gabler* 1970; Vanessa Redgrave — *The Lady from the Sea* 1979; Jane Fonda — in film version of *A Doll's House.*

Another voice is heard with Tennessee Williams, whose work affords another contrast to Ibsen. He viewed man as a Christ figure crucified for his acts suggesting the Kierkegaard image and the image Ibsen was to question in various guises. Williams' forte is in fusing the realistic scene and the symbolic act, concentrating on the existential man trying to live.

His characters attempt to escape the past; for instance, in *The Glass Menagerie,* Tom runs away but is always haunted by the image of Laura, and in *A Streetcar Named Desire* (1947), Blanche can escape only through insanity. With *Cat on a Hot Tin Roof* (1955), there is the attempt to reconcile life and death. Contingent with this idea is the idea of the life-lie, the issue Ibsen focussed on in *Vildanden* and Eugene O'Neill explored in *The Iceman Cometh.*

The question of the play's resolution must have concerned Williams since he wrote two endings to *Cat.* Although the second version was initiated by Elia Kazan, Williams' willingness to rewrite the third act but not discard the first version suggests an ambivalence. In his notes to the play, he asks the reader to decide for himself which end is the more appropriate.

The action of the play involves resolving Maggie's initial concern, which is whether she will be successful in enticing Brick to resume their marriage on a sexual basis. Her frustration gives the play its moving force and her situation is metaphorically reflected in the title of the play; she is the cat on the hot tin roof. However, the sexual act has more significance than a sexual victory for Maggie. It represents a union that has ramifications which are social and economic: the preservation of Brick's regeneration and a satisfaction of Big Daddy's desires.

There are layers of meanings and emotional nuances implicit in the work. In reflecting the tension of the attempt to reconcile life and death, *Cat* goes beyond the obvious; that is, it goes beyond Big Daddy's impending death to the need for Brick to find someone to restore life to him. The animalistic imagery of the dialogue relates to the life and death dichotomy. Whereas the play is associated with animalism, and Maggie refers to herself as Maggie the cat, it is only Brick, a somewhat weak portrayal of the individual, who is free of this imagery. He is dramatized as the moribund one in the family, the wounded one. Maggie and Big Daddy represent the ruthless life force.

Associated with the idea of life and death is the idea of the life-lie. Big Daddy says he can live with lies, Maggie can perpetuate them, and Brick can do neither. Because of his inability to accept the life-lie in any context, he drinks and retreats from the condition of living or "mendacity" as he describes it. In Act II, Brick tells Big Daddy the reason he drinks is "mendacity" and Big Daddy expresses the meaning, "Don't it mean lying and lies"? It is not a single lie but "the whole thing" that eats at Brick. Each man in his own way states the theme of the play — Brick: "Mendacity is a system we live in"; Big Daddy: "Yes, all lies . . . Lying, Dying, Liars."

At the end of the first act, Maggie's determination to have a child even by a recalcitrant husband is clearly articulated. By the end of the second act, Brick has confronted Big Daddy with the truth of his illness. The third act is very important in that *how* the play is resolved changes the shape of the drama. Elia Kazan's suggestion to change the ending was motivated by the fact that he wanted Big Daddy to reappear, Brick to change, and Maggie to be more sympathetic.

In the *first* version, the play ends pessimistically. Maggie is vital to the end and Brick is equally adamant in his rejection of her and very sure of the situation that he is up against. Big Daddy's reconciliation to his death is reduced to an "offstage shriek" and the implication is that Gooper (Big Daddy's other son) and his wife and children will inherit the plantation. Maggie's declaration that she is pregnant is an outright lie and Brick's silence suggests that he may accept the lie. If he does and Maggie is victorious in making the lie a reality, the seduction is more of a rape (his) than a willing compliance.

327

In the *second* version, Big Daddy returns and admits his end is near, "It's time for the wind to blow that ole girl away." Furthermore, Maggie is recognized as a "life-giving force" by Brick. Brick's need for Maggie is also recognized by him. The ending implies a willingness on Brick's part to accept the situation.

In the 1974 production, the third act reflects a compromise. Michael Kahn included Big Daddy in the last act and retained the first ending in the relationship between Maggie and Brick. With *Clothes for a Summer Hotel,* there is not a doubt about the ending. Zelda (in a moment of rationality) locks herself inside the "Sanitarium," separating herself from Scott who has succumbed to "mendacity."

Edward Albee, like Miller, attacks the American dream, shows the emptiness of it and the loss of man's dignity. The absurdity of the 20th century is not that of Kierkegaard — faith by virtue of the absurd — rather, it is related to Camus and the myth of Sisyphus. Man is given a few moments to breathe, not necessarily to live as the fullness of *the Moment* would give. It is enough, say Camus and Sartre, to have the breathing space and to be free. Theoretically, that is true. But, unfortunately, as Ibsen has suggested in his characterization of Maia (*Når vi Døde Vågner*) and Miller and Williams have shown, man is not developed to the highest estate so that humanism is a way of life, a point Isaac B. Singer pointed out in his Nobel Prize speech (1978).

Yet, despite evidence to the contrary, man continues to desire something more from life than mendacity. Audiences have pondered Beckett's *Waiting for Godot* (1953), embraced the sexual revolution, contemplated science fiction, drugs, meditation and jogging, hoping for an encounter of a third kind, one that would heighten their consciousness. Playwrights continue with plays of little interest and much realism. Consider the cerebral problems connected with physical strokes dramatized in Arthur Kopit's *Wings*, 1979 (although a superb performance, there is not even a tragic note on a small scale), or the *recent* blase patticake theatre of Tom Stoppard dialectically connected weakly to Wittgenstein and/or Magritte, technically perfect, impeccably timed,[49] and increasingly trite.

Two other plays on Broadway in 1979, *Whose Life Is It Anyway?* and *The Elephant Man,* are in the same vein as *Wings.* They are plays without a protagonist — sans hero or anti-hero. The first by Brian Clark is about a paralytic's right to die and the other by Bernard Pomerance concerns the plight of a deformed person. Victims of accident and birth can be heroic but such plays are not the stuff of *drama,* much less *tragedy* and they are far removed from *the Ibsen theatre aesthetic* and the comic-tragic.

There is a resurging of interest in Ibsen and Kierkegaard, especially in the young (which would please them both), that suggests that Ibsen and Kierkegaard are communicating with the individual wherever or whoever he is.

Part of the reason that Kierkegaard and Ibsen have not been given more of a hearing in America has been discussed in connection with the receptivity to Ibsen's work. With Kierkegaard, he was not translated until the thirties and the forties, and made his appearance in America, after the fact, so to speak. Whereas Ibsen's dramatic form has been marvelled at, it has not been fully appreciated because of the impediments to the interpretation that the nature of the American scene engendered. The note of optimism in Thornton Wilder's drama reflects the positive aspects of Kierkegaard, the hum of the universe which he shows as enduring. On the other side, Tennessee Williams in *Camino Real* (1953) has Kilroy's heart of gold tossed back at him and Miller's Willy sacrifices himself for his son who does not want that of him and O'Neill's Jim will lose himself in drink.

Reality is spelt with a small *r* in the 20th century. Even though the theatrical scene is, for the most part, muted, there are a few who sit in the wings, and some move about, waiting for the violins to be tuned and the music to begin: Walter

Kerr, Robert Corrigan, Robert Brustein, Peter Brooks and Ingmar Bergman. Bergman is the most positive reflection of the Kierkegaard/Ibsen consciousness in the twentieth century because it is also his own consciousness. All his films show the power of love as the requisite for life. Kierkegaard has said in *Kjerlighedens Gjerninger* that only when it is a duty to love, only then is love made eternally free in blessed independence. He is not excluding self-love, but is expressing the extension of that love — loving your neighbor as yourself.

• • • • •

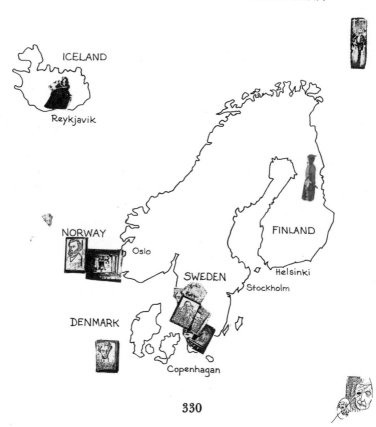

SCANDINAVIA

ICELAND

Reykjavik

NORWAY

Oslo

FINLAND

Helsinki

SWEDEN

Stockholm

DENMARK

Copenhagan

Drama in Northern Europe

Norwegian dramatic activity immediately after Ibsen was "dark" except for Gunnar Heiberg (1857-1920). His most popular work was *Tante Ulrikke* (1883), which is in the style of Ibsen's realistic dramas. Tante Ulrikke is an eccentric, a lonely fighter ruled by a self-interested minority.

The social consciousness that began in the 19th century and constantly grew placed a new emphasis on institutions in conformity with the needs of the present which led to a new individualism running parallel to socialism. Such an individualism is functional, holding that personal talents and powers must be fully developed in the interest of the self and the group.

It was not until the thirties that there was a resurgence of significant dramatic activity. Two significant dramatists are Helge Krog and Nordahl Grieg.

Helge Krog (1889-1962) attained his greatest success with psychological drama. He presents characters who are clear-cut, built up from within. He mastered the art of dialogue and in his plays, it is more important than the play-making. Like Ibsen, he shows women as stronger and more independent. *Underveis* (*On the Way*, 1931) is extremely contemporary. The main character, Cecille, is a doctor; she is independent and has joined a radical group. She becomes pregnant and wants to be a mother, and not to marry the child's father. Her attitude arouses her middle-class family and her ultra-radical friends. She is forced to accept the consequences of her belief — loneliness. The implication at first is that her rejection of conventional values is a denial — dismal, and therefore bad. However, supported by Karsten, a free thinker, she comes to regard loneliness as not being a negative force. Kierkegaard has said in "Nutiden" that the individual who suffers rejection at the hands of the public is benefitted.

Nordahl Grieg (1902-43) is concerned with groups rather than with the individual. His work is of an experimental nature and expressionistic, consisting of short scenes and re-flecting the influence of Russian theatre in the anti-capitalist message, and also the technique of epic theatre. He exploits the shock effect of placing sharply contrasting material side by side. *Vår Aere og Makt* (1935) (*Our Honor and Our Power*) is an anti-war play. It is a protest against war pro-fiteering as carried on by neutrals during World War I. The form consists of fifteen rapidly shifting scenes. Each of the scenes is concerned with essentials — no preliminaries, no slowly approached conclusions. The tableaux are tied together by the use of contrast, incidental music, and symbolistic de-vices with the personae arranged in social groups, each group representing an aspect of the group spirit: the exploiters (the shipowners) and the exploited (the ordinary seaman). Grieg's use of visual effects in contrasting scenes reinforces the play's message: the shipowners' exploitation of Norwegian sailors who died by the thousands during the war because of high profits they were promised.

With Krog the individual must work for society in the framework of some group while with Grieg the individual is functional within the group.

In post-war Norway there is no dramatist of a stature equal to Ibsen, although there are significant literary names who have also written plays — Sigrid Undset,[50] Knut Hamsun, Tarjei Vesaas, Johan Borgen. More recently there is emphasis by women on their situation.[51] Some evidence of a return to the dramatic event is seen in Peder Cappelen's *Lóki*. Self-delusion has also been a theme that has taken its impetus from *Vildanden*, i.e. Finn Bø (1893-1962), for example, *Fordi jeg elsker deg* (*Because I Love You*) which Eiliv Eide says has the Ibsenian form. Another dramatist is Axel Kielland (1907-63) who is concerned with social problems. Eide considers Finn Havervold (1905) who is best known for his radio dramas as being more in the Ibsen tradition than the others mentioned. Whereas there are indications of dramatists writing in the Ibsen tradition, and others such as Jens Bjørneboe, a polemicist — *Fugleelskerne* (*The Bird Lovers*) who focuses on the cruelty of the torturers and their kindness to animals, not one of these playwrights is in the same dimension as Ibsen.

There are indications that "social" plays and happenings in Norway and Sweden constitute the repertoire on the contemporary scene, along with the traditional pieces which Duerrenmatt was to call "museum theatre," and most certainly Ibsen has a place at Nationaltheatret. Sweden with August

Strindberg, Hjalmar Bergman, Pär Lagerkvist, encouraged, with their drama, the kind of a background that allowed the theatricality of Ingmar Bergman to coalesce with the cinematic. Bergman's vision is a distinct reflection of the Ibsen-Kierkegaard consciousness.

In Denmark, the Kierkegaardian perspective is apparent.

The Danish Kaj Munk presents an interesting contrast to Ibsen and Bjørnson with *Ordet* (*The Word,* 1925). A clergyman and a dramatist, Munk wanted to shock his audience. The play ends with a miracle — a dead woman is brought back to life by a young man who has lost his senses as a result of a personal tragedy. Another dramatist, Kjeld Abell, *Melodien der blev vaek* (*The Melody That Got Lost,* 1935) reflects his interest in theatrical experimentation (voices, masks) and makes the point that everyone must find a melody in his life. Carl Erik Soya's ("Soya") plays are written for the stage and radio; his work has a psychological orientation. He tries to be an observer and in one play *Frit Valg* (*Free Choice,* 1948) he presents two conclusions: one shows honesty as causing a series of tragedies; with the other, the dishonesty of one character brings happiness to the others. Gustav Wied is a satirist. His *Efter* (*Afterwards,* 1947) presents a tragic-comic analysis of the weakness people have for rationalization (i.e. the subject is war-profiteering). In more recent times, the situation is similar to Norway and Sweden in that the writers are not primarily dramatists. With Klaus Rifberg's *Hvad en mand har brug for* (*What a Man Needs,* 1966), the form is interesting in that it shifts from the stage reality to the play within a play, not unlike Pirandello's *Six Characters In Search of An Author.* In the seventies, radio and television have preëmpted drama, but the results are not works of lasting interest.

While Aleksis Kivi is considered to be the father of Finnish drama and Minna Canth is referred to as a female Ibsen, Finnish drama is following the tendency of drama elsewhere, but there is a flowering of native drama. Modern Icelandic drama was not regarded as significant until the 1950's when the plays of Agnar Thordarson and Halldor Laxness were written. Laxness, a Nobel Prize winner, is primarily a novelist, his subjects — social criticism. Earlier, Guthmundur Kamban wrote plays concerned with psychological relationships in marriage somewhat in the Ibsen tradition; his themes also concern the nature of justice in a social situation.

334

Other European Drama

In Europe, Ibsen has always been better understood than in America. Germany, Italy, Russia (even China, Japan), found his subject matter significant but controversial. The French appreciated his form from the beginning, as did the Spanish, although the idea of developing exposition backwards was opposed to French logic.[52] Maurice Maeterlinck's dramatic idiom is a language of the soul that admits to the compelling force of love, his intruder (*L'intruse*) is Death. Later, with the advent of Sartre's atheistic existentialism, Ibsen has not enjoyed the same popularity he enjoyed under the auspices of Lugné-Poe who became the avowed Ibsen expert in France. The objectivity of Sartre (*Huis Clos*) and the softness of Giraudoux (*Ondine*) are contrasted by the eroticism of Jean Genet *(Les Bonnes)*, who inverts the immediacy of the Moment in ritualistic drama, the impact of which led Sartre to call him Saint Genet. Samuel Beckett, a Dublin Irishman living in France, writing in French and translating his own work into English, emphasizes an un-Kierkegaardian stasis and dramatizes what happens when nothing happens, epitomized by *Waiting for Godot*.

In Spain, Ibsen's dramaturgy made an impression and left its mark on Spanish dramatic form. But the Spanish audiences do not enjoy psychological and intellectual problems in drama.

The drama of Garcia Lorca is theatrically effective and impeccably constructed, yet is pessimistic and paralyzing in its sense of defeat, even more so than *Når Vi Døde Vågner*. Lorca reiterates in his work the barrenness that thwarts the fulfillment of life, correlating the Castilian code of honor and Catholicism. The resolution does not allow for a multilayered interpretation.

Ibsen was not really acknowledged in Germany until Otto Brahm in 1904 became director of the Lessingtheater in Berlin. Then Ibsen became an integral part of modern German drama. See the Chronology entry on Meiningen.

As has been previously mentioned, George Bernard Shaw (an Irishman by birth) was Ibsen's spokesman in England. His *St. Joan* reflects the significance of *choice* and the ending as having a transcendent intention. T. S. Eliot and W. H. Auden have been similarly appreciative and have written about Ibsen.[53] Eliot demonstrated in *The Cocktail Party* myth on the modern stage, introducing into this play "guardians" who suggest the visitant, Hilde (*Bygmester Solness*). Choice is dramatized and two actions on different levels of reality are shown simultaneously.

Contained in *Beltaine,* the literary journal of the Irish Literary Theatre (1894), is a statement by Edward Martyn, George Moore and William Butler Yeats that acknowledges Norway as an inspiration and an example. Martyn, Moore and Yeats thought highly of Ibsen. Another dramatist, John Millinton Synge, differed in his estimate and called Ibsen joyless and depressing. Sean O'Casey was interested in the fatal part that the "life-lie" played in human existence. O'Casey did not accept the "lie" as constructive. It was his conviction that the lie was a debilitating factor in Irish life and as much an oppressor as the British (Juno and the Paycock).

Each of the dramatic considerations in the preceding discussion illuminates some aspect of the Ibsen aesthetic and marks its individuality.

336

However, it is the comic-tragic that is the essence of modern drama (see Chapter II) and this mode was succinctly articulated by Kierkegaard and Ibsen. While Martin Esslin refers to the tragic-comic as the genre of modern drama, he views tragic-comic plays as both tragedies and comedies, which constantly switch from one form to another within the same play. His designation is an over-simplification and is perhaps understandable since he uses a literary term as his reference point. There are not two forms acting independently — or is it the deliberate admixture of the comic and the tragic that qualifies the nature of modern drama. There is pain in the comic and comedy in the tragic, yet there is not a unity. It is preferable to view the dramatic mode of Ibsen as *comic-tragic* because the pain issues from the bittersweet distortion conveyed by the masks of tragedy and comedy superimposed on each other; the result is dissonance and paradox. Two of the immediate exponents of the comic-tragic mode are Anton Chekhov and Luigi Pirandello.[54]

But, returning to the American scene, because that is the perspective that affords a succinct contrast to this consideration of Ibsen's theatre aesthetic and dramatic art, it is appropriate to say initially the tragic-comic was recognized in Ibsen, not the comic-tragic, and that is the tragedy of the American scene. By initially violating the ending, whether through naiveté, prudence, or misunderstanding, Ibsen has not been fully appreciated and may have even been a distorting focus to some of that which is thought to be modern drama.

The future for modern drama had not been determined and the nature of the American consciousness — its vivacity and spirit, even its gullibility — (which has reached fruition in the musical comedy)[55] is its strength, and this life force suggests that in America the fullness of *the Moment* could occur because in America there is a spontaneity and a hope for the future of the American dream, that — by virtue of the *absurd* — has not dimmed. To go beyond the kind of absurdity of a Eugene Ionesco (comedy arising out of the

337

deadness of life) and the extinction of Samuel Beckett, it may
be that "Bevaegelsen er tilbage."* (See The Dialectic, Chapter III.)

---

* the movement is back

In this interpretation it is *Existence,* not organized religion, that has been the concern of Kierkegaard and Ibsen. The god (Guden) is a personification of that which makes all the difference to them (and in the latter twentieth century, most insistently expressed by Ingmar Bergman's cinematic "theatre")[56] — the quality of life itself — *love.* Even when it seems to be underground, *the qualitative difference,* which gives meaning to existence and to Ibsen's dramatic art, echoes and re-echoes in his theatre.

NOTES TO CHAPTER V

1 Bjørnson speech, 1881 — Norway's Constitutional Struggle.

2 *De Tre* Bergliet Ibsen.

3 Harold Larson, Bjørnstjerne Bjørnson, *"A Study in Norwegian Nationalism."*

4 Martin Lamm, *Modern Drama.*

5 Bjørnson and Ibsen were interested in creating a truly national dramatic art. "Bjørnstjerne Bjørnson Som Teatermann" by Øyvind Anker, Oslo: H. Aschehoug & Company, *Edda* 1960.

6 "The Influences of Shakespeare on Wergeland, Ibsen, Bjørnson" by Francis Bull.

7 "Bjørnson and his Plays" by Kemp Malone.

8 Nobel Prize Speech. In reference to the moral responsibility of the artist, Bjørnson differs from Kierkegaard, Ibsen, and Maritain in one important way. In relation to *purity of heart* as a natural consequence of the life lived and reflected in the poet's work, they did not see it as a contrivance to legislate morals.

9 *En Fallit* — Martin Lamm.

10 The emancipation of women is treated in *Leonarda* (1879), the first feminist play about a woman's right to divorce. Two people who do not love one another are thrown together.

[11] The description of Norway's nationalism is similar to America's in that both are a product of rebellion and a democratic belief as set forth in their Constitutions. Bjørnson shows the paradox that De Tocqueville envisoned in 1853 — the individual and democracy — which Norway has resolved in the 20th century and which America has not, and understandably so.

[12] See Chapter II — "Norway's Constitutional Struggle."

[13] Bjørnson's speech on Norwegian literature. An understanding of the *outcast* in society is the focus Jean Genet dramatizes, his perversity an ethical stance inverted. Sartre referred to him as St. Genet.

[14] "Replique" — line in a play.

[15] He might have added "the replique" in its accompanying condition — indicating other linguistic features: the pauses, inflection, rhythm, rate, stress, mood, et al. *and* the open space which is another dimension in the dramatic idiom.

[16] See Chapter IV.

[17] See footnote 26 also.

[18] Shift in American theatre — classical repertoire to spectacle and melodrama.

[19] American romanticism in art — akin to Norwegian.

[20] American theatrical current became more receptive to continental drama.

[21] *America on Stage,* John F. Kennedy Center for the Performing Arts, 1976.

[22] Fife and Anstensen, "Henrik Ibsen on the American Stage."

[23] Dion Boucicault, quote is from *The Romance of the American Theatre,* Crawford.

[24] "Plays of American Character." See *The Stage in America,* Norman Hapgood, 1901, p. 53.

[25] *Ibid.*

[26] The Syndicate was a monopoly that started in 1895 and lasted for ten years with six men representing different sections of the country.

[27] A requisite of the Syndicate School.

[28] Review, *New York Times,* 1891, May 10. "There is no demand for Ibsen here."

[29] James A.. Herne, 1839-1901, actor-manager-playwright — he saw moral purpose in drama.

[30] English did not accept Ibsen until Archer and Shaw promoted him.

[31] William Archer — Ibsen translator; J. T. Grein — inspired by the example of Antoine founded Independent Theatre Club in London; George Moore — one of original founders of Irish Literary Theatre; Henry James — wrote *The Scenic Art* — scattered writing on theatre; Sir Beerbohm Tree — 1843-1917, founder of Royal Academy of Dramatic Art.

[32] Mme Modjeska had performed the role in Poland the previous year. The play had had its first showing in America in Milwaukee at the Grand Opera House on June 2, 1882. It had been inspired by Professor Rasmus B. Anderson of the University of Wisconsin and the actors were amateurs.

340

[33] *Memories and Impressions,* Helena Modjeska.

[34] *Mrs. Fiske and the American Theatre,* Archie Binns — book on American stage.

[35] World première in America on May 20, 1882 — presented in Norwegian at Turner Hall, Chicago, with Fru Helga Bluhme as Mrs. Alving.

[36] William Dean Howells, "The Ibsen Influence."

[37] *Ibid.* ..

[38] William Winter, "Ibsenites and Ibsenism."

[39] "The Tendencies of the American Stage" by Daniel Frohman.

[40] *Ibid.*

[41] Mrs. Fiske and the American Theatre, Archie Binns, *op cit.*

[42] October 29, 1906 — the first performance in English. Mansfield used his own script.

[43] *Anna Christie* (1921). Anna is a Swedish-American girl, a prostitute who appears to undergo a conversion. The role was recreated by Liv Ullmann on Broadway in 1977, directed by José Quinterro.

[44] The presentation at Lincoln Center, New York City (October, 1979), underplayed the ending.

[45] Cited in *The Plays of Thornton Wilder* by Donald Haberman. In an address to the American Academy of Arts in 1948, he acknowledges Kierkegaard and says, "The artist is under no compulsion to balance the books of good and evil." ..

[46] Miller went to the University in the thirties with the help of Federal support funds. He dedicated his recent book of theatrical essays (1978) to Professor Rowe.

[47] Expression used to describe Ibsen's juxtapositing of the past and the present.

[48] Miller does not consider the loss to be of any significance.

[49] Tom Stoppard's earlier plays are rich verbally and structurally, suggesting intellectual games and theatrical action that is concerned with getting behind the scenes, questioning the nature of the real world. In his first notable play, *Rosenkrantz and Guildenstern are Dead,* the concentration is on the nonentities who were to dispose of Hamlet, rather than on Hamlet. More recently, his work has grown increasingly superficial, especially *Dogg's Hamlet* and *Cahoot's Macbeth.* There is some indication of an attempt to re-establish himself as a credible playwright in *Night and Day.*

[50] Sigrid Undset wrote two plays for the puppet theatre and a play for the radio. The study of these works including analysis, history, interpretation and re-creation in the theatrical milieu and translation is a work by Jane Ellert Tammany in progress, to be published.

[51] For instance, Bjørg Vik's *To Akter for fem Kvinner (Two Acts For Five Women).*

[52] The French production of *Gengangere* and *Vildanden* were first presented by Antoine. Later, Lugné-Poe became the avowed expert of Ibsen. Poe favored the rise of Symbolism against the Naturalism of the day.

[53] Auden in an essay on Kierkegaard says that the act of faith is an

341

act of choice which no one can do for another, p. 178, *Forewords and Afterwords.*

54 Chekhov is often compared to Ibsen. His dramatic idiom is dominated by the pause — the pause before the outburst. Pirandello was drawn to the nature of truth — the reality and illusion of life, and the reality of reason. The elusiveness of truth is demonstrated in the play *Right You Are If You Think You Are.*

55 American musical comedy has been internationally recognized.

56 Essays treating Ingmar Bergman by this author (Tammany): The Figural Reality of Ingmar Bergman's 'Dance of the Dead' (1976) — cinematic art and interpretation; The Theatricality of Ingmar Bergman (1979); Henrik Ibsen and Ingmar Bergman: The Theatrical Aesthetic and the Cinematic Vision (1980); also Ingmar Bergman/August Strindberg — *Drömspelet (A Dream Play), Spöksonaten (The Ghost Sonata)* (1974).

Epilogue

" når vi døde vågner" ...

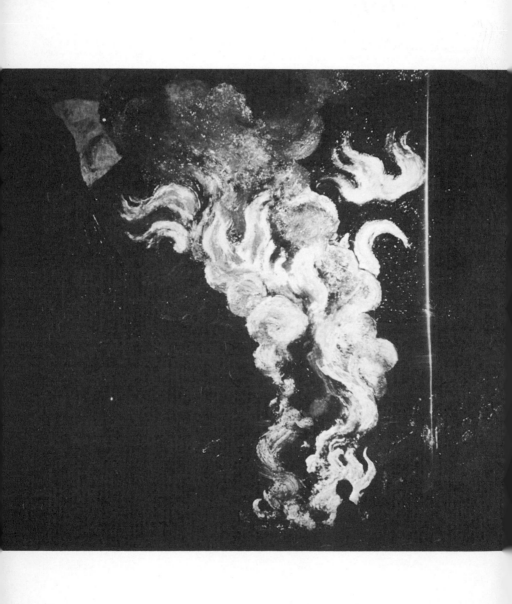

The Future

Ibsen's future is our present and it would appear that the note of disenchantment that ends *Når vi døde Vågner* has gone full cycle. The future that Ibsen posited in *Kejser og Galilaeer* — nobility of mind and spirit — is as far away as it was in his and Kierkegaard's day; contemporary life and "humanism" has supplied the corroboration. In remote places, one or two little glimmers of humanism and spiritual sovereignty exists. In contrast, science and technology and the population have doubled, quadrupled, and exploded. In the bloc view of life, the individual, as Kierkegaard predicted in "Nutiden," has all but been obliterated. In its place, the George Orwell complex, the Big Daddy of Williams' *Cat*, the nihilistic silence of Beckett, the games of Genet, the concentration on self — Sartre, and the fragmented emotional outbursts of "art," the pseudo-logical and technical superiority of Stoppard, the therapeutic drama of Kopit (*Wings*) — almost overwhelm Wilder's celebration of life, the exquisite beauty of a Balanchine ballet, the poetry of Bergman's cinematic theatre, and the perfection of Singer's prose aesthetic.[1]

Kierkegaard wrote in the 1850's that he reads and reads and while there is noise enough, there is nothing but empty noise pretending to be something. Ibsen, in writing about the ballad in 1857, recognizes that the present age is lacking in anything that can be said to be a poetic impulse. That is why he suggests, not a return to the past, but a consideration of an earlier consciousness when life was less complicated, when extraneous things did not overwhelm. He also points out that the ballads are a later form of the mythical poems of ancient times, which is significant to the premise of Chapter II.

The nobility of mind and spirit that Julian envisions is not a pagan-Christian synthesis, but is the fruition of the principles of the *New Testament,* which Kierkegaard calls *existence,* articulated in the theatrical context by Ibsen (and more recently by Ingmar Bergman). In the theatre, its dimension has not been present for a long time, even with Peter Brooks' attempts to return to the "religious" in his theatrical experiments. Ibsen's Julian rejects paganism, philosophy, and Christendom (but not the premise of Christianity). Through a series of misunderstandings and catastrophes, he is bewildered and confused. He, unlike the Kierkegaardian man, cannot experience contemporaneity –– the immediacy of existence through the fullness of the *Moment.* Ibsen has shown the difficulty of extricating one's self from delusion and the impediments to awareness.

The "modernism" that Krutch referred to, and before him Brandes, is that which is different from anything ever entertained before. In point of fact, it is still germinating and it still takes the devastation that Ibsen dramatized in *Kejser og Galilaeer* on a grand scale, and on a personal level in other plays, before the "Ragnarok" or "new birth" can occur.

What audiences today respond to in Ibsen's drama is an essence that is poetic. Strip away the social trappings, the outgrown convention, and the essence is still significant as it is beautiful. When nobility of mind and will is expressed in *Vildanden* as something of the future, it is not the will of force that is meant, but that of love — reflecting *purity of heart* as willing one thing — the god-idea.

Ibsen articulates inversely but consistently (as does Bergman) Kierkegaard's "fellowship of buried lives" — and they suggest that "når vi døde vågner" (when we dead awaken) Julian's third empire can be realized. It is then that the individual will be understood and accepted. Until then there are not any knots to unravel or to hold things together. As Mrs. Alving said in *Ghosts* — there is only machine stitching.[2]

[1] Singer has co-authored a play (based on one of his short stories). It was performed in New York, December 1979 — title — *Teibele and Her Demon*.

[2] In Tennessee Williams' "ghost" play, *Clothes For A Summer Hotel* (1980), the individual is an anachronism. Zelda's pain is intensified because no one really cares. There is not the sorrow that is created by Eugene O'Neill in his last play *Moon for the Misbegotten* (1960); O'Neill's final scene has the prostrate Jim in the loving arms of Josie. With Williams, Zelda's refuge is "the sanitarium" — she is not "waiting for Godot" or looking for an "exit" — and Scott will go back to California where his clothes are appropriate.

Tableaux Vivants
(Levende Bilder)

A Consideration of the Sphere

<u>Staging</u> the Possibility

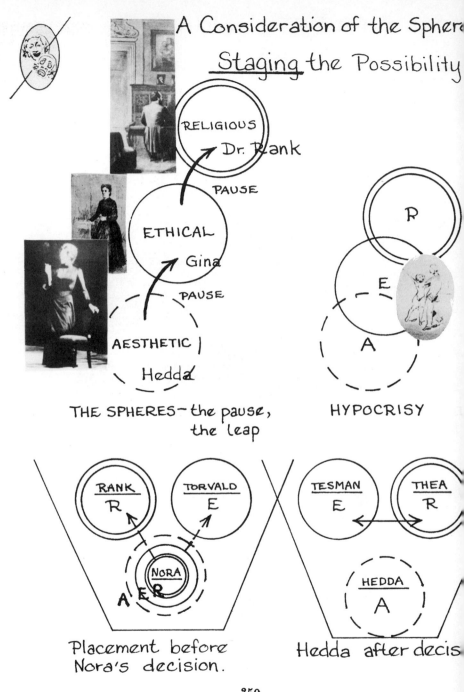

RELIGIOUS

Dr. Rank

PAUSE

ETHICAL

Gina

PAUSE

AESTHETIC

Hedda

THE SPHERES — the pause, the leap

R

E

A

HYPOCRISY

RANK
R

TORVALD
E

NORA

A E R

Placement before
Nora's decision.

TESMAN
E

THEA
R

HEDDA
A

Hedda after decis

350

of Existence and the Theatrical –
and the Actuality.

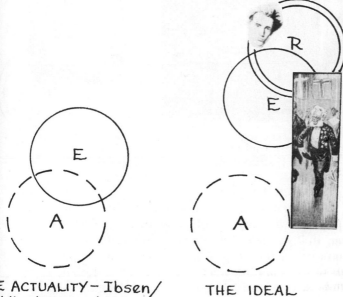

R

E

E

A

A

E ACTUALITY – Ibsen/
Kierkegaard Milieu

THE IDEAL

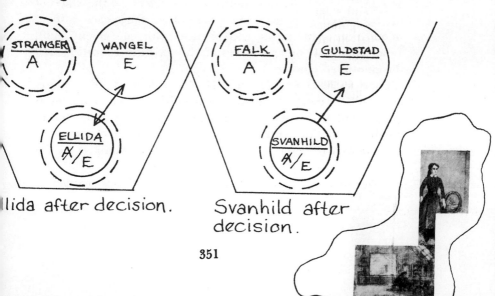

STRANGER
A

WANGEL
E

FALK
A

GULDSTAD
E

ELLIDA
A/E

SVANHILD
A/E

lida after decision.

Svanhild after
decision.

351

"O Du Fornuft-Karrikatur, som draeber
Med Galskabs Hallingdands paa Vennelaeber!"*

The staging brings the spheres of existence that each person
is in into relief (aesthetic, ethical, religious), that is, it indicates the response to a stage of life (*Staadier paa Livets Vei*).
For instance in *Kjaerlighedens Komedie* the religious expression (the fullness of *the Moment*) is missing and the possibility is negated by Svanhild when she chooses Guldstad, and
Falk does not advance on Life's road at all. The division of
the stage in an Ibsen play shows the division within the characterization, the division between characters — the stage of
life the character is at. — the sphere of existence each is in —
in addition to indicating with silence, color, movement, light,
(and sound) — other degrees of the existing condition and
the emotional climate.

Consider *Et Dukkehjem* and *Hedda Gabler* where by placement and staging — the sphere of existence the character is
in is heightened visually, the image commenting upon the individual situation with the drama becoming, at times, a virtual comedy of errors. (See preceding page.) Rank is in the

---

* "The grinning caricature of prudence a deadly danse macabre on
friendly lips."

352

religious sphere, Torvald is on the ethical plane and Nora hovers between the two. Rank disappears (as did Ellida's Stranger and Svanhild's Falk) when the definitive choice is made, while Hedda removes herself and Tesman and Thea advance on life's road.

The Ingmar Bergman production of *Hedda Gabler,* starring Maggie Smith, presents Hedda — cigarette in hand, sensuous against the background of red (not unlike the interior scenes of *Viskningär och rop*)* with the stage space division accentuating her alienation. Bergman uses parallel action, and then by freezing the action of the other characters, he emphasizes the dichotomy between them. When Hedda puts the gun to her head, the act is "live" theatre and even though Brack is incredulous, the audience is not.

The tableaux here are an indication of a point when an individual is in some throes of *Øieblikket/*Øieblikket and as each play demonstrates a stage on life's way — so it is with the tableaux, presenting *levende bilder* that imitate an action.

---

* Cries and Whispers.

355

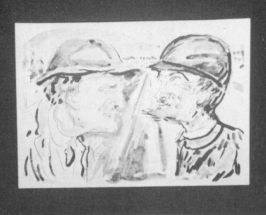

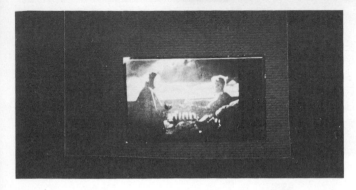

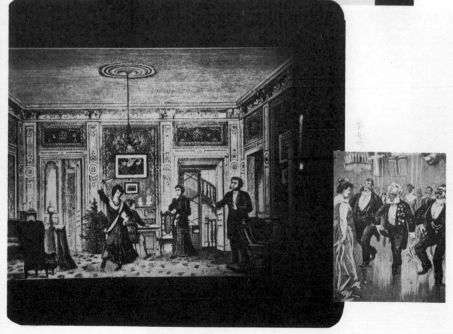

357

361

363

364

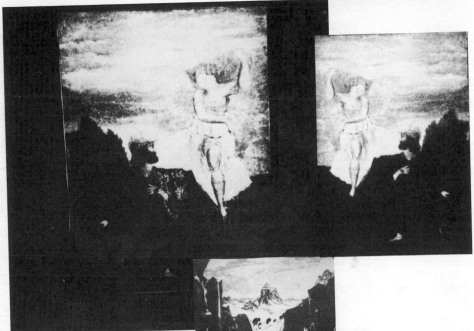

366

SØREN AABYE KIERKEGAARD

SAMLEDE VAERKER

6. BIND

Philosophiske Smuler by Johannes Climacus —
Edited by S. Kierkegaard . Begrebet Angest by
Victor Haufniensis — Edited by S. Kierkegaard   1844
(Philosophical Fragments. The Concept of Dread)
Tre Taler ved taenkte Leiligheder by S. Kierkegaard   1845
(Three Discourses on Imagined Occasions)

7. BIND

Staadier paa Livets Vei. Første halvbind — Edited by
Hilarius Bogbinder   1845
(Stages on Life's Way. First volume)

8. BIND

Staadier paa Livets Vei. Andet halvbind
(Stages on Life's Way. Second volume)

9. BIND

Afsluttende uvidenskabelig Efterskrift. Første
halvbind by Johannes Climacus — Edited by
S. Kierkegaard   1846
(Concluding Unscientific Postscript. First volume)

10. BIND

Afsluttende uvidenskabelig Efterskrift. Andet
halvbind
(Concluding Unscientific Postscript. Second volume)

11. BIND

Opbyggelige Taler i forskjellig Aand by
S. Kierkegaard   1847
(Edifying Discourses of Varied Tenor)

12. BIND

Kjerlighedens Gjerninger by S. Kierkegaard   1847
(Works of Love)

13. BIND

Christelige Taler by S. Kierkegaard   1848
(Christian Discourses)

14. BIND

18. BIND

Om min Forfatter-Virksomhed by S. Kierkegaard 1851
(On my Work as an Author)
Synspunktet for min Forfatter-Virksomhed by
S. Kierkegaard 1848
(The Point of View for My Work as an Author) —
published posthumously 1859
Bladartikler 1842-54
(Newspaper Articles)

19. BIND

Bladartikler 1854-55 I-XX
(Newspaper Articles)
Øieblikket nr. 1-10 — Hvad Christus dømmer 1855
(The Instant no. 1-10 — What Christ's Judgment
is About)
Guds Uforanderlighed by S.K. 1855
(The Unchangeableness of God)

20. BIND

Terminologisk Ordbog ved J. Himmelstrup
(Terminology)

NOTE: The *diagonal* is not used in the translation of *Enten* — *Eller*
(page 1) as is customary (i.e., Either/Or) because the *dash* had a
conceptual significance for Kierkegaard. It represented a *pause*, a thought
mark, rather than *and/or*.

SØREN KIERKEGAARD
Alphabetical List of Titles

Af en endnu Levendes Papirer by S.K.*   1838
(From the Papers of One Still Living)
Afsluttende uvidenskabelig Efterskrift. Første halvbind   1846
   by Johannes Climacus — Edited by S. Kierkegaard
(Concluding Unscientific Postscript. First volume)
Afsluttende uvidenskabelig Efterskrift. Andet halvbind
(Concluding Unscientific Postscript. Second volume)
Atten opbyggelige Taler   1845
(Eighteen Edifying Discourses)
Bladartikler 1842-54
(Newspaper Articles)
Bladartikler 1854-55 I-XX
(Newspaper Articles)
Christelige Taler by S. Kierkegaard   1848
(Christian Discourses)
Dømmer selv: published posthumously   1876
(Judge for Yourself)
En literair Anmeldelse by S.K.   1846
(A Literary Review)
En opbggelig Tale by S. Kierkegaard   1850
(An Edifying Discourse)

---

* The author or editor designations follow Kierkegaard's own writings.

Staadier paa Livets Vei. Andet halvbind
(Stages on Life's Way. Second volume)
Sygdommen til Døden by Anti-Climacus,   1849
   published by S.K.
(Sickness unto Death)
Synspunktet for min Forfatter-Virksomhed   1848
   by S. Kierkegaard
(The Point of View for My Work as an Author) —   1859
   published posthumously
Terminologisk Ordbog ved J. Himmelstrup
(Terminology)
Til Selvprøvelse, Samtiden anbefalet by S. Kierkegaard   1850
(For Self-examination)
To Taler ved Altergangen om Fredagen   1851
   by S. Kierkegaard
(Two Discourses at Communion on Friday)
Tre Taler ved taenkte Leiligheder by S. Kierkegaard   1845
(Three Discourses on Imagined Occasions)
Tvende ethisk-religieuse Smaa Afhandlinger by H.H.   1849
(Two Minor Ethics — Religious Essays)
"Yppestepraesten" — Tolderen" — Synderinden" by
   S. Kierkegaard   1849
("The High Priest" — "The Publican" —
   "The Woman Who Was a Sinner")

373

HENRIK JOHANN IBSEN

PLAYS AND PREMIERES

PLAY	PREMIÈRE DATE
CATILINA Drama i tre Acter af Brynjolf Bjarme 1850 DRAMA I TRE AKTER AF HENRIK IBSEN 1875 presented by Ludvig Josephson, —Nya Teatern i Stockholm —unsuccessful	3 December 1881
KJAEMPEHØIEN	26 September 1850
DRAMATISK DIGTNING I 1 ACT AF BRYNJOLF BJARME 1850 Kristiania Norske Theater Dramatisk Digtning i een Act af Henrik Ibsen 1853	2 January 1854

NOTE: Spelling of titles and textual descriptions of plays are from the SAMLEDE VERKER (Centennial edition). Oslo: Gyldendal Norsk Forlag, MCMXXIII.

	PREMIÈRE
PLAY	DATE

Det norske Theater i Bergen
(revised version 1853)
—less than successful
—two performances
—original title NORMANERNE

NORMA
ELLER (or)
DEN POLITIKERS KJAERLIGHED   Not performed
1851
MUSIK-TRAGEDIE I TRE AKTER
Parody of members of Storting-inspired
by Bellini opera — not intended for
performance.

SANCTHANSNATTEN   2 January 1853
EVENTYRCOMEDIE I TRE ACTER
AF HENRIK IBSEN
1852 (Published in 1909
Efterladte Skrifter)
Det norske Theater i Bergen
produced by Ibsen
—He wrote a prologue asking for leni-
ency; audience not lenient because of expense and disappointment — whistling and
shushing — house empty at next performance

Fru Inger til Østeraad   2 January 1855
Historisk drama i fem Akter
af Henr. Ibsen
1855

SKUESPILL I FEM HANDLINGER
AF HENRIK IBSEN
1874
—failure
—taken off after second performance

Gildet paa Solhoug   2 January 1856
Skuespil i tre Akter af Henrik Ibsen
1856

PLAY	PREMIÈRE DATE

Det norske Theater i Bergen
—his first success in the theatre
—six performances

OLAF LILJEKRANS   2 January 1857
SKUESPIL I 3 AKTER
AF HENR. IBSEN
1857
(Published, in German 1898, in
Norwegian in 1902)
Det norske Theater i Bergen
—not as successful as *Gildet*
—Ibsen producer and costume designer
—last of plays he produced in Bergen

NOTE: ALL THE PLAYS UP TO THIS POINT, EXCEPT FOR THE
FIRST, AND *NORMA* WERE FOR FOUNDATION DAY CELEBRA-
TIONS.

FRAGMENTS:

RYPEN I JUSTEDAL
(*The Ptarmigan in Justedal*)
NATIONALT SKUESPIL I FIRE
ACTER — incomplete — 1 and ½ acts.
AF BRYNJOLF BJARME
1850 (rewritten as *Olaf Liljekrans* in 1857)

FJELDFUGLEN (*The Mountain Bird*)
ROMANTISK OPERA I TRE AKTER
AF HENR. IBSEN
1859
Incomplete — first act and part of second.

SVANHILD
Komedie i 3 Akter
AF HENRIK IBSEN
1860
It was rewritten later as *Kjaerlighedens
Komedie*

BRAND
UTKAST I EPISK FORM —
a fragment 1864-65

PLAY	PREMIÈRE DATE

HAERMAENDENE PAA HELGELAND 24 November 1858
SKUESPIL I FIRE HANDLINGER
AF HENRIK IBSEN
1858, 1873
Det norske Theater i Kristiania
—house full
—success

Kjaerlighedens Komedie 24 November 1873
Komedie i tre Akter af
Henr. Ibsen (1862)
*première ten years later
artistic director Ludvig Josephson
Christiania Theater
—popular success
—based on short prose version written 1860

Kongs=Emnerne
Historisk Skuespil i fem Akter 17 January 1864
af Henr. Ibsen
1863

KONGS=EMNERNE
HISTORISK SKUESPIL I FEM AKTER
AF HENRIK IBSEN
1870
produced by Ibsen
—well received
—eight performances

BRAND June 1867
ET DRAMATISK DIGT AF
HENRIK IBSEN
1866
*première or production nearly twenty
years later — although Act IV had appeared to mark jubilee or benefit
occasions — 1866, 1867
1st Student's Union (1866)

| | PREMIÈRE |
| PLAY | DATE |

2nd Christiania Theater (June 26, 1867)
Première of entire performance in
Stockholm
Nye Teatern
Stockholm première in Swedish
translation
Nye Teatern (Ludvig Josephson)
—performance from half-past six
in the evening until a quarter past one
in the morning

PEER GYNT   24 February 1876
Et Dramatisk Digt af Henrik Ibsen
1867
Christiania Theater
—cut
—Grieg score
  —produced by Ludvig Josephson

DE UNGES FORBUND   18 October 1869
Lystspil I Fem Akter
af Henrik Ibsen
1869
1st performance Kristiania Theater
—well received
—demonstrations and counter-demonstra-
tions at second and third performance,
i.e. political implications
—The play was to become the most popular of his works in Kristiania in the
nineteenth century

KEJSER OG GALILAEER   5 December 1896
Et Verdenhistorisk Skuespil
af Henrik Ibsen
1873
Dramatic reading by Andreas Isachsen
in 1873

PLAY	PREMIÈRE DATE

1st performance 1896
Stadttheater in Leipzig
—4 hour performance
—adaptation by Leopold Adler
6 acts, 1st 4 devoted to Caesar's Apostasy
(omitting apparently the second act,
set in Athens)
Norwegian première Nationaltheatret
March 20, 1903

SAMFUNDETS STØTTER   18 November 1877
SKUESPIL I FIRE AKTER
AF HENRIK IBSEN
1877
Opening performance Det Kongelige
    teater, København
—reported earlier performance Odense by
a Danish company which had performing
rights for the provinces
Norwegian première
Det norske Theater i Bergen   30 November 1877

ET DUKKEHJEM
SKUESPIL I TRE ACTER   21 December 1879
AF HENRIK IBSEN
1879
Première Det Kongelige Teater,
København Norwegian première —
Kristiania Theater   20 January 1880

GENGANGERE   20 May 1882
ET FAMILJEDRAMA I TRE AKTER
AF HENRIK IBSEN
1881
Première in America in original
Norwegian
Aurora Turner Hall, Chicago with
Helga von Bluhme as Mrs. Alving

	PREMIÈRE
PLAY	DATE

presented by Danish-American Society
—Scandinavian theatre would not touch it
—August Lindberg, Swedish actor-manager responsible for bringing it to
Scandinavia — Aug. 28, 1883,
Helsingsborg, Sweden
Norwegian première — Møllergaten   17 October 1883

EN FOLKEFIENDE   13 January 1883
Skuespil i fem Akter
af Henrik Ibsen
1882
1st performed at Christiania Theater
—received favorably but not a greatly
enthusiastic reception in Scandinavia
in its early days

VILDANDEN   9 January 1885
SKUESPIL I FEM AKTER
AF HENRIK IBSEN
1884
1st performance Bergen
Den Nationale Scene
11 January, Christiania Theater
In Rome, 1892, howled down by audience

ROSMERSHOLM   •17 January 1887
SKUESPIL I FIRE AKTER
AF HENRIK IBSEN
1886
1st performed in Bergen
Den Nationale Scene
—moderate success
—baffled critics

FRUEN FRA HAVET   12 February 1888
Skuespil i fem Akter
af Henrik Ibsen
1888

PLAY	PREMIÈRE DATE

Christiania Theater — with
Laura Gundersen as Ellida
—première simultaneously in
Kristiania and Weimar
—failed on stage

HEDDA GABLER   31 January 1891
Skuespil i fire Akter
af Henrik Ibsen
1890
première at the Residentztheater
in Munich
—not well done
—Ibsen present — displeased with
declamatory manner of Marie Ramlo
—audience baffled
—hissing
—Ibsen took a curtain call
—at Kristiania Theater   26 February 1891

Bygmester Solness   19 January 1893
SKUESPIL I TRE AKTER
AF HENRIK IBSEN
1892
two premières simultaneously
Lessing Theater in Berlin   January 1893
and in Trondhjeim which had provincial
rights (William Petersen's Company)
It failed in Berlin
—1st successful production in London
with American-born actress,
Elizabeth Robins

LILLE EYOLF   12 January 1895
SKUESPIL I TRE AKTER
AF HENRIK IBSEN
1894

| | PREMIÈRE |
| PLAY | DATE |

Deutsches Teater Berlin
Norwegian Kristiania Theater   15 January 1895
—36 performances

JOHN GABRIEL BORKMAN   10 January 1897
Skuespil i fire Akter
af Henrik Ibsen
1896
—one performance in London
14 December at Avenue Theatre
—première Helsinki, Finland at both
Swedish and Finnish theatres
—Norwegian performance (première)
Drammen by August Lindberg's part-
Swedish and part-Norwegian company
—sold out   19 January 1897
—Kristiania performance 25 January
with Ibsen present on first night

NÅR VI DØDE VÅGNER   26 January 1900
En dramatisk epilog i tre Akter
af Henrik Ibsen
1899
Hofteater in Stuttgart
—in Norway, presented after Copenhagen
at Nationaltheatret   6 February 1900
—not a great success

AMERICAN PREMIÈRES

Date		Performance in America
1850	CATILINA	
1850	WARRIOR'S BARROW (originally *The Norseman*)	
1855	LADY INGER OF ØSTRÅT	
1856	THE FEAST AT SOLHOUG	
1857	OLAF LILJEKRANS	
1858	THE VIKINGS AT HELGELAND Empire Theatre, New York (March 22) Matinee given by the students of the American Academy of Dramatic Art	1907
1862	LOVE'S COMEDY Hudson Theatre, New York (March 23)	1908
1863	THE PRETENDERS Given by an amateur dramatic club (Review of Reviews 34:39)	1904
1866	BRAND New Theatre, New York (April 3) Act IV, scene between Brand and the mayor omitted	1909
1867	PEER GYNT Grand Opera, Chicago (October 29)	1906
1869	LEAGUE OF YOUTH	
1873	EMPEROR AND GALILEAN	

1877 THE PILLARS OF SOCIETY 1879 (G)   1891
March 6, 1891 — the first performance in
English in America was given by Frank-
lin Sargent's students aided by several
professional artists.

Date	Performance in America

1879 A DOLL'S HOUSE   1883
Macauley's Theatre, Louisville, Kentucky
Mme. Modjeska gave a performance of
the play and changed the name of it and
the heroine to THORA. The ending was
also changed — a happy ending.

1881 GHOSTS   1882 (N)   1894
May 20, 1882 — world première
in America — presented by Norwegian-
Danish society at Turner Hall,
Chicago, with Fru Helga Bluhme as
Mrs. Alving.   .
The first English performance in
America in 1894 in New York
(Goodfriend and company (with Mrs.
Ida Jeffreys as Helene Alving.

1882 AN ENEMY OF THE PEOPLE   1895
Abbey's Theatre, New York (April 8)
March at Chicago Grand Opera House

1884 THE WILD DUCK   1895 (G)   1918
Plymouth Theatre, New York (March 11)
The first Broadway production in
English; presented by Arthur Hopkins;
designer Robert Edmond Jones;
Nazimova as Hedvig. Play described as
"shallow idealism"

1886 ROSMERSHOLM   1895 (G)   1904
Princess Theatre, New York
(March 28, 1904 one week)
Given by the Century players; the first

English production in the United States.
Director — Sydney Rosenfeld.

1888 THE LADY FROM THE SEA   1905 (G)   1906
(In New York in German, Nov. 12)

Date			Performance in America
1890 HEDDA GABLER Fifth Avenue Theatre, New York (March 30) One performance — matinee Elizabeth Robins as Hedda	1892 (G)		1898
1892 THE MASTER BUILDER Hooley's Theatre, Chicago (March 25) Student performance — the pupils of Miss Anna Morgan from the Chicago Conservatory	1893 (N)		1895
1894 LILLE EYOLF June 1895 — LILLE EYOLF was presented on many stages, reached Chicago in the Spring. Nov. 20 — Elizabeth Robins — gave several matinees, successful performances	1895 (G)		1896
1896 JOHN GABRIEL BORKMAN Criterion Independent Theatre's production at Hoyt's Theatre, New York, Nov. 18			1897
1899 WHEN WE DEAD AWAKEN KNICKERBOCKER THEATRE Irene played by Florence Kahn; Rubek by Frederick Lewis			1905

G = German
N = Norwegian
Information based on IBSEN IN AMERICA, Annette Andersen, 1931.
Commentary and updating added by the author using theatre/history
sources.

Chronological List of Writings

Henrik Ibsen

		Date	Première Date
Catilina	Catiline	1850	1881
Kjaempehøien	Warrior's Barrow	1850	1850
Norma	Norma	1851	not performed
Sancthansnatten	St. John's Eve	1852	1853
Fru Inger til			
Østeraad (Østråt)	Lady Inger	1855	1855
Gildet paa (på)			
Solhoug	Feast at Solhoug	1856	1856
Olaf Liljekrans	Olaf Liljekrans	1857	1857
Haermaendene paa			
(på) Helgeland	Vikings in Helgeland	1858, 1873	1858
Kjaerlighedens			
Komedie	Love's Comedy	1862	1873
Kongs=Emnerne	The Pretenders	1863	1864
Brand	Brand	1866	1867
Peer Gynt	Peer Gynt	1867	1876
De Unges Forbund	League of Youth	1869	1869
Digte	Poems	1871	
Kejser og Galilaeer	Emperor and Galilean	1873	1896
Samfundets Støtter	Pillars of Society	1877	1877
Et Dukkehjem	A Doll's House	1879	1879
Gengangere	Ghosts	1881	1882
En Folkefiende	Enemy of the People	1882	1883
Vildanden	Wild Duck	1884	1885
Rosmersholm	Rosmersholm	1886	1887
Fruen fra Havet	Lady from the Sea	1888	1888
Hedda Gabler	Hedda Gabler	1890	1891
Bygmester Solness	Master Builder	1892	1893
Lille Eyolf	Little Eyolf	1894	1895
John Gabriel			
Borkman	John Gabriel Borkman	1896	1897
Når Vi Døde Vågner	When We Dead Awaken	1899	1900

NOTE: Fragments: *Rypen i Justedal (The Ptarmigan in Justedal)* 1850
Fjeldfuglen (The Mountain Bird) 1859
Svanhild 1860
Brand — Utkast i Episk form — a fragment 1864-65

Spelling of the titles is from the *Samlede Verker* (Centennial edition). Oslo: Gyldendal Norsk Forlag, MCMXXVIII.

BIBLIOGRAPHY

Andersen, H. C. *Mit Livs Eventry* I. København: Gyldendalske, Boghandel, 1951.

Anderson, Annette. Ibsen in America (Bibliography). University of Iowa Press, 1936.

Anker, Øyvind. *Bjørnstjerne Bjørnson.* Aulestad, Follebu, 1955. "Scenekunst gjennom 150 år" *Dette er Norge.* Redaksjon: Johan T. Ruud, et al. Gyldendal Norsk Forlag, Oslo, 1964.

—— "Bjornstjerne Bjørnson Som Teatermann in *Edda.* Oslo: H. Aschehoug & Company, 1960.

Anstensen, Ansten. *The Proverb in Ibsen.* New York: Columbia University Press, 1936.

Antoíne, André. *Mes Souvenirs sur le Théâtre-Libre.* Paris: B. Grasset, 1928.

Archer, William. *Play-Making.* Boston: Small, Maynard & Co., 1912.

Aschengren, Erik. "Engang den mest Spillede (Studier i Eugene Scribes teater i Frankrig og Danmark) *Studier fra Sprog-og Oldtidsforskning.* København: G.E.C. Gads Forlag, 1969.

Auden, W. H. *Brand* (foreword). New York: Doubleday & Company, Inc., 1960.

Auden, W. H. *Forewords and Afterwords.* New York: Vintage Books, 1974.

Auerbach, Erich. *Mimesis.* New Jersey: Princeton University Press, 1953.

Balice, Vincent J. *Ibsen's Feminine Mystique.* New York: Vantage Press, 1975.

Barker, Harley Granville. *Dramatic Method.* New York: Dover, 1928.

Bellows, Henry Adams. *Poetic Edda.* New York: The American-Scandinavian Foundation, 1923.

Bentley, Eric. *The Playwright as Thinker.* New York: Harcourt & Brace, & Co., 1946.

Bergman, Ingmar. *Bergman om Bergman* (Interview with Ingmar Bergman). New York: Simon & Schuster, 1973.

Binns, Archie, *Mrs. Fiske and the American Theatre*. New York: Crown Publishers, Inc., 1968.

Bertelsen, Jes. *Kategori og afgørelse*. Højberg: J. Bertelsen, 1972.

Bjørnstjerne, Bjørnson. "Norway's Constitutional Struggle" in *Scribner's Monthly Magazine*, XXI. New York, 1881.

Blanc, T. *Christiania theaters historie*, 1827-77. Christiania: J. W. Cappelens Forlag, 1899.

Brandes, Georg. *Henrik Ibsen, Critical Study*. New York: Benjamin Blom, 1964.

Brandes, Georg. *Reminiscences of My Childhood and Youth*. New York: Duffield & Co., 1906.

Brandt, Frithiof. *Søren Kierkegaard*. Copenhagen, 1963.

Bredsdorf, Elias, Brita Mortensen, R. Popperwell. *Scandinavian Literature*. Cambridge: At the University Press, 1951.

Brockett, Oscar G. and Robert R. Findley. *Century of Innovation*. Englewood Cliffs: Prentice-Hall, 1973.

Brown, John Mason. *The American Theatre as Seen by Its Critics 1752-1934*. New York: Cooper Square, 1967.

Brustein, Robert. *The Culture Watch*. New York: Alfred A. Knopf, 1975.

Bukdahl, Jorgen, et. al. *Scandinavia Past and Present*. Arnkrone, Denmark: Edvard Henriksen, 1959.

Bull, Francis. *Ibsen: The Man and the Dramatist*. Oxford: Clarenden Press, 1954.

Bull, Francis. "The Influence of Shakespeare on Wergeland, Ibsen, Bjørnson." *Norseman* 15:88-95 (1957), London.

Chesnais, P. G. "Ibsen disciple de Kierkegaard" in *Edda* 21. 1934. Oslo.

Clark, Barrett H., and George Freedley. *A History of Modern Drama*. New York: Appleton-Century-Crofts, Inc., 1947.

Clurman, Harold. *Ibsen*. New York: Collier Books, 1977.

Cole, Toby. *Playwrights on Playwriting*. New York: Hill & Wang, 1960.

Contemporary Approaches to Ibsen. Oslo: Universitetsforlaget, 1965.

Corrigan, Robert W. *The New Theatre of Europe* (edited with an introduction by Robert W. Corrigan). New York: Dell Publishing Company, 1968.

Crawford, Mary Caroline. *The Romance of the American Theatre*. New York: Halcyon House, 1913.

Crites, Stephen. *Crisis in the Life of an Actress (Krisen og en Krise i en Skuespillerindes Liv)*. New York: Harper & Row, 1967.

Dannenburg, Joseph. "Playing Ibsen in the Bad Lands" in *Theatre*. New York, 1906.

Dinesen, Isak. *Daguerretotypes and Other Essays* (tr. P. M. Mitchell and W. D. Paden). Chicago: University of Chicago Press, 1979.

Downs, Brian. *Ibsen The Intellectual Background*. Cambridge: University Press, 1948.

Drews, Elizabeth Monroe. *The Higher Levels of Human Growth*. New York: Philosophical Library, 1979.

Dru, Alexander. *The Journals of Søren Kierkegaard* (Chronology). New York: Oxford University Press, 1938.

Duerrenmatt, Freidrich. "Problems of the Theatre" in *Playwrights on Playwriting* (edited by Toby Cole). New York: Hill & Wang, 1960.

Duve, Arne. *Symbolikken i Henrik Ibsens Skuespill.* Oslo: Nasjonalforlaget, 1945.

Ebbell, Clara Thue. *I Ungdomsbyen med Henrik Ibsen.* Grimstad: Ibsenhuset og Grimstad bymuseum, 1966.

Edda. [on Knut Hamsun] Universitetsforlaget, (Hefte 6), 1972.

Eide, Eilin. *Modern Nordic Plays.* Olso: Universitesforlaget, 1974.

Eitrem, H. *Ibsen og Grimstad.* Oslo: H. Aschehoug & Company, 1940.

Erbe, Berit. *Bjørn Bjørnson's Vej mod realismens teater.* Bergen: Universitetet i Bergen, 1973.

Ericksen, Valborg, "Søren Kierkegaard og Henrik Ibsen" in *Edda,* XIX. Oslo: Nordisk tidsskrift for litteratur forskning, 1929.

Esslin, Martin. *An Anatomy of Drama.* New York: Hill and Wang, 1976.

Fasting, Kåre. *Så Vidunderlig Det Er.* Oslo: Gyldendal Norsk Forlag, 1973.

Fergusson, Francis. *The Idea of a Theater.* New York: Doubleday & Company, 1949.

Fife, Robert Herndon, and Ansten Anstensen. "Henrik Ibsen on the American Stage," *American Scand. Review* 16:218-28, 1928.

Finch, R. C. *The Saga of the Volsungs.* London: Thomas Nelson and Sons, Ltd., 1965.

Flom, George T. "Søren Kierkegaard" in *Scandinavian Studies and Notes* Vol. VI. University of Illinois, 1920.

Frohman, Daniel. "The Tendencies of the American Stage" in *The Cosmopolitan.* New York, 1904.

Genung, C. H. "Ibsen and Bjørnson" in *The Book Buyer.* Vol. XX. New York: Charles Scribner's Sons. 1900.

Gosse, Edmund. *Ibsen.* London: Hodder and Stoughton, 1907.

Gran, Gerhard. *Henrik Ibsen-Liv og Verker.* Kristiania: H. Aschehoug & Company, 1918.

Gray, Ronald. *Ibsen — A Dissenting View.* London: Cambridge University Press. 1977.

Grimsley, Ronald. *Søren Kierkegaard and French Literature.* Cardiff: University of Wales Press, 1966.

Haakonsen, Daniel. "The Function of Sacrifice in Ibsen's Realistic Drama" in *Ibsenårbok.* Oslo: Universitetsforlaget, 1974.

Haberman, Donald. *The Plays of Thornton Wilder.* Middletown, Connecticut: Wesleyan University Press, 1967.

Haecker, Theodor. *Kierkegaard the Cripple.* New York: Philosophical Library, 1950.

Halvorsen, J. B. *Bibliografiske oplysninger til Henrik Ibsen's Samlede vaerker.* København: Gyldendal, 1901.

Hansen, Peter. *Den Danske Skueplads.* Kjøbenhavn: Ernst Boyensen, 1914.

Hapgood, Norman. *The Stage in America.* New York: MacMillan Co., 1901.

Heiberg, Gunnar. *Ibsen og Bjørnson paa scenen.* Kristiania: H. Aschehoug & Company, 1918.

Heiberg, Hans. *fodt til Kunster, et Ibsen Portrett*. Oslo: H. Aschehoug & Company, 1967.

Hendersen, Archibald. *Interpretations of Life*. New York: Kennerly, 1911.

Herford, C. H. "Ibsen's Earlier Work" in *Lippincott's Monthly*, Vol. 49. Philadelphia: Lippincott, 1892.

Heusler, Andreus. *Codex Regius of the Elder Edda*. Copenhagen: Levin and Munksgaard, 1937.

Hollander, Lee M. *The Poetic Edda*. Austin: University of Texas Press, 1964.

Holm, Søren. *Filosofien i Norden før 1900*. København: Munsgaard, MCMLXVII.

Hong, Howard V. and Edna H. Hong. *Søren Kierkegaard Journals and Papers (Papirer)*. Bloomington, Ind. and London: Indiana University Press, 1967.

Hornblow, Arthur. *A History of Theatre in America*, Vol. 2. New York: Benjamin Blom, 1919, 1965.

Høst, Else. *Vildanden av Henrik Ibsen*. Oslo: Aschehoug & Company, 1967.

Howard, Bronson. *The Autobiography of a Play*. New York: Dramatic Museum of Columbia University, 1914.

Howells, W. D. "The Ibsen Influence" in *Harpers Weekly*, Vol. 39. Northfield, Minn., 1937.

Hughes, Catherine. "Ibsen? Yes, Ibsen" in *American, March* 27, 1971, New York.

Huneker, James G. "Ibsen the Individualist" in *Iconoclasts*. New York: Scribner's, 1906.

Hurt, James. *Catiline's Dream*. Chicago: University of Illinois Press, 1972.

Ibsen, Bergliot. *De tre*. Oslo: Gyldendal Norsk Forlag, 1948.

Ibsen, Henrik. *Brevveksling med Christiania theater 1878-99*. Oslo: Gyldendal Norsk Forlag, 1965.

Ibsen, Henrik. *Samlede Verker*. Hundreårsutgave. 21 vols. Ed. Frances Bull, Halvdan Koht, and Didrik Arup Seip. Oslo: Gyldendal Norsk Forlag, 1928-57.

Jaeger, Henrik. *Henrik Ibsen*. Chicago: A. C. McClure and Company, 1890.

James, Henry. *The Scenic Art* (edited by Allan Wade). London: Rupert Hart-Davis, 1949.

Johnston, Brian. *The Ibsen Cycle*. Boston: Twayne, 1975.

Kalen, T. E. "Ghosts" *Time Magazine*. New York, May 1971..

Ker, W. P. *Epic and Romance*. New York: Dover Publications, 1957.

Kerr, Walter. "The Quiet Makes the Horror Great" in *The New York Times*, April 22, 1973.

—— *Tragedy and Comedy*. New York: Simon and Schuster, 1967.

Kierkegaard, Søren. *Papirer* (Udgivet af Det danske Sprog-og Litteraturselskab or Søren Kierkegaard Selskabet). København: Gyldendal, 1911, 1968.

Kierkegaard, Søren. *Samlede Vaerker*. Copenhagen: Gyldendal, 1963.

Koht, Halvdan. *Life of Ibsen*. New York: Benjamin Blom, 1971.

—— "Shakespeare and Ibsen" *Festschriften* 6, 41-51.

Krutch, Joseph W. *Modernism in Modern Drama*. New York: Cornell University Press, 1953.

Lagerkvist, Pär. *Dramatik*. Stockholm: A. Bonnier, 1946.

Lamm, Martin. *Modern Drama*. New York: Philosophical Library, 1953.

Larson, Harold. *Bjørnstjerne Bjørnson A Study in Norwegian Nationalism*. New York: Kings Crown Press, 1944.

Lawson, John H. *Theory and Technique of Playwriting*. New York: G. P. Putnam's Sons, 1936.

Leatham, James. *The Blight of Ibsenism*. London: The Cottingham Press, 1915.

Lewis, Allan. *The Contemporary Theatre*. New York: Crown Publishers, 1971.

Liden, Hans-Emil. "The Excavation of Maere Church in Trondelag" in *Norwegian Archaelogical Review*. Oslo: Universitetsforlager, 1969.

Lorentzen, Bernt. *Det første norske teater*. Bergen: John Griegs Forlag, 1949.

Lucas, F. L. *The Drama of Ibsen and Strindberg*. London: Cassell, 1962.

Lumley, Frederick. *New Trends in 20th Century Drama*. New York: Oxford Press, 1972.

Maehle, Leif. *Ibsens rimeteknikk*. Oslo: Mallingska 3, boktr., 1955.

Malone, Kemp. "Bjørnson and his Plays" in *Forum*. Houston: Univ. of Texas, 1961.

Maritain, Jacques. *Creative Intuition and the Practical Intellect*. New York: The World Publishing Company, 1954.

Marker, Frederick J. *Hans Christian Andersen and the Romantic Theatre*. Toronto: University of Toronto Press, 1971.

Martin, Robert A. *The Theatre Essays of Arthur Miller*. Baltimore: Penguin Books, 1971.

McFarlane, James. *Henrik Ibsen*. Baltimore: Penguin Books, 1970.

Meserne, Walter J. *American Drama* (Reference Book). Totowa, New Jersey: Littlefield, Adams & Company, 1965.

Midbøe, Hans. "Max Reinhardts iscenesettelse av Ibsens *Gespenster*" *Det kongelige norske videnskabers selskab*. Trondheim: F. Bruns Bokhandel, 1960.

Mitchell, P. M. *A History of Danish Literature*. New York: The American-Scandinavian Foundation, 1971.

Mohr, Otto Lous. *Henrik Ibsen som maler*. Oslo: Gyldendal Norsk Forlag, 1953.

Moore, George. *Impressions and Opinions*. London: D. Nutt, 1891.

Morris, William. *Volsunga Saga*. New York: Collier Books, 1962.

Mosfjeld, Oskar. *Henrik Ibsen og Skien*. Oslo: Gyldendal Norske Forlag, 1949.

Munch, Edward. *Editions Beyelser Basel*. Berne: Banteli, 1965.

Naess, Arne. *Hvilken verden er den virkelige?* Oslo: Universitetsforlaget, 1969.

Naess, Harald S. "Tre engelske Ibsenintervjuer i 90-årene" in *Ibsenårbok*. Oslo, 1957-59.

—— *Norwegian Literary Bibliography* Madison: University of Wisconsin, 1972.
New York Times. "Ghosts," 1899.
New York Times. "Ibsen's Wild Duck and Mme Alla Nazimova," March 17, 1918.
New York Times. "The Wild Duck" April 12, 1978.
Nissen, Ingjald. *Sjelelige kriser i menneskets liv Henrik Ibsen og den moderne psykology.* Oslo: Aschehoug, 1931.
Norden, August 25, 1880. tidskrift for det Norske Amerika. [Dramatic criticism by P. P. Iverslie.]
Northam, John. *Ibsen's Dramatic Method.* London: Faber and Faber, 1952.
Nygaard, Knut. *Ibsen på festspillscenen.* Bergen: J. W. Eide Forlag, 1969.
Olrik, Axel. *Nordisk Aandsliv.* København: Gyldendalske Boghandel, 1927.
Overskou, Thomas. *Den danske Skueplads.* København: Gyldendalske, 1876.
Paasche, Fredrik. *Ibsen og nationalromantiken.* Oslo: Samtiden, 1909.
Paulson, Arthur. *North-American Reaction to Ibsen and Bjørnson.* University of Iowa, 1928.
Phillpotts, Bertha S. *The Elder Edda and Ancient Scandinavian Drama.* Cambridge University Press, 1920.
Rappoport, Angelo S. "Ibsen, Nietzsche, and Kierkegaard." *The New Age,* September 19, 1908.
Rohde, Peter P. *Søren Kierkegaard.* København: Thaning & Appel, 1960.
Røine, Eva. *Vandring i Nationaltheatret.* Oslo: Hausmann & Jensen Boktrykkeri, 1968.
Rudler, Roderik. "Levende bilder på scenen i Henrik Ibsens Tid" in *Kunst and Kultur,* Vol. 48. Oslo: Glydendal Norsk Forlag, 1965.
Schlauch, Margaret. *Romance in Iceland.* New York: American-Scandinavian Foundation, 1934.
Scott, A. C. *The Theatre in Asia.* New York: Macmillan Publishing Co. Inc., 1972.
Shaw, George Bernard. *The Quintessence of Ibsenism.* New York: Hill and Wang, 1957. (1891)
Singer, Isaac Bashevis. Nobel Prize Speech, December 10, 1978, Stockholm, Sweden.
Stampenbourg, Baron de. "The Passing of Ibsen" in *The Independent,* Vol. 53. New York, 1901.
Stack, George. *Kierkegaard's Existential Ethics.* Alabama: University of Alabama Press, 1977.
Steene, Birgitta. *The Greatest Fire.* Carbondale: Southern Illinois University Press, 1973.
Steinberg, Erwin R. "Gregers as Loki" in *Papers on Language and Literature.* Alton: Southern University Press, 1970.
Steiner, George. *The Death of Tragedy.* New York: Hill and Wang, 1961.
Strindberg, August. *The Inferno.* Mass.: Peter Smith.

—— *Letters to Harriet Bosse*. London: Owen, 1966.

Strømme, Arnulf M. *Strukturen i Ibsens Dramaer*. Oslo: Cammtermeyers Boghandel, 1951.

Stuart, Donald Clive. *The Development of Dramatic Art*. New York: Appleton & Co., 1928.

Tammany, Jane Ellert. "The Dramatic Nature of *The Poetic Edda*," (thesis). The Catholic University of America, Washington, DC, 1970. Essays on Ingmar Bergman: see page 342. *Henrik Ibsen's Theatre Aesthetics and Dramatic Art as a Reflection of Kierkegaardian Consciousness — Its Significance for Modern Dramatic Interpretation and the American Theatre* (doctoral dissertation). Ann Arbor: University Michofilms International, 1979.

Tennant, P. F. D. *Ibsen's Dramatic Technique*. Cambridge: Bowes & Bowes, 1948.

Theatre. New York, 1917.

Thoresen, Magdalene. *Memoir og breve*. København: August Bangs Forlag, 1971.

Time. "Ghosts." June 20, 1977.

Unamuno, Miguel de y Juga. *Perplexities and Paradoxes*. New York: Philosophical Library, 1945.

Valency, Maurice. *The Flower and the Castle*. New York: The Universal Library, 1963.

Vowles, Richard. "The Square Root of Ibsen" in *Modern Drama* 4. Lawrence, Kansas, 1962.

The Washington Post, June 5, 1976. "The Master Builder." Washington, DC.

Weigand, Hermann J. *The Modern Ibsen*. New York: E. P. Dutton & Co., 1925, 1953.

Weightman, John. "Ibsen and the Absurd" in *Encounter*. Oct. 1975.

Welland, Dennis. *Arthur Miller*. Edinburgh: Oliver and Boyd, 1961.

Winter, William. "Ibsenites and Ibsenism" in *The Wallet of Time*. New York: Moffat, Yard & Co., 1913.

Ziff, Larzier. *The American 1890's: Life and Times of a Lost Generation*. New York: The Viking Press, 1966.